KIPLINGER'S

INVEST
YOUR WAY TO
WEALTH

How ordinary people can accumulate extraordinary amounts of money

BY THEODORE J. MILLER
EDITOR,
*KIPLINGER'S PERSONAL
FINANCE MAGAZINE*

KIPLINGER BOOKS, Washington D.C.

KIPLINGER
BOOKS

Published by
The Kiplinger Washington Editors, Inc.
1729 H Street, N.W.
Washington, D.C. 20006

Library of Congress Cataloging-in-Publication Data

Miller, Theodore J.
Kiplinger's invest your way to wealth : how ordinary people can accumulate extraordinary amounts of money / by Theodore J. Miller.
p.   cm
Includes index.
ISBN 0-938721-16-X : $21.95
1. Investments. 2. Speculation. 3. Finance, Personal.
I. Title.
HG4521.M463   1991
332.6'78--dc20

91-5032
CIP

This publication is intended to provide guidance in regard to the subject matter covered. It is sold with the understanding that the author and publisher are not herein engaged in rendering legal, accounting, investment, tax or other professional services. If such services are required, professional assistance should be sought.

Printed in the United States of America.

First edition. First printing.

Book and dust jacket design by S. Laird Jenkins Corp.

ACKNOWLEDGMENTS

Creating this book was a humbling experience, chiefly because the process underscored for the author how dependent I am on the talents and efforts of others. Access to the considerable human and institutional resources of the Kiplinger organization made it possible to develop for these pages the highest caliber of investment guidance—based not on the experience of one person, but on that of dozens; and based not on the lessons learned by one generation of financial journalists, but on the lessons of three. The long, ink-stained line of Kiplinger reporters and editors stretches back to 1923, and in a way this book has been in the making all those years.

More immediately, it owes its existence to Knight Kiplinger, the editor in chief and publisher of *Kiplinger's Personal Finance Magazine*, who has long wanted a book of investment guidance as part of the Kiplinger bookshelf. In addition, Knight drew on his own experience as a collector to write the section on collectibles in Chapter 11. Other direct contributions of copy include Chapter 16, written by Kevin McCormally, tax editor of the magazine, and Chapter 9, most of which was contributed by Priscilla Thayer Brandon, chief of research. Sarah Young gets the credit for careful fact-checking and updating of the manuscript. David Harrison, the director of and driving force behind Kiplinger Books, was a great help—a flexible project manager and a fine editor, to boot. Dianne Olsufka did an excellent job as proof reader, manuscript coder and liaison with the typesetter. Dayl Sanders was indispensable in getting the project organized and keeping it on track. I am grateful to all these people.

I am also grateful to the writers and editors of *Kiplinger's Personal Finance Magazine*, the evidence of whose work is stamped clearly on these pages: Janet Bodnar, Kristin Davis, Fred Frailey, William Giese, Sherry Harowitz, Nancy Henderson, Ed Henry, Jeff Kosnett, Andrea Meditch, Dan Moreau,

Ronaleen Roha, Manny Schiffres, Mark Solheim, Melynda Dovel Wilcox. Thanks to all of you, and to the research reporters who assist you.

To my wife, Carolyn Clark Miller, and to my son, Jason, who saw precious little of me while this book was being written: Thanks for your patience. Carolyn also served as a valuable non-expert reader, helping me to clarify difficult concepts.

This book is dedicated to the readers of *Kiplinger's Personal Finance Magazine* (formerly *Changing Times*)—past, present and future. You are why we are here, and it is for you that we toil.

Ted Miller
October 1991

CONTENTS

Introduction by **Knight A. Kiplinger**

Editor in Chief, *Kiplinger's Personal Finance Magazine*

PART 1

THE ROOTS OF INVESTMENT SUCCESS

PART 2

STEPPING UP THE RISK

Introduction

By **Knight A. Kiplinger**
Editor in Chief
Kiplinger's Personal Finance Magazine

———————— ∎ ————————

IN THE 1980s, making money in investments seemed as easy as hitting the broad side of a barn.

Starting from depressed levels in 1980, the major stock market indexes racked up average annual total returns in the high teens—well above their historical performance. Single-family homes appreciated strongly in most parts of the country. Even tangible assets such as art, antiques and collectibles, which aren't investments in the true sense of the word, enjoyed strong price gains.

All of this was happening during the longest peacetime economic expansion in U.S. history. No wonder many investors developed unrealistic expectations . . . a belief that everything they owned would increase in value every year, never missing a beat.

That assumption was shaken by the stock market crash in the fall of '87, but the Dow Jones industrial average managed to finish that year fractionally ahead of its January 1 level. But then came the sobering bear market of 1990, when the major indexes really did decline, for the first time in nearly a decade.

On top of that, many homeowners in once-hot cities found that their homes were declining in value, after all those years of rapid appreciation.

What's going on here? Is the American Dream becoming a nightmare? Is the chance to accumulate wealth flitting away? Not at all. The message of this book is simple: There is still time, brother and sister. You can still accumulate substantial wealth—if you know how. After a rocky start, the '90s will be a decade of solid growth, filled with great opportunities for the savvy investor.

We at Kiplinger have been providing personal-finance advice and business forecasting information to our readers for nearly 70 years, through years of modest growth and booms, recessions and depression. And through it all, those who have followed our advice have prospered.

We don't offer fast ways to vast riches, or secrets only we know. Quite the opposite. The Kiplinger way to wealth comes not from get-rich-quick schemes, playing the markets or speculating for fast profits. It consists instead of participating in the steady, long-term growth of carefully selected assets.

When it comes to smart investing, there's really very little new under the sun. The fundamental key to creating wealth—buying a broad mix of quality assets and giving them time to grow—has never changed.

But some things *have* changed—and changed radically—in the past few decades. For one thing, there has been an explosion in the sheer number and kinds of assets that are readily available for the average investor to consider. There are vastly more small-company stocks, mutual funds, real estate trusts and even "securitized debts": mortgages, consumer installment loans, and short-term corporate debts that are bundled together to be bought and sold like bonds.

One of the best illustrations of this proliferation of investment choices is the mutual fund industry. In 1950 there were fewer than 100 funds selling shares to the public; today investors have more than 2,000 stock and bond funds to choose from, plus another 1,000 or so money-market funds.

Another big change in the investment climate has been the very pace of change itself. The fortunes of even the most solid companies can shift fundamentally in a short time. The rapidity of technological change has shortened the life cycle of high-tech products, making yesterday's leading-edge design tomorrow's unwanted dog.

Still another challenge comes from the globalization of business. While this adds new dimensions for investment opportunity, it also means that tough competition can come out of left field with little warning, not to mention the risk of changes in currency valuation, international trade laws, government regulation, and so on.

For decades we at Kiplinger have been tracking these changes—in fact, anticipating most of them—in the pages of *The Kiplinger Washington Letter* and *Kiplinger's Personal Finance Magazine* (formerly *Changing Times*). This book was written by the Magazine's editor, Ted Miller, to help you be a smart investor. It is designed to enable you to sort through these choices and understand the investment environment, so you can make intelligent decisions and be prepared to act when necessary to enhance your financial well-being—or to protect it.

But being *prepared* to act is not the same as being *compelled* to act. More often than not, what looks like a significant development really isn't, and it doesn't warrant a shift in investment strategy. The smart investor is not a financial dervish, responding frantically to the daily headlines. The hallmarks of competent investing are patience, informed calmness and skepticism of fad and fashion.

Smart investing does not involve lots of transactional activity—calling your broker every day, trading actively, selling short, switching frequently among mutual funds, using exotic hedging techniques. In fact, this kind of approach is pseudo-sophistication, at least as practiced by most individual investors. The truly smart investors, whatever their income, occupation and investment experience, are the ones who calmly make a plan, select the right investments to implement that plan and give it time to work. (Of course, some active traders make good money, but only those who are willing to make an enormous commitment to the daily tracking of all their investments. Most people are unwilling or unable to do this, preoccupied as they are with family, career and hobbies.)

This book will help you make and implement your plan, whatever your investment goals. With it at your side, you'll be ready for the Global '90s—an exciting time for the investor, full of pitfalls for the impetuous and opportunities for the well informed. There will be substantial growth in the world economy, as trade barriers decline and nations jockey for position in emerging industries. The United States, as the world's most open economy and biggest exporter—open to foreign capital, immigration and products—will benefit enormously from the growing openness of other nations.

The self-education of the individual investor is a never-ending journey; we look forward to helping you along the way.

Knight Kiplinger

Washington, D.C.
October 1991

PART 1

THE
ROOTS OF
INVESTMENT
SUCCESS

CHAPTER

1

THE FIVE KEYS TO INVESTMENT SUCCESS

T HE TIME HAS COME to talk sense about investing for personal and family wealth, starting with two simple truths.

First, investing requires taking some risks. Your hope for investment success depends in part on your ability to reduce those risks without passing up reasonable rewards. And reasonable rewards, over time, are probably enough to generate the wealth you seek.

Second, the best opportunities for building wealth occur in healthy, growing economies. Thus your personal prosperity also depends in part on the prosperity of the world's economies—for we truly live, work, save and invest in a world economy, not just an American economy.

This book will show you how to minimize your risks without sacrificing a reasonable reward, and it will argue that the years ahead offer more opportunities for more people to acquire meaningful wealth in their lifetimes than perhaps any other span of years in history. The chapters that follow will describe those opportunities and recommend ways to profit from them.

The experience of the Kiplinger organization in reporting,

analyzing, interpreting and forecasting the ups and downs of the world's economies dates back to 1923—a period that spans the Roaring Twenties and the Great Depression, World War II and the Cold War that followed, years of growth and years of recession, double-digit inflation, stock market booms and stock market busts. Those years of experience applied to the economic forces at work in the world today lead us to conclude that the next decade or so is shaping up as a period of potential economic boom.

It will be a worldwide boom; America will share in it and in many important ways will help to create it. The course won't be perfectly straight and uninterrupted—it never has been. But the general direction will be clear. Chapter 2 lays out the reasons we believe this.

If you're in a hurry to cash in on the boom, this book won't help you. Buy a lottery ticket or enter a magazine subscription sweepstakes instead. All you risk is the price of the ticket or the price of the stamp and the envelope, and you have a pretty good idea of your chances.

But if you're patient, the economic climate of the years ahead, coupled with a nearly inexhaustible supply of ways to get in on the action, can make the next decade or so uniquely profitable for people like you. This book will show you how to accumulate a six- or seven-figure chunk of money while you still have enough lifetime left to enjoy it. Getting rich this way takes you along a path that's short on thrills, but it's short on spills, too. And the nice green scenery along the way keeps you interested in the trip.

You can devise a plan to achieve this goal regardless of your current style of saving and investing. If you tend to neglect your finances, you should create a plan with neglect in mind. Lots of successful investors put their portfolios on autopilot, spending only a few hours each year monitoring performance. Others like to pay close attention to what's happening to their money.

Whichever description fits you, you can accumulate remarkable sums of money by applying the following five keys to investment success. Note that we call these *keys,* not *secrets.* In fact there are no investment secrets. The methods employed by successful investors are well known to those who follow money matters closely, but they tend to get lost in the clutter and clamor of the day-to-day action. This chapter will provide an arms-length look at the methods behind the apparent madness. Later chapters will show you how to apply them to your own investments.

You'll probably be familiar with most of the investment terms used in these pages. If you come across any that stump you, you can consult the glossary in Chapter 18.

KEY # 1: MAKE INVESTING A HABIT
How to have $500,000 or more in 20 years or less

Your task is not to devise the most ingenious investment plan ever conceived. Rather your task is to create a plan that suits you and stick with it. For most people who start with a small amount, the best chance to acquire measurable wealth lies in developing the habit of adding something to the pot on a regular basis and putting the money where it can do the most for you.

The rewards can be considerable compared with a lackadaisical approach to saving and investing. Suppose you take $5,000 and stick it in the bank, where it earns a nice, safe, sedate 5.5% interest. Twenty years later you come in to claim your deposit and discover that it has grown to a not-very-impressive $14,500.

Meanwhile, your brother-in-law socks $5,000 in one-year certificates of deposit (CDs) at the same bank, with instructions to roll over the proceeds into a new certificate every 12 months. In addition, every month he buys another CD for $100 and issues the same instructions. Over 20 years he earns an average of 8% interest. His nest egg: more than $80,000.

That's a lot better, but it's not going to finance a worry-free retirement. Suppose your goal is a lot loftier than that? Suppose you'd like to have a nest egg of half a million dollars? You've got 20 years to get there and $5,000 with which to start. You're willing to investigate investment alternatives that should boost your return above what you'd earn in a bank account. What's a reasonable return to plan on and how much will you have to contribute along the way?

For reasons you'll find discussed in Chapter 4, Kiplinger thinks an average annual return of 15% over the long run is a reasonable expectation for individuals who apply the principles laid out in this book. At that rate, with $5,000 to start, you'll reach your $500,000 goal if you contribute $320 a month to your investment account.

Less ambitious plans can also work wonders. Starting from zero, putting just $50 a month into an investment that pays a compounded average annual total return of 15% for 20 years will get you a nest egg of better than $65,000. Stick to the plan for 30 years and you'll have more than $275,000. Double your contribution and you'll double the size of your nest egg. For a look at the results of a variety of regular investment amounts earning different rates of return, see Chapter 17.

Starting small and gradually increasing your monthly investment amount as your income grows is another possibility. For instance, you can start with nothing, put $100 a month into your investment account for five years, raise it to $200 a month for the next five, $300 a month for years 11 through 15 and $400 a month for years 16 through 20. At the end of the period you'll have nearly $227,000. Boost your monthly amount to $500 for years 21 through 25 and your fund will grow to almost $500,000, assuming you earn an average of 15% per year.

How common is an average annual return of 15%? For the 10-year period through 1990, no fewer than 45 different mutual funds delivered that much or more. You'll find some of them listed in Chapter 5, along with lists of other outstanding funds that can help you achieve your goals. (Were the 1980s typical for investors? No, they weren't. The Dow Jones industrial average tripled during the decade—a remarkable performance, though not unique. The Dow also tripled in the ten-year span from 1942 to 1952, and again from 1953 to 1963. We don't believe that it will triple in the 1990s, but a mediocre market would be enough for it to double, ending the decade in the neighborhood of 6000. But helping you achieve mediocre investment results isn't the goal of this book. If you follow the plan, you should do better than that.)

These examples are oversimplified, of course, because they don't take taxes or commissions into account. But the point is the same: Making investing a habit is an important key to making investing a success.

KEY # 2: SET EXCITING GOALS
Why not a condo on the golf course?

Investment goal-setting is an intensely personal affair that will be guided by your own style and preferences. But if you set nebulous, generalized goals, such as "financial security" or "a comfortable retirement," you're going to have trouble measuring your progress along the way. You may even struggle to maintain interest in the project. Vaguely defined investment goals can lead to half-hearted efforts to achieve them.

Better to set goals you can grab onto, goals that excite you. Instead of "financial security," why not "a million-dollar net worth by age 60?" Instead of "a comfortable retirement," why not "a two-bedroom condo on a golf course on Hilton Head Island, plus an investment portfolio that will yield $3,000 a month to supplement my pension?" Now *that's* a goal.

Setting investment goals is a lot like reading a map: Before you can get to where you want to go, you've got to figure out where you are. The easiest way to find out where you are now is to fill out the personal balance sheet on page 8. It's largely self-explanatory. You may have to do a little guesstimating about the value of your furniture, jewelry and so forth, but don't spend a lot of time trying to be precise about those numbers. It's the financial portion of your balance sheet that

WHERE YOU STAND NOW: YOUR PERSONAL BALANCE SHEET

Use this worksheet to calculate your current assets, liabilities and net worth. When you know where your current net worth comes from, you can see where your financial position is strong and where it is weak. This worksheet, along with the investment-mix worksheet on page 22, lay the necessary groundwork for setting your investment goals and making plans to reach them.

ASSETS	
Cash in savings accounts	$
Cash in checking accounts	
Cash on hand	
Certificates of deposit	
Money-market funds	
U.S. savings bonds	
Market value of home	
Market value of other real estate	
Cash value of life insurance	
Surrender value of annuities	
Vested equity in pension plans	
Vested equity in profit sharing	
401(k) or 403(b) plans	
Individual retirement accounts	
Keogh plans	
Stocks (individually owned)	
Bonds (individually owned)	
Mutual funds:	
Stocks	
Bonds	
Real estate investment trusts	

Other investments:	$	
Collectibles		
Precious metals		
Estimated market value of:		
Household furnishings		
Automobiles and trucks		
Boats, recreational vehicles		
Furs and jewelry		
Loans owed to you		
Other assets		
Total Assets	$	(A)
LIABILITIES		
Balance owed on mortgages	$	
Auto loans		
Student loans		
Home-equity credit line		
Other credit lines		
Credit card bills		
Other bills		
Total Liabilities	$	(B)
CURRENT NET WORTH: (A minus B)	$	

should concern you the most: money in savings accounts, stocks, bonds and mutual funds, real estate and the like, plus your equity in pension plans and other sources of current and future income.

Another approach is to pose a few basic questions: How much money could you raise if you were to liquidate everything you own and pay off all your debts? How difficult would it be to get your hands on that money? And where would that money come from? What you learn about *where* your money is will also influence your goal-setting and the routes available to get to your goals.

Your goals should affect your investment choices. There are no "right" or "wrong" investment goals. They can be whatever you want them to be and naturally will be influenced by your income and job security, your ability to take risks, your age and your financial prospects in general. In addition, the time you have to achieve your goals should influence the kinds of investments you might consider. Most people have several goals at once.

■ *Short-term goals.* Suppose, for instance, that a vacation in Europe is one of your goals and that you want to go next summer. Such a short time horizon suggests that the stock market wouldn't be a good place to invest the money you're setting aside for the trip. The market is subject to wide swings, and you wouldn't want to be forced to sell your stocks in a downswing just because the time had come to buy your tickets. Don't put into the stock market any money you think you might need in the next three to five years. Certificates of deposit that mature about the time you'll need the cash, or a money-market fund that allows you to withdraw your cash instantly by writing a check would be a better choice for this goal.

■ *Medium-term goals.* Maybe you'd like to buy a larger house within three or four years. With more time, you have more flexibility. Safety is still important but you are in a better position to ride out bad times in the financial markets. For medium-term goals like these, you should consider longer-term CDs that pay more interest than the short-term certificates you would buy to help finance your vacation trip. You could even consider mutual funds that invest in stocks that pay good dividends but don't tend to fluctuate much in price (See Chapter 6). That would give you high income (for reinvesting in more fund shares), a chance to ride along if the stock market zooms, and pretty good protection against all but a catastrophic drop in stock prices.

▮ *Long-term goals.* A comfortable retirement is probably the most common of all financial goals—so common, in fact, that it gets its own chapter in this book. A college education for the kids is another common goal (it gets its own chapter, too). For long-term goals like these, consider a wide range of possibilities: stocks, corporate and government bonds, and long-term CDs among them. You should also take maximum advantage of tax-sheltered plans such as individual retirement accounts (IRAs), in which earnings accumulate tax-free and contributions to which may be tax deductible, and 401(k) plans offered by your employer, which provide many of the same advantages as IRAs. These are described in detail in Chapter 14.

With several years and sometimes decades ahead of you, financial assets that aren't strictly investments also come into play: home equity, pension plans and social security, for example. Your investment goals and choices should be influenced by the size and accessibility of those assets, as we'll discuss in later chapters.

Your goals are likely to change, so it's important to reassess them from time to time. For instance, the kinds of growth-oriented investments that might be perfectly appropriate while you are accumulating a retirement nest egg and have a long-term horizon could be inappropriate after you retire and need income to pay the bills. Luckily, the investment universe is so vast—not just stocks and bonds and certificates, but also hybrids too numerous to mention here—that you'll never be at a loss for choices.

KEY #3: DON'T TAKE UNNECESSARY RISKS

There are two times in a man's life when he shouldn't speculate:
when he can't afford it, and when he can. — **Mark Twain**

Most people would say that risk is the chance you take that
you'll lose all or part of the money you put into an investment.
That's true as far as it goes, but it doesn't go far enough. A
more complete definition of risk acknowledges the availability
of investments carrying virtually iron-clad guarantees that you
will get all your money back plus the interest promised you:
savings accounts in federally insured banks, savings and loans,
or credit unions, for instance. These are and will remain safe
despite the recent problems of some institutions and the fund
that insures their deposits. Also, with all investments, even
government-guaranteed ones, you run the risk that your return
will be less than the inflation rate.

In fact, savings accounts, certificates of deposit, Treasury
bills, savings bonds and a handful of other government-
backed investments establish a useful benchmark for measuring risk.

Risk is the chance you take that you will earn less from an
investment than the rate of inflation or less than the interest
available at the time from insured savings certificates or U.S.
Treasury-backed obligations.

To put it another way, risk is the chance that you will earn
less than 5% or 6% on your money. If you can't reasonably
expect to do better than that, then there's no sense in taking the
risk.

Controlling your exposure to risk. It's difficult to pick up a book
on investing without running into something called the pyramid
of risk, and this book will be no exception. If the pyramid of risk
is familiar to you, feel free to skip this section and go right to the
next. If it isn't familiar, the following short discussion could be
the most important part of the book for you.

The pyramid of risk is a useful visual image for a sensible
risk-reducing strategy.

The pyramid is built on a broad and solid base of financial security: a home; money salted away in insured savings accounts or certificates; plus insurance policies to cover your health, your car, your home, your life and your ability to earn an income (that is, disability insurance). As you move up from the pyramid's base, the levels get narrower and narrower, representing the space in your portfolio that is available for investments that involve risk. The greater the risk of an investment, the higher up the pyramid it goes and, thus, the less money you should put into it.

The image itself is more important than some of the specifics of what belongs on each level of the pyramid. Weak real estate markets in some places in recent years have raised the question of whether homeownership still belongs at the base of the pyramid. We believe that it does—for security as much as for wealth.

How much should you have in savings? Three to six months' living expenses should be your goal. Bank, savings and loan or credit union accounts are good places to keep this money, but look for opportunities to earn more than the 5% or 5½% these institutions tend to pay on their run-of-the-mill deposit accounts. If you can't do better than that in local institutions, consider a money-market fund for at least part of your rainy-day money. Such funds aren't federally insured, but they are prudent, conservative places to put your money and they pay a higher return. Chapter 3 describes them and recommends several other low-risk ways to step up the return from your savings.

Once you've built the base of your pyramid, you're ready to move up and become an investor. One level up from savings, insurance and homeownership is the appropriate place for mutual funds that invest in low-risk, dividend-oriented stocks and top-quality government and corporate bonds. Individual stocks and bonds that you pick yourself are on the same level. Most experts would put investment real estate on the next level up from stocks. At the very top of the pyramid go investments few people should try, such as penny stocks, commodities futures contracts and most limited partnerships. We recommend against these and several other risky ventures and explain why in Chapter 12.

Thus, the pyramid, which is broad and solid at the bottom and gets narrower and smaller as you move up, is the perfect image for the sensible deployment of your financial resources. As long as you remember that, you'll never stray too far out of your risk zone.

How much risk should you take? Controlling risk means more than being "comfortable" with an investment. Certainly you should never invest in something that makes you uncomfortable or in something you don't understand, but it is our frequent observation that too many investors seem perfectly comfortable with entirely too much risk—until the bottom falls out.

Late in the summer of 1990, a remarkable scene took place in a meeting room in Englewood, Colo. Investors had gathered to hear their portfolio adviser report on recent performance. This adviser's specialty was buying and selling stock options, a technique that greatly magnifies the effect of movements in the price of the underlying stock (See Chapter 12). If you choose the right option, you can make more money than if you had actually owned the stock. If you choose wrong. . . . well, the advisor chose wrong—so wrong that he lost an estimated $100 million of his clients' money and didn't have the nerve to show up at the meeting. Instead he sent a videotape, on which he explained how his mistaken opinion about the direction the price would move on a single stock (UAL Corp.) had resulted in massive losses to the people in the room. The adviser may have misjudged the stock, but he knew exactly how his clients would react to the news: To keep the peace, security guards patrolled the room as his videotaped message was played.

More than 1,000 investors were thought to have been hurt by this single miscall. They had been drawn into participating in this terribly risky (but perfectly legal) investment strategy by dreams of extraordinarily high returns, or by ignorance of what the advisor was doing, or both.

These luckless investors are a sad reminder of the most enduring truth about the risk-reward relationship:

The bigger the promised reward, the bigger the risk. Conversely, the bigger the risk of the investment you undertake, the bigger the potential reward should be.

This risk-reward relationship applies no matter what the investment, who the investment adviser, what the condition of the financial markets or the phase of the moon. The landscape is littered with the discarded portfolios of investors who forgot that basic fact.

Does this mean you should avoid all high-risk investments? No. It means you should confine them to the top of the pyramid—to the attic, where they can never occupy a very significant portion of your investment portfolio. Invest only as much as you can afford to lose, because there is a good chance you *will* lose it. You should also learn to recognize the risks involved in every kind of investment.

▌ *Risks in stocks.* A company's stock may decline in price because the company hits the skids or isn't being managed well and the shareholders lose faith. It may also decline in price because large numbers of investors decide to move into bonds or cash on a particular day and sell millions of shares of stock of all kinds, thus driving the market down and taking dozens of companies along without bothering to differentiate the good from the bad.

▌ *Risks in bonds.* Bond prices tend to move in the opposite direction from interest rates, rising in price when rates fall and vice versa. But individual bond issues can be hurt even if interest rates in general are falling. All it takes is for one of the rating services—Standard and Poor's and Moody's are the major ones—to downgrade its opinion of the company's financial stability. A bond issue that's paying an interest rate noticeably higher than that of other bonds with a similar maturity date is probably forced to pay it to compensate investors for the higher risk inherent in a lower safety rating. That, in a nutshell, is the situation with "junk" bonds: low ratings, high interest, high risk of default.

▋ *Risks everywhere.* Real estate values go up and down in sync with supply and demand in *local* markets, regardless of the health of the national economy. Gold and silver, which are supposed to be stores of value in inflationary times, have been decidedly unrewarding in times of tolerable inflation. Even federally insured savings accounts carry risks—not that the government won't cover insured deposits, but that their low interest rate won't be enough to protect the value of your money from the combined effect of inflation and taxes.

What is a prudent risk? It depends on your goals, your age, your income and other resources and your current and future financial obligations. A young single person who expects his or her pay to rise steadily over the years and who has few family responsibilities can afford to take more chances than, say, a couple approaching retirement age. The young person has time to recover from market reversals; the older couple may not. A more complete discussion of risk appears in each of the chapters devoted to specific investment alternatives.

KEY #4: KEEP TIME ON YOUR SIDE

$10,000 today, or $10,000 a year from today?

A penny saved is a penny earned—or so the saying goes. In fact, a penny saved may be more or less than a penny earned, depending on when it is earned and how it is saved. The reason is rooted in a concept called the time value of money (and its close cousin, opportunity cost).

Which would you rather have, $10,000 today or $10,000 a year from today? Of course you'd choose the take the money now—anyone would. Besides possessing the sure knowledge . that a bird in the hand is worth two in the bush, you understand that the value of that $10,000 you have to wait a year for will be eroded by a year's worth of inflation and a year's worth of lost interest on the money. To put a dollar figure on it, if inflation is 5% and you could earn 7% interest in a year, the thrill of being handed $10,000 today is worth about 12%, or $1,200, more than the thrill of being handed $10,000 a year from today.

The time value of money works against you if you're the one waiting to collect the money, but it works in your favor if you're the one who has to pay. Success with your money often lies in being able to identify the winning side of the time value equation.

Let's say you're a big winner on *Jeopardy!*. For your prize you are offered the choice of $25,000 in cash or an annuity worth $50,000. Which should you take?

The answer depends on how long you'd have to wait to collect the $50,000. Annuities are contracts that pay a certain sum of money in regular installments over a period of time, often 10 or 20 years, rather than in a lump sum. Stretching out the payments creates a big benefit for the company that owes the money because it collects interest on the unpaid amount while the recipient waits to collect. For instance, if the $50,000 were paid out in annual installments stretched over 20 years, and the company earned 8% on the unpaid amount, all it would need to meet that schedule of future payments would be about $25,000 today. Thus your choice of prizes would really be no choice at all; you'd just be picking a collection schedule.

It is the time value of money that permits state governments and other sponsors of sweepstakes and lotteries to promise fabulous payouts that actually exceed the amount of money they take in by selling tickets. Consider two sweepstakes, both of which promise a million-dollar prize. One pays it right away and the other, which advertises an "annuity value" of a million dollars, pays you $50,000 a year for 20 years. That's a million dollars, all right, but it doesn't cost the sweepstakes sponsor nearly that much. In fact, the sponsor can purchase an annuity contract from an insurance company that will fulfill its obligation for about $490,000—less than half the eventual payout.

Clearly, the sweepstakes that pays right away offers a much more valuable prize. You could use it to purchase the same annuity and waltz to the bank with more than half a million dollars in change—not counting taxes, of course.

You don't have to win a lottery or a quiz show to contemplate whether you're headed for the winning or the losing side of the time value equation. If you keep in mind one basic principle—that a dollar you pay or receive today is worth more than a dollar you pay or receive tomorrow—you'll wind up on the winning side more often than not. A couple of examples illustrate why:

▎ *Paying the kids' college bills.* Your future rocket scientist faces education costs exceeding $100,000 when she enters Stanford or MIT in 18 years. That's a huge sum, but because you're familiar with the time value of money, you know the smart thing to do is to find a way to pay those bills today, when your dollars are worth more than they will be in 18 years. Assuming a time value for the money of 10% per year (meaning you could earn that much on the money between now and the time you have to pay it) the value of the $100,000 you need 18 years from now is a shade under $18,000 today. Salt that away in an investment earning 10% a year and you've got the bills covered. If you haven't got $18,000, gather as much of it as you can and get the time value of money working for you, easing at least some of the burden when the college bills come due. Or raise your sights a bit. If you could manage to earn 12% on the money, you'd need just slightly over $13,000 today to have $100,000 by your daughter's freshman year. Chapter 14 describes some ways to achieve such a goal.

▎ *Paying off the mortgage.* Ignorance of the time value of money can cause you to think you're doing something smart when you're not. For instance, you have probably heard praises sung for the 15-year mortgage. Because you pay it off sooner than a 30-year loan, you pay less interest and thus save tens of thousands of dollars. But the homeowner with the 15-year mortgage parts with the money sooner than the

30-year buyer, and the time value of money suggests some caution may be in order before making extravagant claims of savings. You need the answers to two questions: What else might you do with the extra money you'd be spending on the higher monthly payments required by the 15-year mortgage? How much could it earn if you invested it in something other than mortgage payments?

Suppose it costs you an extra $200 a month to pay off the loan in 15 years instead of 30. That's $200 a month not available for something else—investing in a mutual fund, for example. Say the mortgage rate is 10% and the mutual fund earns 12%. You could benefit from that 2% difference by putting the money in the fund instead of paying off the mortgage. $200 a month earning 2% compounded for 15 years grows to almost $42,000. That's your *opportunity cost* to pay off your mortgage early, and before you crow about how much you've saved over taking a 30-year mortgage, you need to subtract it from your savings.

Opportunity cost is the cost of doing one thing and not another. To make sure you don't overlook it, ask yourself before you make any investment or spending choice: "What *else* could I do with the money?"

KEY #5: DIVERSIFY

There's more to it than putting your eggs in different baskets

There are at least three good reasons to diversify your investments. First, it's common sense not to put all your eggs in one basket. Our grandmothers taught us that. Second, no investment performs well all the time; as a rule, when something is down, something else tends to be up. And third, some investment experts believe that you can actually increase your return with a sensible strategy of diversification.

Riding the ups and downs. The *Chase Investment Performance Digest,* published by Chase Global Data & Research, Inc., put together comparisons of the ups and downs of various investment markets since 1960. Here's a snapshot of selected recent years, plus inflation figures. The investment figures are total returns, which means they include price changes and assume that all earnings from the investment, if any, are reinvested.

	1975	1979	1985	1989
Inflation rate	6.9%	13.3%	3.8%	4.6%
Dow Jones industrials	44.8	10.6	33.6	32.2
Shearson Long-term Treasuries	8.3	-0.5	31.6	18.9
Donoghue's Money Market Index	na	12.8	7.2	8.1
Gold	-24.9	126.6	6.9	-2.0
Real Estate Investment Trusts	27.3	18.3	0.8	-21.9

Stocks and money-market funds managed positive returns in each of the four years. Two highly touted investments —gold and real estate—soared, struggled or nearly collapsed, depending on the year that you're looking at. A different selection of years would have shown a different pattern from the one shown above. For instance, even with dividends included, the Dow Jones industrials turned in a dismal performance in 1973, 1974 and 1977. Gold soared in each of those years, while real estate investment trusts fell so sharply in 1973 and 1974 that their survival as an investment vehicle was actually in doubt.

The lesson here isn't hard to find: Invest in whatever you want, but invest in something else, too.

Spreading the risk. One way to hedge your bets is to select a number of investment vehicles you like and divide your money equally among them. That's the approach adopted by Bailard, Biehl & Kaiser, an investment management firm based in San Mateo, Cal. BB&K's recommendation is to invest an equal amount in a five-part "fixed mix" portfolio consisting of cash (money-market funds, CDs, Treasury bills); bonds; U.S. stocks; foreign stocks; and real estate. Once a year, adjust the mix to maintain the dollar balance. You do that by taking the gains from the winners and spreading them out among the losers so that your asset distribution stays the same. Other than that, sit back and forget it.

For example, if you had stuck with this fixed-mix approach from 1965 to 1990, and your selection of stocks, bonds and real estate had matched the average market experience for those investments, your cumulative return would have been a shade under 950%. Looked at another way, $1,000 invested in 1965 would have grown to $9,500 by 1990. The same amount invested in U.S. stocks would have grown to about $8,700 measured by the Standard & Poor's 500 Composite Index. The most spectacular returns during that period came from a portfolio of international stocks, which rocketed a phenomenal 2,477%, turning $1,000 into $24,770.

The results work out to an average annual return of 10.2% for the diversified portfolio over 25 years. That's not bad, but it's not much better than the historical return generated by the stock market alone.

Dividing your portfolio equally among domestic stocks, foreign stocks, bonds, real estate and cash equivalents is only one approach to diversification. Another formula, which is popular with many successful investors seeking to prosper while controlling their risks, is the 40–40–20 portfolio: 40% in stocks, 40% in bonds and 20% in cash equivalents. Either mix creates a good diversified portfolio, but thinking about a portfolio in such terms can lure you into a misleading sense of permanence about what is actually a very fluid situation. As stock prices and interest rates go up and down, the proportions in your portfolio will shift without your lifting a finger. In addition, there will be times when you want to shift more money into stocks or bonds or cash, for reasons described in Chapters 4 and 5. It is more realistic to think in terms of ranges rather than fixed percentages. Use the worksheet on page 22 to discover how your investments sort out today. The results will suggest moves you should make to get them more in line with the kind of mix you'd like.

This is the range of portfolio mixes Kiplinger recommends

for investors seeking long-term growth, moderate risk and ease of access to their money:

> Stocks: 40% to 80%
> Bonds: 20% to 50%
> Cash: 10% to 25%

This is the *core portfolio*. It should form the bedrock of your investment plan. That doesn't mean you should always be invested in stocks, bonds and cash to the exclusion of everything else, just that they should compose the bulk of your invested capital. You could keep 50% of your investments in stocks, 20% in bonds, 10% in cash and the remaining 20% in something else—real estate, for example. Real estate is left out of the core portfolio not because we don't think it can deliver solid gains but because achieving those gains requires specialized knowledge of *local*, not national, marketplaces. The beaten-down values in many markets as the 1990s began could eventually generate lucrative profits for investors well-informed and well-heeled enough to take advantage of them. Real estate investing is the subject of Chapter 9.

Some investors consider their collectibles—antiques, automobiles, stamps, baseball cards—to be part of their investment portfolios. We don't think they are, for reasons set out in Chapter 11. If you have specialized knowledge of a particular field, enjoy collecting and have access to the kinds of information and markets that can make collecting a profitable venture, fine. But we wouldn't include collectibles in the core portfolio.

Gold is often cited as an inflation hedge that belongs in everyone's portfolio. We don't believe that the inflation outlook for the rest of this century supports that position, and we address the subject in Chapter 11.

Another thing about the core portfolio: By "stocks," we don't necessarily mean individual shares. As later chapters will show, mutual funds are often the best way to own stocks, although knowing how to select a promising stock will make you a better picker of promising funds as well. By "bonds," we

HOW ARE YOUR INVESTMENTS DEPLOYED?

Complete this worksheet at least once a year so you'll know how your invest-ment mix is changing and can take action, if necessary, to bring it back into line with a mix that matches your goals and your risk tolerance. A good year for stocks, for instance, could cause them to become a larger portion of the mix than you'd like, prompting you to sell some shares and redeploy the profits into bonds or Treasury bills.

	MARKET VALUE	% OF TOTAL
CASH		
Savings accounts		
Money-market funds		
Treasury bills		
Total Cash	$	
STOCKS		
Individual shares		
Mutual funds		
Total Stocks	$	
BONDS		
Individual bonds		
Mutual funds		
Unit trusts		
Total Bonds	$	
RENTAL REAL ESTATE	$	
LIMITED PARTNERSHIPS	$	
PRECIOUS METALS	$	
OTHER INVESTMENTS	$	
COLLECTIBLES	$	
Total Investments	$	100%

don't necessarily mean only corporate or municipal securities that are so labeled. Variations on the bond theme—mortgage-backed securities, for instance (See Chapter 10)—can perform the same function for your portfolio, often at a more attractive return. These investments are described in later chapters.

Keep these points in mind as you read through the chapters that follow. The core portfolio is intended not as a hard-and-fast formula but as guidance for constantly changing investment markets. Your exact mix should also take into account your age, income and investment goals. For instance, as you approach retirement it's natural to shift more of your assets into income-producing investments such as bonds or utility stocks and out of stocks that have long-term potential but are subject to market reversals.

Other ways to diversify. Diversifying among different kinds of investments is a classic strategy that has served many people well. But in fact it is only the beginning of investment wisdom. Alert investors perform at least two other kinds of diversification.

▉ *Diversify within investment categories.* Stocks come in so many shapes and sizes that to say "Put 60% of your money in stocks" is not very helpful advice. Which stocks? There are blue-chip stocks, small-company (emerging growth) stocks, income-oriented stocks, foreign stocks, regional stocks. These and other kinds of stocks are explored in depth in Chapter 4. A well-designed portfolio includes more than one kind.

▉ *Diversify according to time horizons.* In the investment markets, a month or two can be a long time. Interest rates move up and down. The stock market churns and boils, achieving new heights in July, new depths in August. National and world events can change the investment climate overnight.

You can protect your portfolio against the effects of such uncertainty by spreading your holdings across the calendar. Don't overcommit to either the long term or the short term. Mix the maturities of your bonds and certificates of deposit and continue to make regular contributions to your investment program *especially* when market prices are down. They will bounce back and you will be sitting pretty when they do.

Failing to apply the concepts described in this chapter won't necessarily deny you investment success, but the success you do manage to achieve will be due largely to pure dumb luck. If you apply these five keys to success, you'll need no more than your fair share of luck to succeed, no matter what your goals. You can be sure that every investor needs *some* luck. The idea is to rely on it as little as possible.

2

THE INVESTMENT CLIMATE IN THE YEARS AHEAD

■

Whe you invest money in a company, you're casting a vote of confidence not only in the prospects for the company itself but also in the prospects for the economy in which the company must sell its products or services. Most of this book is devoted to describing successful techniques you can apply in your search for companies worthy of your confidence. This chapter describes why we think the American economy deserves that confidence as well.

After you've set aside the Japan-bashing and the America-bashing; after you've examined the evidence supporting the claims and the counterclaims; when you've dug through the statistics and analyzed the trends . . . when you've done all that, in our opinion, you face three overriding and inescapable facts about the current state of the world's economy and America's place in it.

■ *First, the global economy has clearly arrived.* It is not on the horizon; it is already here. In the global economy, the competitor who is located six time zones away is potentially as serious a threat as the competitor six blocks away. This is what high-speed communication and transportation have done to the world's commerce, and there's no turning back.

▮ *Second, America's ability to prosper in the years ahead will depend on its ability to compete successfully in the global economy.* This is so obvious that it seems almost pointless to state it. Whether it's banks or burritos, chemicals or cosmetics, cars or computers, televisions or tractors, the companies that can do the job faster, cheaper and better will take markets away from those who lag, and national borders aren't going to stop them.

▮ *Third, America is marvelously well equipped to compete in the global economy.* This is perhaps the most controversial of our conclusions, but in fact it is probably safe to say that the *majority* of the world's business economists share that opinion.

Let's examine these conclusions.

THE AGE OF THE GLOBAL ECONOMY

That the global economy is here hardly needs documentation for anyone who can read the nameplates on the cars on our highways and on the VCRs in our living rooms. But this consumer's-eye view is woefully incomplete. The list of generic products traded around the world is almost endless—electric parts, plywood, finished metal shapes, fish, corn, pharmaceuticals, plastic materials, industrial machinery, newsprint—forming a vast commercial linkage among nations that none of them wants to break.

The volume of imports and exports involving the U.S. totals nearly a trillion dollars a year. And that's just products; it doesn't include tens of billions of dollars worth of services such as insurance, engineering and banking that move across our borders each year.

Yet another aspect of the global economy intertwines nations for their common good: joint ventures. The number of joint ventures with Japan alone is an impressive example of the growing interdependence of multinational companies. To cite only a few: General Motors joins with Toyota and Ford joins with Mazda to build cars; IBM and Matsushita combine forces to build computers; Kodak and Canon sign on together to produce copiers and photographic equipment; Boeing and Mitsubishi build airliners together.

More evidence of the global economy can be found in the direct investment by one country in the assets of another. Although Japanese acquisitions of American businesses and real estate get most of the attention, in fact, Great Britain owns nearly twice the value of U.S. assets as the Japanese do. The Netherlands, Canada and Germany also have multibillion-dollar stakes in the American economy. U.S. companies, for their part, own nearly as much property in foreign countries as all foreign companies *combined* own here. And that almost certainly understates the value of such holdings, which are often carried on U.S. companies' books at original cost. That would often assign them market values of 30 or 40 years ago, while U.S. property acquired by foreign corporations would have more current values. At any rate, U.S. assets owned by foreign companies gives them a substantial stake in our prosperity, just as our ownership of their assets gives us a substantial stake in theirs. (In mid 1991, the U.S. Commerce Department estimated the value of foreign-owned assets at about $2 trillion.)

Finally, another very tangible commodity ties together the fates of the world's economies: money. Businesses all over the world need it to expand. They need a place to invest it, a place to park it between long-term commitments, a decent rate of return on it and an assurance of economic stability in the place where it's being kept. These last two considerations especially are what have drawn billions and billions in foreign capital into the U.S. financial markets—winding up chiefly in bank deposits, corporate stocks and bonds and U.S. Treasury bonds. In turn, U.S. capital plays an important role in the financial markets of other nations.

This situation worries some Americans. What if foreign investors were suddenly to pull out of U.S. markets? What if they yanked their deposits out of our banks, sold their stocks and bonds and took their money home? Because of the rapidity of electronic order-taking and funds transfers, that could theoretically be accomplished in a single day, and it would surely be a catastrophe. With billions of dollars worth of indiscriminate sell orders flooding the market and major sources of capital drying up, the value of stocks would plunge, interest rates would soar and property values would take a dive.

But why would foreign investors do such a thing when they have such a large stake in real estate, industrial plants, equipment and other business property whose value would plunge, too? The more interdependent the world's economies become, the less likely it is that a foreign pullout will happen. The nations of the world have a growing interest in the prosperity of other nations. That's why the global economy is not worrisome but good. It creates new markets and new opportunities for prosperity throughout the world.

The promise of those new markets is a major reason why the world is moving toward more interdependence, not less. Through the Single European Act, usually called "Europe 1992," trade barriers among 12 different nations are coming down (See Chapter 7). The U.S., Canada and Mexico, historically major buyers of each others' goods and services, are finding ways to strengthen that relationship, working to create a North American common market that will be better equipped to compete with a unified European market. (Canada is a *much* bigger trading partner for the U.S. than is Japan, and Mexico is our third largest trading partner.) The nations of the Pacific Rim—Japan, Taiwan, Korea, Singapore, Indonesia and others —need our consumer markets if they are to thrive. New consumer markets, in Eastern Europe, the Soviet Union and Latin America, lie ahead.

In the years to come, there will be efforts at protectionism, short-sighted attempts at home and abroad to close borders to trade in the interest of protecting jobs and markets. Some will no doubt succeed. But for the long run, the die is cast. The global economy is here to stay.

CAN AMERICA COMPETE?

Yes, America can compete. American companies *are* competing successfully on many fronts, although they have lagged in some of the most visible areas, virtually abandoning leadership to foreign competitors in home electronics, for instance. But in Chapter 7 you'll find descriptions of several American companies that are thriving in foreign markets. They aren't flukes, and the techniques explained in Chapter 4 as well as Chapter 7 can help you find others. A bigger question is this: Can the American economy create and sustain the kind of conditions that lead to prosperity in a global economy? Can a nation that has lately been spending more wealth than it has been creating, making up the difference with borrowed money, find a way to mend its spendthrift ways?

Again, we believe that the answer is yes, not because Americans have changed in any basic way but because they haven't. The core of this apparent paradox lies in significant shifts in the country's population mix. Together with the streamlining of American business that has been taking place largely unnoticed for the past couple of decades, these shifts will constitute the most important influences on the American economy for the rest of this century and well into the next.

Middle-aged boomers. Baby-boomers are moving into middle age. They may not like the idea very much, but business economists are absolutely wild about it. The effects of the aging of this gigantic segment of the population can be expected to reverberate for the good throughout our economy for years to come. You'd have to assume a sea change in Americans' spending and saving habits to conclude otherwise.

The effects aren't difficult to grasp if you forget the big numbers for a moment and consider the various economic stages of a person's life. In the early years you're completely dependent on your parents for support, a stage that ends when you finish school and start supporting yourself. You don't make much money at first, so you tend to spend it all on rent, car payments, food and clothes, probably relying on a lot of credit to get you through. As you move into your thirties, you're still in what might be called the acquisition phase of your life. Somehow all the money gets spent. Statistics say that you've gotten married along the way and it takes the income of both you and your spouse just to keep the household running. You're doing a lot of spending supported by a lot of borrowing. Multiply yourself by about 70 million and you'll have a pretty good idea of what was happening to the American economy for much of the 1970s and '80s.

Now, as you approach your mid- to late-thirties, your priorities begin to change. You're further along in your career and making more money, but the demands on it are different. You've become a parent, and as the kids grow the reality of college expenses looms larger. The thought of retiring someday takes on meaning. As a result, you look for ways to save and invest money you used to spend without a second thought. You have entered the nest-egg-building years. Multiply yourself by about 70 million and you'll have a pretty good idea of what's going to be happening in the American economy for the next couple of decades:

■ The number of households headed by people between 35 and 44 years old will grow by about 20% by the year 2000, reaching nearly 24 million.

■ The number of households headed by people between 45 and 54 will grow by about 50% in the same period, reaching 20 million by the year 2000.

■ Households headed by 35- to 54-year-olds spend more on food, housing, clothes and practically every other category, *including* financial products and services (stocks and bonds, for instance) than households headed by any other age group.

■ The households closest to the 35- to 54-year-olds in terms of their volume of spending and saving are those that bracket both sides of that age group: They are headed by 55- to 64-year-olds and 25- to 34-year-olds. Both of those age groups are growing, too.

Enough jobs? Clearly the markets will be there for the goods and services that American companies sell. At the same time, demand can be expected to increase for the kinds of financial products people use to fund their college and retirement savings and investment plans. But a question remains: Where will they get the money to support all this spending and saving? Can the economy create enough jobs with incomes high enough for the new generation of middle-agers to afford to follow the pattern of past generations of middle-agers?

Again we say the answer is yes, and again the reason lies largely in the very population shifts just described. One effect of the huge number of baby-boomers hitting the job market in the 1970s and '80s was a clumping-up of workers at and near the entry level. This influx of inexperienced workers was responsible in part for the relatively poor productivity gains America experienced during those decades. (We say "in part" because the failure of American business to invest in new plants and equipment also played an important role in our relatively weak productivity growth.) Workers were plentiful—too plentiful, really—contributing to the dual problems that developed in the '80s: sluggish wage increases and high unemployment.

As the boomers have grown older, the pressure on the economy to generate millions and millions of entry-level jobs year after year has subsided because the younger population groups following behind the boomers are much smaller. This slower growth of the labor force tends to keep unemployment low and wages and salaries up. It's probable that the economy will generate more jobs than there are American-born workers to fill them, creating a growing demand for immigrants—a traditional source of strength for America.

Corporate America. Meanwhile, corporate America has been restructuring itself with the global economy in mind. For instance, the emphasis on quality by auto manufacturers is beginning to pay off. Although it will take a while longer to change public perceptions, U.S. cars should soon begin to win back buyers and regain market share.

The list of American companies that have slimmed down and reoriented themselves to compete in the global marketplace includes several that seemed to be in big trouble only a few years ago: Xerox, which has slashed the cost of manufacturing copiers; Cummins Engine, which has doubled productivity in its plants; Caterpillar, which managed to boost sales by a third while cutting its payroll by thousands. This abbreviated list doesn't include American companies that never lost their stature as world leaders in their fields: Boeing, Coca Cola, Hewlett-Packard, IBM, Merck, McDonald's and other global giants whose names are known everywhere.

As investments, companies such as these are worth investigating, applying the criteria explained in Chapter 4. The purpose of citing them here is to make a different point: that the rumors of America's death as a world economic power are greatly exaggerated. We are the world's leading exporter as well as the world's leading importer, and likely to retain both honors for as far into the future as anyone can see.

THE INVESTMENT CLIMATE AHEAD

Strong companies rooted in strong economies make good investments. When you assess the forces converging in the American economy in the years ahead, this is the picture that emerges:

■ *Inflation will be relatively tame,* thanks to a number of factors. Chief among them: a plentiful supply of oil that will keep energy prices in check not just for America but for the world; and fierce global competition that will keep prices in check. Figure on an average inflation rate of about 4% per year. That's something to be concerned about and to account for your investment plans, but 4% is a manageable level. For comparison, inflation averaged 7.4% per year in the 1970s and 5.2% in the '80s.

■ *Business productivity will rise* as the payoff from a decade of

reducing work forces and refocusing effort. Despite perceptions to the contrary, the U.S. is the world's leader in manufacturing productivity, and it solidified its hold on the top
position in the '80s, actually cutting labor costs while Japan's
soared when measured in terms of the dollar.

▌ *Interest rates will remain moderate.* Increased levels of saving
and investment will infuse the financial markets with enough
capital to finance business expansion without pushing rates
up. Meanwhile, marginal banks and thrifts will be weeded out,
taking pressure off stable institutions to compete for depositors
by offering higher-than-healthy rates on certificates.

▌ *Net: Our living standards will rise* as these trends take hold
and the global economy provides a growing marketplace for
the goods and services we want to buy and sell. This in turn
will generate growing profits for companies that compete
successfully—and for investors who can spot them in advance.
The rest of this book will help you do that.

3

How to Get More from Your Savings

I N CHAPTER 1, we recommended setting aside three to six months' living expenses in a safe place where the money earns interest and is easily accessible in case of an emergency. These are your savings, not your investments, and it's important to distinguish between the two. No one has ever explained the difference better than Will Rogers did: Forget about a return *on* my investment, he said, what I want is a return *of* my investment.

The key to a successful saving strategy is finding ways to increase the return on your money without having to worry about the return *of* your money.

A lot of people stash this rainy-day cash in a federally insured bank, credit union or thrift account and let it go at that. They may be a little uneasy about the relatively puny amount of interest adding up, but they're willing to live with less in exchange for the peace of mind that comes with knowing their money will be there when they need it.

Some states have created their own deposit insurance plans for savings and loan associations and credit unions operating within their borders. The spectacular collapse of state systems covering some savings and loan associations in Ohio and Maryland in 1985, and the sudden closing of state-insured credit unions in Rhode Island in 1991 serve as loud warnings: Do not put your money in any bank or savings and loan that is not insured by the Federal Deposit Insurance Corporation (FDIC), or in any credit union that is not insured by the National Credit Union Administration.

A safety-above-all-else approach to saving makes sense for a portion of your savings, but relying on it exclusively short-changes you and your family. You generate less money to transfer to an investment account, where you have the chance to earn a greater return. Sometimes such a practice can even cause you to *lose* money after inflation and taxes have taken their share of your earnings.

THE COST OF DOING NOTHING

If you've been letting a lot of your money languish in a minimum-interest savings account, welcome to a very large club. As America headed into the 1990s, savers had $215 billion sitting in passbook or statement savings accounts that were earning around 5%. If all the country's savers were to move all that cash to bank money-market accounts paying about 6%, they'd earn an additional $2.15 billion a year. If they switched all of their savings from passbook accounts to money-market funds yielding around 7%, they'd be $4.3 billion richer in a year. And if they all transferred their passbook money to certificates paying 8%, as a group they would soon be nearly $6.5 billion richer.

Lucky for you, it's not going to happen. If passbook savers suddenly started moving great gobs of their money into higher-paying accounts, those accounts would soon be paying less. But because most people won't take the trouble to do it, the opportunity is yours. Somewhere in the spectrum of low-risk savings vehicles, you can almost certainly find one that will pay you more than you're earning now without measurably increasing your risk.

HOW TO GET THE MOST FROM CERTIFICATES OF DEPOSIT

Certificates of deposit, or CDs, are a staple of many savers' and investors' portfolios. Available at banks, savings and loans, and credit unions, CDs are insured up to $100,000 and they pay a higher-than-passbook rate of interest in return for your commitment to leave the money on deposit with the institution for a specified time, commonly from a minimum of a month or so to a maximum of five years. The longer you commit your money, and in some cases the more money you commit, the more you earn. The interest rate is usually fixed but may be variable, pegged to a market rate, such as the prime rate. Minimum denominations are often $500 to $1,000.

CDs have a lot to offer the safety- and yield-minded saver. Virtually the only catch is that if you need the money before the CD matures, you'll pay a penalty that could eliminate the advantage you thought you were getting from the higher rate.

By shutting down so many unhealthy banks and savings and loans that were paying sky-high rates to attract desperately needed depositors, federal regulators have taken the pressure off healthy institutions to offer similar rates. That makes the job of locating higher yields a little tougher. It can be worth the effort, though: Interest rates for CDs with similar maturities can vary by a percentage point or more. On large amounts especially, the added interest can make a big difference.

▋ *Shop around.* You can often find a better deal simply by shopping around in your local area, either by reading the ads in the paper or telephoning local institutions.

To get an idea of rates being paid around the country, consult the Friday *Wall Street Journal,* which publishes a list of representative rates supplied by Banxquote Money Markets. You can contact the institutions listed there for information about making a deposit, or you can use the information as a negotiating tool with your bank if its rates are significantly lower. Suggest that you will send your money away unless your bank offers a better rate.

■ *Know the bank.* Actually, you should think twice about sending your money out of town in quest of a higher yield. Don't do it for a fraction of a percentage point on a relatively modest amount of money. Your deposit isn't any more at risk in a federally insured institution in some other state, as long as it doesn't exceed the FDIC's ceiling of $100,000 per person per institution. But it's difficult enough to determine whether a local bank is solvent, let alone an out-of-state bank. If the institution is taken over by another, the new institution has the option of lowering the rate on your CD, and it probably will. There is usually a two-week grace period, although federal regulators have allowed rates to drop immediately in some cases. You could withdraw your money if that happens, which could cost you a few days' interest while you find someplace else to put it. To reduce that risk, keep your out-of-town money in short-term accounts—say, three months or less.

You can find names of banks and s&l's paying the most generous yields in specialized publications that gather such information. Three of the best known are *100 Highest Yields* (P.O. Box 088888, N. Palm Beach, Fla. 33408; phone 407-627-7330); *Rate Watch* (P.O. Drawer 145510, Coral Gables, Fla. 33114; phone 305 441-2062); and *RateGram* (253 Channing Way, Suite 13, San Rafael, Cal. 94903-2605; phone 415-479-3815). Names of institutions you get from those publications can be checked for financial stability through Veribanc (800-442-2657), which will tell you its safety rating of financial institutions over the telephone for a charge of $10 for one, $3 for each additional rating. *Rate Watch* will also send you its evaluation of all the banks and s&l's in your state for $25 ($35 for Texas or Illinois), or one institution's rating for $10.

■ *Buy from a broker.* A brokerage firm can generally offer you an above-average yield on a federally insured CD: about half a percentage point to a point or more higher than average, depending on the market at the time and on the maturity of the certificate. Because issuing banks pay a fee to brokers who parcel out their CDs this way, the customer usually doesn't

DEPOSIT INSURANCE FOR ORGANIZATIONS

Q: *I am on a church board, and we are "shopping" for a new bank. We're going into a building program, and will have big deposits. This question came up in the process: Are we insured?*

A: Yes. Funds deposited by a corporation, partnership or unincorporated association are insured up to a maximum of $100,000. Such funds are insured separately from the personal accounts of the stockholders, partners, or members.

have to pay a commission. And because brokerage firms that do this sort of packaging usually maintain an active secondary market for their CDs, you can often sell them back before maturity without paying the penalty a bank or s&l would charge for early withdrawal.

There are two possible traps here, and both are avoidable:

First, in the search for an attractive yield, the broker packaging the deal may buy up CDs from institutions you'd rather not do business with yourself. To avoid this situation, ask the broker where the CD originated and what the brokerage firm knows about the stability of the issuing institution and the status of its federal deposit insurance. And beware: As this book was going to press, Congress was threatening to terminate federal insurance coverage for brokered CDs.

Second, the privilege of cashing in your CD early with no penalty may bear a different price. If interest rates rise between the day you purchase the CD and the day you cash it in early, you won't get back as much as you paid for it. (On the other hand, if rates have fallen, you should get more.) This is because a CD in the secondary market is in many respects a short-term bond, and the usual relationship between bond values and market rates will be at work: When interest rates rise, the value of outstanding bonds falls; when rates fall, bond values rise.

For more on this relationship, see Chapter 5.

■ *Take advantage of gimmicks.* Some banks and s&l's have devised yield-boosting gimmicks to attract new money. A popular one is the "bump-up" CD. On a bump-up, banks promise to increase the rate they're paying on your CD if interest rates rise during the CD's term. Another kind of bump-up promises a yield a fraction of a percentage point higher every time you roll over the original six-month CD into a new one. In the latter deal, your initial rate is almost surely lower than the rate being offered on a CD without the bump-up feature. You'd probably be better off locking in the higher rate to begin with.

In assessing a bump-up, it's important to be aware that the deal is usually crafted to favor the bank. Whether the rate goes up, and by how much, may be entirely at the bank's discretion. A better deal is one in which you have the option to switch to the higher rate if the bank boosts the rate it's offering on a CD with the same maturity as one you're holding. In that kind of arrangement, it's up to you to keep track of the bank's current CD rates.

An even better deal on a bump-up is one on which the rate is tied to an independent index rather than one that's controlled by the bank or by you. But it's still up to you to keep track of which way rates are headed and decide when to lock in a new, higher rate.

■ *Protect yourself by staggering maturities.* The best way to maintain the liquidity of your savings, boost yield and protect yourself against rapid rate changes is to stagger the maturity dates of your CDs. Sometimes called "laddering," staggering maturities is really a form of diversification. You spread your money over several different maturities: say, one fourth of your CD funds in certificates maturing in three months, one fourth in CDs maturing in six months, one fourth in CDs maturing in a year and one fourth in CDs maturing in two or three years. (A profitable rule of thumb based on the history of interest rate movements: If five-year CD rates ever reach 10%, stock up on them.)

Normally, the longer maturities pay more interest, so why not just concentrate on those? In fact, that would be a splendid strategy if you could accurately predict the direction of interest rates and your prediction was that they were going to fall. But what if they rise? By staggering your maturities, you have protected yourself in either case. If rates rise, your short-term CDs will mature in time for you to reinvest the principal at the new, higher rates. If rates fall, or stay flat, you'll be sitting pretty because you've locked in the current two- or three-year rate. By the time those certificates mature, rates could well have turned in the other direction again.

THE LIMITED APPEAL OF MONEY-MARKET DEPOSIT ACCOUNTS

One place to get federal insurance plus interest that's somewhere between a passbook account and a CD is in a money-market deposit account (MMDA). Banks and thrifts like to boast about the higher rates paid by these accounts, but in fact they don't compete very well with certificates, which routinely pay a couple of percentage points more.

In fact, MMDAs probably compete more directly with low-rate savings accounts and interest-paying checking accounts, except for all the strings attached. You can write a limited number of checks on the account and make a limited number of withdrawals; if you exceed the limit, you pay a penalty. These limits on liquidity, coupled with the low rates generally paid by MMDAs compared with money-market mutual funds, add up to a high premium to pay for federal insurance, considering the excellent safety record of the uninsured money-market funds.

WHY YOU SHOULD USE MONEY-MARKET FUNDS

The reason you want to have a piece of the money market through a money-market fund is that it normally pays two or three percentage points higher than savings accounts with no appreciable increase in risk. Minimum initial investment is often $1,000 or less, for which you get a slice of a portfolio containing a number of investments you could never afford on your own.

Money-market mutual funds take your cash and invest it in the money market, which is a collective name that describes all the different ways in which governments, banks, corporations and securities dealers borrow and lend money for short periods. Money-market loans may be due in a few days, a few weeks or a few months, but never more than a year. Thus, short-term certificates of deposit are considered to be in the money market. Treasury bills, which mature in three, six, nine or 12 months, are money-market instruments; Treasury bonds, which mature in ten or more years, are not.

A typical money-market portfolio contains a variety of short-term investments. *Certificates of deposit* are among the favorites, along with *commercial paper* (short-term corporate IOUs); *Treasury bills and notes* (government IOUs) within a few months of maturity; *federal agency securities* (short-term debts issued by agencies such as the Federal National Mortgage Association); and a couple of somewhat esoteric instruments known as *banker's acceptances* (used to finance international commercial transactions) and *repurchase agreements,* often called repos, which are ways of selling financial holdings for a day or two with a pledge to buy them back at a higher price. Money funds also invest in Eurodollar CDs (issued by the foreign branches of U.S. banks), and Yankeedollar CDs (issued by U.S. branches of foreign banks). Some pay tax-free earnings because they invest exclusively in short-term municipal bonds issued by state and local governments.

One of the most attractive features of money funds is that you can sell your shares anytime by writing a check drawn on your account. You pay no sales fees either buying or selling. The funds' managers, who decide which money-market instruments to buy, charge a modest management fee, on the order of 1% or so. All that makes the funds liquid, convenient and relatively economical to own. But money-market funds often engage in transactions that individual savers and investors comprehend only dimly, if at all. Thus it is important to know what could go wrong with them, how likely it is to happen and how you might be hurt if something does go wrong.

Are they safe? Actually, money-market funds have a reputation for being about the safest uninsured, non-Treasury investment around, and it's a well-earned reputation. Since they were created in 1972, no investor has lost a cent of principal in any of the hundreds of funds you now have to choose from. So safe are they thought to be that savers and investors have stashed some $400 billion into them.

This safety record was built partly on restrictions that govern the funds and partly on the fund sponsors' determination to keep the public's faith in funds strong.

Securities laws dictate that the average maturity of a money fund's holdings may not exceed 120 days, and any individual debt instrument owned by a fund must mature within 12 months. Short maturities help insulate the value of money funds from movements in interest rates. (Prices of interest-paying investments such as bonds fall when rates rise, and vice versa; the shorter the maturity, the smaller the move.)

This relative stability allows money funds to keep the value of their shares constant from day to day (almost always $1), even though, in fact, net asset values do fluctuate a little. Under a widely accepted accounting procedure known as "penny rounding," a fund may report a value of $1 a share as long as its actual value does not drop below $0.995 per share or rise above $1.005.

The short maturities also make it unlikely that a fund will be caught holding the debt of an issuer that gets into financial trouble. If a fund buys 30-day commercial paper issued by an apparently healthy company, chances are slim that the firm's financial condition will deteriorate so quickly that it defaults before the debt matures.

continued on page 47

MONEY-MARKET FUNDS: A STARTER KIT

Here is a sampling of the hundreds of money market funds available to investors today. The funds on this list are among the largest in each category and most have well-established track records for safety and performance. The best way to choose a fund you'll like is to identify several that fit your objectives, telephone for prospectuses and make your choice based on investor services that fit your needs.

GENERAL TAXABLE FUNDS	Minimum Initial Deposit	Minimum Check Size
American Express Daily Dividend 800-872-1166	$ 2,500	$ 250
Cash Equivalent 800-621-1148	1,000	250
Centennial Daily Cash Accumulation 800-525-7048	500	250
Dean Witter/Sears Liquid Asset 800-869-3863	5,000	500
Dreyfus Liquid Assets 800-782-6620	2,500	500
Dreyfus Worldwide Dollar Money Market 800-782-6620	2,500	500
Fidelity Cash Reserves 800-544-8888	2,500	500
Fidelity Spartan Money Market 800-544-8888	20,000	1,000
IDS Cash Management 800-222-9700	2,000	500
Kemper Money Market 800-621-1048	1,000	500

GENERAL TAXABLE FUNDS	Minimum Initial Deposit	Minimum Check Size
Kidder, Peabody Webster Cash Reserve 212-510-5050	$ 1,500	no checks
Merrill Lynch CMA Money 800-262-4636	20,000	no minimum
Merrill Lynch Ready Assets Trust 800-221-7210	5,000	500
Oppenheimer Money Market 800-525-7048	1,000	100
PaineWebber Cash 800-762-1000	5,000	500
Prudential-Securities MoneyMart Assets 800-225-1852	1,000	500
Reserve 800-223-5547	1,000	500
Schwab Money Market 800-227-4444	1,000	no checks
Scudder Cash Investment Trust 800-225-2470	1,000	100
T. Rowe Price Prime Reserve 800-638-5660	2,500	500
Vanguard Money Market Reserves Prime 800-662-7447	3,000	250

continued

GOVERNMENT-ONLY FUNDS	Minimum Initial Deposit	Minimum Check Size
Capital Preservation 800-472-3389	$ 1,000	100
Cash Equivalent Fund/Government 800-621-1048	1,000	250
Dreyfus 100% U.S. Treasury 800-782-6620	2,500	500
Fidelity U.S. Government Reserves 800-544-8888	2,500	500
Merrill Lynch USA Government Reserves 800-221-7210	5,000	500
Vanguard Money Market Reserves Federal 800-662-7447	3,000	250

TAX-FREE FUNDS	Minimum Initial Deposit	Minimum Check Size
American Express Daily Tax-Free 800-872-1166	$ 2,500	250
Calvert Tax-Free Reserves 800-368-2748	2,000	250
Merrill Lynch CMA Tax-Exempt 800-262-4636	20,000	500
Dreyfus Municipal Money Market 800-782-6620	2,500	500
Fidelity Tax-Exempt Money-Market Trust 800-544-8888	5,000	no minimum
USAA Tax-Exempt Money Market 800-531-8181	3,000	250
Vanguard Municipal Bond/Money Market 800-662-7447/800-662-2739	3,000	250

Default risks. But a slim chance doesn't mean no chance. In June 1989, Value Line Cash Fund and Liquid Green Trust, two smallish money-market funds, found themselves holding large amounts of suddenly worthless commercial paper issued by Integrated Resources, Inc., a financial services company that defaulted on some $1 billion worth of short-term debt. Then, in March of the following year, ten other money funds got stuck with more than $75 million in commercial paper issued by Mortgage & Realty Trust (MRT) when that real estate investment trust defaulted and filed for reorganization under the bankruptcy laws.

T. Rowe Price's huge Prime Reserve money-market fund held $41.7 million of MRT paper, representing 0.8% of the fund's assets. Alliance Money Reserve fund owned $8.7 million worth of MRT paper in its $1 billion portfolio. Another fund, Heritage Cash Trust, was hit even harder, holding $12 million worth of short-term MRT IOUs, representing 1.6% of the fund's assets.

In each case, the fund's sponsor bought back the failed debt at face value and swallowed the losses so that shareholders wouldn't be hurt, keeping the money-market fund industry's safety record intact.

But what if a sponsor didn't have the money to bail out a floundering fund? William Donoghue, publisher of *IBC/Donoghue's Money Fund Report* and a leading booster of money funds, says he has been told privately that the industry would arrange a bailout or acquisition of any sponsor that couldn't make the grade. Industry officials deny it—perhaps because it's not true, perhaps because they don't wish to hand fund managers the same kind of blank check to make risky investments that the government's deposit insurance gave to the owners of savings and loans.

After the Integrated Resources and MRT defaults, many managers began weeding out all but the highest-rated commercial paper—that rated A-1 by Standard & Poor's and P-1 by Moody's Investors Service. That is no guarantee that some won't be caught again, but it has served to reduce the chances.

Interest rate risks. There is another way funds can get clobbered—by a sudden spike in interest rates. When rates soar upward, even the relatively short-term holdings of money funds can suffer a decline in value so severe that the fund has difficulty maintaining its net asset value. The longer the average maturity of the fund at the time of the spike, the greater the danger. If investors flee from the fund in search of higher yield elsewhere, forcing a sale of holdings at distress prices, the problem is compounded.

In 1980 a money fund called Institutional Liquid Assets lengthened the average maturity of its assets just as a quick run-up in interest rates was starting. The fund suffered a $2 million loss on its $1.4 billion portfolio after institutional customers bailed out in droves. In this case, the fund's distributor and adviser came up with the cash to maintain the fund's $1 share value.

The experience hasn't deterred all fund managers from betting heavily on the direction rates will move. One of the top-performing money funds in 1989, Harbor Money Market Fund, achieved its rank by extending its average maturity at one point to 116 days, just four days short of the maximum permitted by the SEC. Then, as rates began to fall, Harbor was able to maintain its higher yield longer than funds with much shorter average maturities. Had rates climbed instead of falling, the fund's yield would have fallen noticeably behind the competition.

Impact of a rate spike today. What would happen if a fund got caught in a rate bind these days? What would it take to do real damage? A fund with an average maturity of 60 days could suffer a half-cent loss of net asset value if short-term rates were to quickly ratchet up three percentage points, according to Standard & Poor's. In fact, says S&P, short-term rates in the U.S. have surged as much as four percentage points in as few as five days. The share value of a fund with an average maturity of 100 days would drop a half cent if rates jumped two points within a few days.

For all this, the odds of losing principal in a money fund remain very slight. A fund would have to suffer several defaults among its holdings or own a portfolio with an extremely long average maturity at a time when rates suddenly skyrocketed. Furthermore, the fund's sponsor would have to abandon the industry's unwritten policy of bailing out money funds in the event of a loss. Even in such circumstances, losses to investors would be modest, probably on the order of 1% or 2%. That's a small enough chance to take compared with the dead certainty of losing out on one, two or more percentage points of yield by keeping all your money in a savings account or a bank money-market deposit account.

Playing it super safe. To diminish the risks even further, follow these routes to the safest money-market funds. As you do, remember that each restriction you place on a fund can, under certain market conditions, hold down the yield. Government-only funds, for instance, pay slightly less than others because their portfolios are safer. For a list of money-market funds that fit the descriptions below, see pages 44-46.

▌ *To limit the risk of default,* check the prospectus carefully to see what kinds of debt the fund will buy. If the fund invests in commercial paper, make sure that it is limited to issues receiving the highest ratings (they will be labeled A-1 and P-1) from the major rating services. Call the fund and ask about its current policy, which may be more or less conservative than is permitted by the prospectus. Standard & Poor's follows several dozen money-market funds and ranks them for safety. For a list of the ratings, write to Standard & Poor's, Mutual Fund Rankings Group, 20th Floor, 25 Broadway, New York, N.Y. 10004.

▌ *To eliminate the default risk entirely,* look for funds that invest only in government securities. Some of these invest in a variety of government-backed issues, such as Treasury bills, debts of government agencies such as the Federal Farm Credit Bank, and repurchase agreements backed by Treasury issues. Another type of government-only fund buys just Treasury bills—the ultimate in credit safety.

■ *To control interest rate risk,* look into the fund's policy on average maturity of its portfolio. Most prospectuses allow money funds to extend maturities to the maximum 120 days. As a matter of policy, however, many funds keep average maturities at 40 to 60 days. You can also find current average maturities in tables of money-fund yields, which are published weekly in many newspapers.

SHIFT SOME CASH INTO SHORT-TERM TREASURIES

If you have accumulated more than $10,000 in savings, you should consider eliminating the management fees charged by money-market funds by owning Treasury bills yourself. T-bills and other securities issued by the U.S. Treasury are even safer than CDs because they're backed by the full faith and credit of the federal government. For that reason, they generally yield a little less than CDs, but they still have a couple of advantages.

For one thing, rates are determined by the market rather than by a rate-setting committee at a bank. For another, Treasuries are exempt from state and local income taxes, which can be a definite benefit in high-tax states such as California, Massachusetts and New York.

How to buy them. You can buy T-bills from a bank or a broker for a modest fee, and there is one good reason to consider doing so. Banks and brokers are selling bills from their own inventory, which is likely to contain a variety of maturities. New bills mature in three, six, nine or 12 months. That's a nice variety, but the timing may not be to your liking. Suppose you know you're going to need the money in three weeks? Or five months? Theoretically, a bank or a broker should be able to find you a bill that matures within a few days of when you want your money back.

If timing isn't that important, you can save the $25 or so a broker would charge by buying directly from the Treasury. To purchase T-bills, which come in maturities of one year or less, you fill out a simple form and send a certified check or cashier's check for $10,000 (the minimum investment) to the government. For information on how to do this and on purchasing other securities directly from the government, see the more detailed discussion and the list of Federal Reserve banks and branches in Chapter 5.

One note of caution: Although Treasury securities that you buy yourself are not subject to state and local taxes, you can't assume the same is true for dividends earned through a U.S. government securities mutual fund. At least five states—Connecticut, Mississippi, North Dakota, Pennsylvania and Tennessee—don't exempt fund earnings from state tax. In states that do, only funds that limit their investments to securities issued directly by the Treasury and certain government agencies qualify for exemption.

SAVING WITH SAVINGS BONDS

The Series EE savings bond is also an excellent saving vehicle. As long as you hold it for at least five years, it pays a market rate of interest, which is guaranteed not to fall below 6%. Interest is free of state and local taxes and federal taxes can be deferred until you cash it in. Interest earned on bonds purchased in your name may escape income taxes entirely if you use the proceeds to pay college tuition and fees for your children and meet certain income tests, which are described in Chapter 13.

Because savings bonds must be held for at least five years, they don't meet the liquidity test you should apply to your emergency fund. But they can be a valuable part of your long-term savings and investment strategy and are described in greater detail in Chapter 5.

THE WAY TO WEALTH
WITH STOCKS

I F IT'S WEALTH you want, look to the stock market. No other investment available to intelligent amateurs with average resources, an average willingness to take risks and a limited amount of time to spend on active management delivers as well as stocks over the long run. Not real estate. Not gold. Not bonds. And certainly not savings accounts. Stocks aren't the only things that belong in your investment portfolio, but they are the most important.

Probably the best study of comparative investment results ever undertaken was done by Roger Ibbotson and Rex Sinquefield, who delved into records going back to 1926. They calculated the compound annual returns (including reinvested dividends and interest) of large- and small-company stocks, corporate and government bonds, and Treasury bills. Ibbotson and Sinquefield then matched all the returns against each other and, for good measure, against the inflation rate.

The graphs on page 55 show the results through 1990, a period that includes the two biggest stock market crashes in history, plus the Great Depression. Stocks win by a large margin, with small-company stocks edging out those of big companies by a couple of percentage points. Even that small difference looms large when it is compounded over the years: $1,000 growing at 10% a year for 20 years becomes about $6,700. At 12%, it becomes $9,600. During the 65-year period covered by the graph, $1,000 invested in a representative sampling of big stocks would have grown to an eye-catching $490,000. That same $1,000 riding along with small stocks would have become more than $1,500,000.

That's quite impressive, but unless your main concern is the financial welfare of your great grandchildren, you'd probably prefer a somewhat faster pace. So here's the good news: *These results actually understate the long-term return you can reasonably expect to earn from stocks.*

Why is this so? Because the 10% return from big-company stocks is based on the performance of all the companies in the S&P 500 Composite Index and a similar, earlier index, with no attempt to separate the good companies from the bad. Same goes for the 12% return from small-company stocks. It is the average from a representative portfolio of stocks of the smallest companies the authors could find, whether they performed well or terribly. If you can pick better-than-average stocks, you will beat the average return.

What's more, the payoff from even mediocre stocks often beats the long-term averages, which, remember, cover bad times as well as good. From 1985 through 1989, the return on the 30 big-company stocks that make up the Dow Jones industrial average topped 22% per year with dividends reinvested, and the 500 stocks in the S&P 500 followed close behind. For the '80s as a whole, Dow stocks returned 18% per year (the S&P 500 returned 17%), and in the 15-year period from 1975 through 1989, both the Dow and the S&P returned an average of about 16% per year.

This chapter will show you how to pick good stocks that can reasonably be expected to beat the averages during a decade in which it is reasonable to expect the stock market to generate better-than-average returns. You don't have to beat the market

STOCKS ARE THE LONG-TERM WINNERS

Whether you take the long-term view represented by the graph on the top or the extra-long-term view, shown in the graph on the bottom, it's clear that stocks beat other financial assets, and that the stocks of small companies tend to outperform the stocks of large companies. Since 1961, small-company stocks returned 13.5%, on average, while large-company stocks topped 10%. The figures reflect <u>total return</u>, which means that any dividends or interest paid by the investment being measured were plowed back into the same investment.

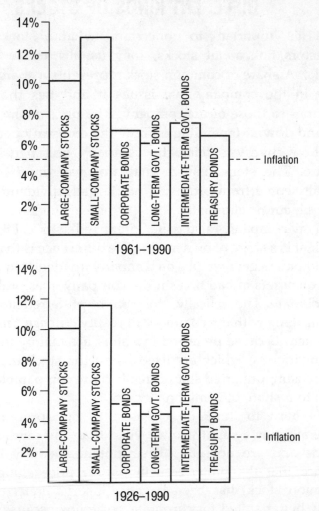

Source: Ibbotson Associates

by much to prosper over time. A reasonable target is to do five percentage points better than the market. By that measure, you ought to be able to earn an average return of 15% to 17%—not every single year, but on average. There is risk involved, as there is in all investments, but if you stick to the techniques described in this book, you can minimize those risks.

DIFFERENT KINDS OF STOCKS

First it's important to understand what a stock *is*. When investors talk about stocks, they usually mean "common" stocks. A share of common stock represents a share of ownership in the company that issues it and ties the investor's fortunes to those of the company. The price of the stock goes up and down, depending on how the company performs and on how investors *think* the company will perform in the future. The stock may or may not pay dividends, which usually come from profits. If profits fall, dividend payments may be cut or eliminated.

Many companies also issue "preferred" stock. Like common stock, it is a share of ownership. The difference is that preferred stockholders get first dibs on company dividends in good times and on assets in bad times if the company goes broke and has to liquidate. Theoretically, the price of preferred stock can rise or fall along with the common. In reality it doesn't move nearly as much, because preferred investors are mainly interested in the dividends, which are fixed when the stock is issued. For this reason, preferred stock is really more comparable to a bond than to a share of common stock.

It's hard to think of a reason to buy preferreds. They generally pay a slightly lower yield than the same company's bonds and are no safer. Their potential equity kicker (the chance that the preferred will rise in price along with the common stock) has been largely illusory. Preferred stock is really better suited for corporate portfolios because a corporation doesn't have to pay federal income tax on most of the dividends it receives from another corporation. This chapter will concentrate on common stocks.

Stocks are bought and sold on one or more of several "stock markets," the best known of which are the New York Stock Exchange (NYSE) and the American Stock Exchange (AMEX), or through a widely dispersed telecommunications system known as Nasdaq, which stands for the National Association of Securities Dealers Automated Quotation System. There are also several regional exchanges, ranging from Boston to Honolulu. Stocks sold on an exchange are said to be "listed" there; stocks sold through Nasdaq are called "over-the-counter" (OTC) stocks.

There are lots of reasons to own stocks and several different categories of stocks to fit investors' goals. Sometimes the reasons for buying a particular kind of stock are obvious from the definition of the category.

■ *Growth stocks* have good prospects for growing faster than the economy or the stock market in general. Investors buy them because of their good record of earnings growth and the expectation that it will continue generating capital gains over the long haul. More stocks seem to fit this definition than you can shake a stick at, ranging from the very well known and much commented-upon, such as ketchup-maker H.J. Heinz and department store operator Wal-Mart Stores, to the comparatively obscure, such as Luby's Cafeterias, which operates only in the Sunbelt states.

■ *Blue-chip stocks* are a more loosely defined universe, including solid performers that could also be classified as growth stocks, such as IBM and Coca-Cola. Investors with an eye on the long term and little tolerance for risk buy these stocks for their undeniable high quality. They tend to generate decent dividend income, some growth and, above all, safety and reliability.

■ *Income stocks* worthy of the name pay relatively high dividends and raise them regularly. Electric utilities, automobile manufacturers and banks often fall into this category, which is favored by retirees and others in need of a relatively high level of income from their stocks.

▌ *Cyclical stocks* are called that because their fortunes tend to rise and fall with those of the economy at large, prospering when the business cycle is on the upswing, suffering in recessions. Automobile manufacturers are a prime example, which illustrates the important fact that these categories aren't mutually exclusive. Other industries whose profits are sensitive to the business cycle include airlines, steel, chemicals and any business dependent on homebuilding.

▌ *Defensive stocks* are theoretically insulated from the business cycle because people go right on buying their products and services in bad times as well as good. Utility companies fit here (another overlap), as do companies that sell food, beverages and drugs. The major problem with this category is that to maximize profits, you need to buy them on the verge of an economic downturn, which requires an ability to predict that is rare even among experts.

▌ *Speculative stocks* don't pass the usual tests of quality (such as those laid out later in this chapter) but for some reason or another attract investors anyway. They may be unproven young companies (which may be dubbed "emerging growth" stocks). They may be erratic or down-at-the-heels old companies exhibiting some sort of spark, such as the promise of an imminent technological breakthrough or brilliant new product. Buyers of speculative stocks have hopes of making a killing but almost never do. Most speculative stocks don't do well, so it takes big gains in a few to offset your losses in the many.

KIPLINGER'S WAY TO BUY STOCKS

The secret to choosing good common stocks is that there is no secret to it. The winning techniques are tried and true; it's how you assemble and apply them that makes the difference. The techniques don't work all the time, but they work often enough so that the methods employed by successful stock investors tend to be more alike than they are different.

Information is the key. Having the right information about a company and knowing how to interpret it are more important than any of the other factors you might hear credited for the success of the latest market genius. Information is even more important than timing. When you find a company that looks promising, you don't have to buy the stock today or this week or even this month. Good stocks tend to stay good, so you can take the time to investigate before you invest.

You get the information you need to size up a company's prospects in many places, and a lot of it is free. The listing on the following pages offers a guide to the most readily available sources of the data described below.

What You Need to Know

The Kiplinger way to succeed in the stock market is to invest for growth and "value." That means concentrating the bulk of your portfolio in stocks that pass the tests described below and holding them for the long term—three, five, even ten years. For those in search of income, not growth, it means applying the same tests so that you don't make any false and risky assumptions about the stocks you buy. The Kiplinger way is *not* based on buying a stock one day and selling it the next. It does *not* depend on your ability to predict the direction of the economy or even the direction of the stock market. It *does* depend on your willingness to apply the following measures before you place your order. If you do that, you'll find most of your choices falling into the growth, income and blue chip categories described above. The aim: an average 15% to 17% annual return on your investments when the market is performing in its historical range, plus the opportunity for much bigger gains when the economic forces described in Chapter 2 push it to much greater heights.

You'll have no trouble finding candidates for your investment dollars. Brokers are full of suggestions, of course, and

continued on page 62

WHERE TO GET THE FACTS YOU NEED

This chapter recommends using certain key facts about a company to size up prospects for its stock. Here's where to find those facts. In most cases you won't need more than one or two of the sources listed.

Source	What's in it and where to get it
Company's annual report	Basic information about the company, including audited financial data for the most recent year and summaries of prior years. Available from: Brokers, investor relations offices of the company.
Form 10K	Extensive financial data, required to be filed annually with the Securities and Exchange Commission. Includes two years' worth of detailed, audited financial balance sheets, plus five-year history of stock price, earnings, dividends and other data. Available from: The SEC in Washington, D.C. To order copies ($30 each), call Disclosure Information Services at 800-638-8241.
Analysts' Report	Commentaries by brokerage firms' research departments, containing varying amounts of hard data to accompany the analysts' recommendations to buy, sell or hold stocks followed by the firm. Available from: Brokers.
Value Line Investment Survey	A vast collection of data, including prices, earnings and dividends, stretching back as far as 16 years, along with analysis and several unique features, such as a "timeliness" rating for each stock. Follows 1,700 stocks. Available from: Libraries, or from Value Line for $525 a year (trial subscriptions are $65): Order from the company, 711 Third Ave., New York, NY 10017, or call 800-633-2252.
Standard & Poor's	S&P *Stock Reports* offer a wealth of current and historical data in 12 loose-leaf volumes. The monthly S&P *Stock Guide* is a compendium of similar data on more than 5,000 stocks, but with no analyst's commentary. At $112 for a year's subscription (often discounted), the *Guide* provides most of the hard data you need to check out a company.

Source	What's in it and where to get it
	Available from: Libraries, brokers or by subscription from S&P, 25 Broadway, New York, NY 10004, phone 800-221-5277.
Moody's Investors Services	*Moody's Manuals* are eight volumes containing current and historical data on thousands of companies. The *Handbook of Common Stocks* covers about 1,000 stocks, and the *Dividend Record* keeps track of current dividend payments of most publicly traded companies. The *Handbook of Dividend Achievers* is widely used by individual investors.Available from: Brokers, libraries or from Moody's, 99 Church St., New York, NY 10007, phone 800-342-5647, ext. 0435.
Financial newspapers	The stock listings of the *Wall Street Journal, Barron's* and *Investor's Daily* contain current information on prices, dividends, yields and price-earnings ratios, as do the stock listings of most daily newspapers. What sets these three apart is the accompanying depth of coverage of the investment markets. Available from: Newsstands, libraries or by subscription.
Computer on-line databases	There are several, the best known of which is probably Investext, which provides historical and current data, information on file at the Securities and Exchange Commission, market news, analysts' reports and other features. Available from: Dow Jones News/Retrieval and Compuserve database services or by subscription from Thomson Financial Networks (800-662-7878). Users pay about $2 a minute, plus a per search charge. The Prodigy on-line service offers an extensive stock databank for a flat monthly charge (800-776-3449).

you may come across intriguing products or companies while walking through a store or leafing through a newspaper. Or your eye may be caught by one of the gorgeous "corporate image" ads that run in upscale magazines. Most of the information you need to check out these possibilities is readily available from the sources listed on pages 60 and 61 or can be calculated from the data you find there.

You'll quickly discover that the number of stocks that meet all these tests at any given time will be low. So what you're really looking for are stocks that exhibit most of the following signs of value and come close on the others.

Earnings. This is the company's bottom line—the profits earned after taxes and payment of dividends to holders of preferred stock. Dividing earnings by the average number of common stock shares outstanding during the period being measured gives you *earnings per share,* a key number for evaluating any company. Earnings are also the company's chief resource for paying dividends to shareholders and for reinvesting in business growth. In the annual report, check to be sure that earnings come from routine operations—say, widget sales —and not from one-time occurrences—say, the sale of a subsidiary or a big award from a patent-infringement suit. The exhaustive stock listings in *Barron's* give the latest quarterly earnings per share for each stock, plus the date when the next earnings will be declared. Historical earnings figures are available in annual reports as well as the S&P, Moody's and Value Line publications.

Value Sign #1: Look for companies with a pattern of earnings growth over at least five years and a habit of reinvesting at least 35% of earnings in the expansion of the business. The reinvestment rate can be determined by comparing earnings per share with the dividend payout. The portion that isn't paid out to shareholders gets reinvested in the business.

Price-earnings ratio. The price-earnings ratio is probably the single most important thing you can know about a stock. It is the price of a share divided by the company's earnings per share. If a stock sells for $40 a share and the company earned $4 a share in the previous 12 months, the stock has a P/E ratio of 10. Simply put, the P/E ratio tells you how much money investors are willing to pay for each dollar of a company's earnings. It is such a significant key to value that it's listed every day in the papers along with every stock's price.

Any company's P/E needs to be compared with those of similar companies and with broader measures as well. Market indexes such as the Dow Jones industrials and the S&P 500 have P/E's, as do different industry sectors, such as chemicals or autos. Knowing what these are can help you decide on the relative merits of a stock you're considering. Standard & Poor's 500-stock index tends to have a P/E in the low teens—that's the combined price of its 500 component companies divided by their combined earnings. Analysts would say that a stock with a P/E, or "multiple," of 10 trades at a *discount* to the market, because its P/E ratio is lower than that of the market as a whole. By the same token, a stock with a P/E of 20 is said to be trading at a *premium*, which means that its P/E is higher than the market's.

In addition to allowing you to judge a stock's comparative worth, knowing the P/E of the S&P 500 or the Dow Jones industrials can give you a clue to the bigger picture. A typical range for the P/E of the S&P 500 is 13 to 15 during a rising, or bull, market and 8 to 10 in a declining, or bear, market. When the S&P sports a P/E of 22 or thereabouts, as it did shortly before the stock market crash of October 1987, it's wise to cut back on new stock purchases or even lighten up on your holdings in expectation of a fall to a more sustainable level.

As you might expect, investors are willing to pay more to own shares of companies they think will increase their profits faster than the average company. But high-P/E stocks carry the risk that if the company's earnings disappoint investors, its share price may plunge quickly. Just one poor quarter—or

TRACKING THE MARKET'S PRICE/EARNINGS RATIO

*The price/earnings ratio of a stock is a key measure of its value, as explained
in this chapter. The P/E ratio of the stock market as a whole can also be a useful tool for judging how high stock prices are in relation to historical levels.
This graph shows the P/E ratio of the Standard & Poor's index of 500 stocks.
Note that when the ratio climbed too far above the average for the 15-year
period being measured, it fell abruptly. That "correction" began with Black
Monday—the market crash of October 1987. This graph shows the P/E ratio
of the index at the end of each year.*

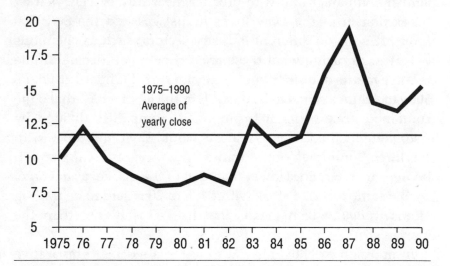

a rumor of one—can mean a vicious pounding for a stock with
a premium multiple.

By contrast, investors don't expect a low-P/E company to
grow as rapidly and are less likely to desert the company on
mildly unfavorable news. If profits rise faster than expected,
investors may bid up that low P/E. The combination of higher
earnings and a growing P/E can push a stock's price up fast.

P/Es serve yet another useful function: Other things being
equal, analysts often recommend the stock with the lowest P/E
in its industry if they like the business and if several companies look good. For example, the auto and truck industry
normally trades at a P/E of around 5 or 6, while the food
processing industry usually has a multiple of about 15.

Therefore, if General Motors has a P/E of 4, it is actually selling at a slight discount to its industry and is thus relatively cheap. If General Mills has a P/E of 15, it is right in line with its industry, neither expensive nor especially cheap at that time. (Caution: A low P/E is not by itself a sign of value. A stock's price may be low relative to its earnings because investors have little faith in the reliability of those earnings, and investors could be right. A good example of this was the low premium investors were willing to put on shares of banks just before their earnings evaporated in 1990.)

You don't make any money from the stellar performance of a company *before* you buy its stock. You want it to do well *after* you buy it. So look not only at the "trailing" P/E, which is based on the previous 12 months' earnings, but also at P/Es based on analysts' future earnings estimates. Those could be wrong, of course, but they are another piece of information on which to base your decision to buy or not to buy. Brokers will happily provide the forecasts of their firms' analysts.

There are other factors to weigh before deciding which stocks to buy. But P/E ratios are the natural starting point because they provide a quick way to separate stocks that seem overpriced from those that don't.

Value Sign #2: Look for companies with P/E ratios ranging from under 10 to no more than about 12 or 13.

Dividend yield. This is the company's dividend expressed as a percentage of the share price. If a share of stock is selling for $30 and the company pays $2 a year in dividends, its yield is 7%. In addition to generating income for shareholders, dividends are a good indicator of the strength of a company compared with its competitors. A long history of rising dividends is evidence of a strong company that manages to maintain payouts in good times and bad. Even better is a company with a history of rising dividends and rising earnings per share to match. A stock's current dividend payout and yield are included in the daily stock listings in the newspaper.

TRACKING THE MARKET'S DIVIDENDS

This graph shows how the dividend yield of the stock market as a whole (represented here by the Standard & Poor's index of 500 stocks) can offer clues to what may lie ahead. The higher the market's dividend yield, the more likely it is to attract investors, which in turn serves to push prices up. If the dividend dips too low, other investments look more attractive and stock prices often soften. When matched against stock market prices, this graph shows that the relatively high dividends of the early 1980s coincided with the bull market that ran for most of the decade. When dividend yields dipped and flattened, prices began to fall. (Yields shown are the average for the year being measured.)

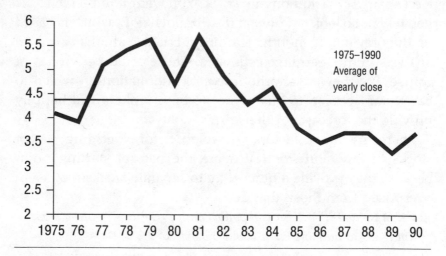

For historical information, the S&P *Stock Guide* and *Value Line* are excellent sources.

Analysts' dividend forecasts play an important role in creating expectations for a stock's future performance. If analysts expected the $30 stock mentioned above to raise its quarterly dividend to 55 cents, its price might creep upward in anticipation of the increase. Then, if the company's profits rose only enough to permit it to pay 52 cents per share, disappointed investors might sell, thus causing the stock's price to fall even though profits and dividends rose!

Sometimes the opposite can happen. Shortly after the death

of its nonagenarian founder, Armand Hammer, Occidental Petroleum announced a dividend cut and its price quickly *rose*. Analysts deemed the move (which was part of a larger plan to close down some unprofitable operations and write off debts) a smart step toward a stronger company in the future. Thus, a dividend cut isn't always a sign of weakness in a company. It's important to know what's behind it.

Although occasionally dividends are paid in the form of additional shares of stock, they are usually paid in cash; you get the checks in the mail and spend the money as you please. Many companies encourage you to reinvest your dividends automatically in additional shares of the company's stock and have set up programs that make it easy to do. Such arrangements, called dividend reinvestment plans, or DRIPs, are described later in this chapter.

Value Sign #3: Look for a pattern of rising dividends supported by rising earnings, and look for a dividend yield of at least 3% or 4% to generate income to reinvest in the company.

Book value. Also called shareholders' equity, book value is nothing more than the difference between the company's assets and its liabilities (which includes the value of any preferred stock the company has issued). *Book value per share* is the company's book value divided by the number of shares of common stock outstanding.

Normally, the price of a company's stock is higher than its book value, and stocks may be recommended as cheap because they are selling below book value. Such stocks have often attracted takeover bids from big investors and corporate raiders, which in turn attracted other investors who bid up the price of the shares. But the hope of a profitable takeover is not a good enough reason to buy such shares. A company's stock may be selling below book value because the company shows little promise, and you could wait a long time for your profits to materialize.

Still, the idea of buying shares in a company for less than

they are really worth does have a certain appeal. At any given time, dozens of stocks will be selling below book value for one reason or another, and they aren't all dogs. Some may be good small companies that have gone unnoticed or good big companies in an unloved industry. How can you tell? If the company has a low P/E ratio (under 10), a 3% or 4% dividend with plenty of earnings left over to reinvest in the business and no heavy debts, then it may be a bargain whose down-and-out status is a temporary condition that time and patience will correct.

On the other end of the scale, you want to stay away from companies whose price is too far above book value per share. It's difficult to say what's too high because the standards vary so much depending on the industry, and in some industries —insurance and finance, for instance—book value per share isn't considered particularly significant. In general, when the figure is available, you want it to be on the low side.

Value Sign #4: Look for stocks selling at a price no higher than 1.3 times book value per share.

Return on equity. This number is the company's net profits after taxes divided by its book value, and it can usually be found in the annual report. It shows how much the company is earning on the stockholders' stake in the enterprise. If return on equity is growing year after year, the stock's price will tend to show long-term strength. If the number is erratic or declining even though profits are steady, you may have uncovered problems with debt or profit margins and you should stay away from the stock.

Value Sign #5: Look for a return on equity that is consistently high compared with other companies in the same industry, or that shows a strong pattern of growth. A steady return on equity of more than 15% is a sign of a company that knows how to manage itself well.

Debt-equity ratio. The debt-equity ratio shows how much leverage, or debt, a company is carrying compared with

STOCK SPLITS

Q: *A friend recommended that I buy some stock in a company because he thinks it is going to split 3 or 4 to 1. Should I? Is the price of a stock likely to rise after a split?*

A: A company will split its stock if it thinks a lower price will attract more investors, but a split by itself is meaningless to the value of the stock. If you own 100 shares of a $40 stock, it's worth $4,000. If the stock splits 4 for 1, you have 400 shares of a $10 stock, which is worth $4,000. Stocks sometimes experience short-term jumps when a split is announced, especially when it's in combination with a hike in the dividend. Over the longer term, though, the company's fundamentals—earnings, cash flow, business prospects—will determine the share price.

shareholders' equity. For instance, if a company has a billion dollars in shareholders' equity and $100 million in debt, its debt-equity ratio is .10, or 10%, which is quite low. In general, the lower this figure the better, although the definition of an acceptable debt load varies from industry to industry. You'll find data on debt in annual reports, Value Line, Moody's and S&P publications.

Value Sign #6: Stick with companies whose debts amount to no more than 35% of shareholders' equity.

Price volatility. Probably the most widely used measure of price volatility is called the *beta*. It is calculated from past price patterns and tells you how much a stock can be expected to move in relation to a change in the S&P 500-stock index, which is assigned a beta of 1.00. A stock with a beta of 1.50 historically rises or falls half again as much as the index. A stock with a beta of .50 is half as volatile as the index; it would be expected to go up only 5% if the market rose 10% or down 5% if the index fell 10%. A few stocks have negative betas, meaning they tend to move in the opposite direction from the market.

Betas are published by several stock-tracking services such as those mentioned on pages 60 and 61 and are usually available from a broker. The key thing to remember about betas is that the higher the beta the bigger the risk.

Value Sign #7: For the most part, stick with stocks with betas of around 1.0. If you're going to assume the risk that goes with an oversized beta, it should be in the expectation of an oversized reward.

MORE CLUES TO VALUE IN A STOCK

There you have the numbers-crunching, balance-sheet approach to finding value in the stock market. Those numbers are extremely important, but they aren't the only facts you need. If the stock meets the above tests, look for these additional signs of value.

∎ *The company's industry is on the rise.* Even though you can make lots of money in a declining industry (Philip Morris has managed to maintain profitability in part by taking market share away from other companies as cigarette sales dropped), you're more likely to succeed in big and growing markets than in small or shrinking ones. Exciting new industries such as personal computers, biotechnology and long-distance telephone services may still offer exciting profit potential, but the staying power of any particular company is hard to predict. The best long-term prospects lie with established companies in large industries that meet the tests in the previous section.

∎ *The company is a leader in its industry.* Being number one or two in its primary industry gives a company several advantages. As an industry leader it can influence pricing, rather than merely reacting to what others do. It has a bigger presence in the market: When the company introduces new products, those products stand a better chance of being accepted. Also, it can afford the research necessary to create those new products.

∎ *The company invests in research and development.* Any company worthy of your investment dollar should be concerned about product development and future competitiveness. Compare what the company spends on research and development —both in actual dollars and as a percentage of earnings and sales—with that of other firms in its industry. If expenditures seem quite low, think twice about buying the stock.

LOW-RISK STRATEGY #1:
Dollar-Cost Average

Now that you know how to find good stocks, you have to address the question of how to go about buying them. One of the biggest worries is timing. Suppose you're unlucky enough to buy at the very top of the market? Or suppose something unexpected happens to dash the price of your shares overnight? Is there any way to protect yourself against bad things happening to good stocks while you're holding a basketful of them?

Yes, there is. Dollar-cost averaging is a time-tested method of smoothing out the roller-coaster ride that awaits those who try to time the market. You don't have to be brilliant to make it work, and you don't even have to pay especially close attention to what's happening in the market or in the economy. With dollar-cost averaging, you simply invest a fixed amount on a regular basis, depending on your saving schedule. The trick is to keep to your schedule, regardless of whether stock prices go up or down.

Because you're investing a fixed amount at fixed intervals, your dollars buy more shares when prices are low than they do when prices are high. As a result, the average purchase price of your stock will be lower than the average of the market prices over the same time.

For example, say you invest $300 a month over a six-month period in SureThing Enterprises, a stock that ranges in price from a low of $20 to a high of $30. Here's a look at what dollar-cost averaging would do. (This example ignores brokerage commissions, which can be distressingly high on small trades such as these. See Chapter 15 for help in reducing brokerage fees.)

First month: The stock is trading at $30 a share. Your $300 investment buys ten shares of SureThing.

Second month: The market has taken a tumble and the price of your stock has fallen to $25. You buy 12 shares.

Third month: Things have stabilized. The price of your stocks is still $25, and you buy another 12 shares.

Fourth month: On news of a takeover bid by another company, the price soars to $33. Your $300 buys you only nine shares, with a little change left over.

Fifth month: The takeover bid falls through and the price dips back down to $25. You pick up another 12 shares.

Sixth month: Uh-oh. An earnings report that falls short of analysts' expectations causes a couple of mutual funds to bail out of your stock, pushing the price down to $20 a share. You acquire 15 shares.

Let's add it up: So far you've spent, in round numbers, $1,800 (not counting commissions) and you own 70 shares of SureThing, for which you paid an average of $25.71 a share. Compare that with other ways you could have acquired the stock: If you had bought ten shares during each of those six months, you'd own 60 shares at an average price per share of $26.33. If you had invested the entire $1,800 at the start of the period, you'd own 60 shares at $30 per share. You can begin to see the advantages of dollar-cost averaging. The only reliable way to beat it over the long haul is to buy consistently at the bottom and sell at the top, which is not a very realistic expectation.

Now, you should have noticed that at the end of the sixth month you were holding stock for which you paid an average price of nearly $26 in a market that was willing to pay you only $20 a share. What now? Should you sell and cut your losses? Not necessarily. Now is a good time to reassess your faith in SureThing with another careful examination of the fundamentals described earlier in this chapter. If the fundamentals still justify your faith, this dip in the price represents a good opportunity to acquire more shares.

Dollar-cost averaging won't automatically improve the performance of your portfolio. But don't underestimate the value of the added discipline, organization and peace of mind it gives you. It's natural to be frightened away from owning stocks when prices head down, even though experience has shown that such times can be the best to buy.

Because they charge no sales commissions, no-load mutual funds (See Chapter 6) are actually better suited for dollar-cost averaging than stocks. You'd incur relatively large commissions to buy a small number of shares of stock, and your fixed monthly investment might not buy whole shares. You can buy fractional shares in a mutual fund. Many funds will let you arrange to have money transferred regularly from a bank account, and some can arrange payroll deductions.

Although dollar-cost averaging lets you put your investments on autopilot, you shouldn't leave them there indefinitely. Inflation and increases in your salary make your fixed-dollar contribution less meaningful over time, and you shouldn't continue to buy any stock merely out of habit. Reexamine the company's investment prospects on a regular schedule—at least once a year—and adjust your investment accordingly.

If you have a lump sum to invest, such as a pension payout or an inheritance, you can take advantage of dollar-cost averaging by parking the sum in a money-market fund and taking some of it out in regular installments to buy stocks.

LOW-RISK STRATEGY #2:
Reinvest Your Dividends

Another investment strategy that, like dollar-cost averaging, pays little attention to the direction of prices uses corporate dividends to boost profits over the long haul. It's called the dividend reinvestment plan, or DRIP. About 1,000 companies offer these special programs. Instead of sending you a check for dividends your shares earn, the company automatically

reinvests your money in additional shares. Since most companies pay dividends quarterly, your portfolio grows every 90
days without your having to lift a finger.

In a DRIP, shares are held in a common account. You receive
regular statements but no stock certificates unless you request
them. Companies seldom promote their DRIPs, so unless you
ask about them you may not know that they exist. But most
big-name firms, from AT&T to Xerox, have them. DRIPs are
loaded with advantages:

■ Three out of four charge no commission. Every penny you
earn goes toward increasing your holdings.

■ Small dividends buy fractional shares, a boon to small
investors.

HOW TO READ THE STOCK LISTINGS

A A small "s" next to the listing means the stock was split or the company
issued a stock dividend within the last year. This is your signal that the year's
high and low prices have been adjusted to reflect the effect of the split.

B An "x" indicates that the stock has gone "ex-dividend." Investors who buy
the stock now won't get the next dividend payment, which has been declared but not paid. Most listings stick the "x" next to the figure in the volume column.

C Sometimes so few shares of stock are sold that day that the actual number
will fit in the space in the "Vol" (volume) column, which usually lists how
many hundreds of shares traded hands. When the actual number is listed,
you see the little "n."

D The dividend listed is the latest annual dividend paid by that stock.

E The yield is the stock's latest annual dividend expressed as a percentage of
that day's price.

F The price/earnings ratio is the price of the stock divided by the earnings
reported by the company for the latest four quarters.

G Prices—and price changes—are reported in 1/8-point increments. An
eighth of a dollar is 0.125 cent.

■ The majority of DRIPs let you make additional investments on your own. A handful of companies sweeten the pot further by offering DRIP shares at discounts of 3% to 5% from the market price, though few permit the discounts on additional purchases.

■ When you're ready to sell, most of these companies will buy back the shares directly, again saving you the expense of brokerage commissions.

■ You reduce risk by investing via a DRIP because it's a form of dollar-cost averaging.

Some plans charge small fees, such as a maximum $2.50 administrative fee per transaction, or $1 to $15 if you want possession of stock certificates. Brokers who hold stocks that

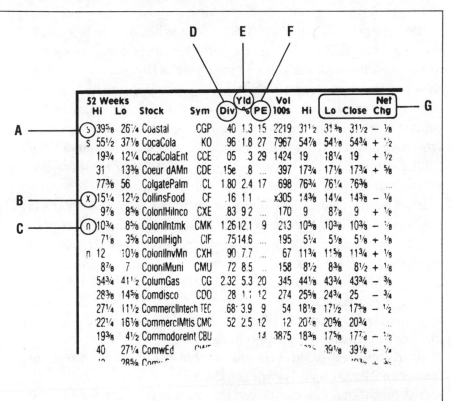

Listing taken from the *Wall Street Journal*

are in a DRIP either make no charge or make a modest one to add these shares to your account each dividend period.

How you join. Joining a DRIP is easy. Call the company's shareholder relations department for a prospectus and application and send back the completed form. You must already own some stock before you can sign up.

You'll have to buy your first shares through a broker, register the stock in your own name (not in the broker's "street" name), and then transfer it to the DRIP. Only a few companies will handle an initial purchase directly. They include Citicorp, Control Data, W.R. Grace, Great Northern Nekoosa, Johnson Controls, and Kroger.

How you get out. DRIPs can be a drag when it's time to sell. Since most DRIP investors are long-termers, companies are not geared toward sales. It can take weeks to get your money. In some cases you need only write a letter stating the number of shares you wish to sell and the company will send you the proceeds. But other firms merely mail you a stock certificate, which you must then sell through a broker. A few also limit selling to specified amounts, such as 100-share lots. But selling needn't be troublesome if you plan ahead.

If you don't plan to hold the stock for at least five years, a DRIP may not be for you. Remembering the rules of each plan can be confusing if you belong to several, and there's no guarantee those rules won't change. You may be limited to buying additional shares only at monthly or quarterly intervals that coincide with dividend payment dates. Money for voluntary cash purchases is often held by the company—at no interest—until the plan's purchase dates.

All reinvested dividends are taxable for the year they are paid, even though you don't see the money. And if the shares were bought at a discount from the market, the amount of the discount is included in your taxable income in the year of your purchase.

How to pick a DRIP. Don't buy a stock just because it offers a dividend reinvestment plan. Evaluate the company's fundamentals, and consider the following points.

▮ Stocks with good track records of steadily rising dividends make the best choices. Companies offering DRIPs that also have outstanding dividend-raising records include American Business Products, H&R Block, Emerson Electric, Lance (snack foods), Minnesota Mining & Manufacturing, and Pfizer. These companies may or may not be good buys right now based on fundamentals.

▮ If you plan to invest additional cash through a DRIP, check the limits. Some companies will let you kick in amounts as little as $10 per month. Others have higher minimums. Nearly all have maximums, ranging from $1,000 to more than $5,000 per month. AT&T, for example, permits optional cash purchases of up to $50,000 a year. Plans with the lowest minimums will be more attractive to small investors. Ask for the company's dividend record dates, when dividends are recorded on the books. By sending voluntary payments just before the record date you can cut down on waiting time for reinvestment. The same applies when you first sign up.

▮ DRIPs change. Some companies that once offered a discount no longer do. Overall, the number of firms offering shares at a discount has diminished in recent years. If you're shopping for a discount, check to see if it is still being offered.

▮ A few plans let you receive part of your dividends in cash and have part reinvested. Check the prospectus.

For a list of companies offering dividend reinvestment plans, plus details of those plans, consult the most recent edition of the *Directory of Companies Offering Dividend Reinvestment Plans,* by Sumie Kinoshita. It sells for $28.95, including postage, from Evergreen Enterprises, P.O. Box 763, Laurel, Md. 20725.

WHEN TO <u>SELL</u> A STOCK

Deciding when to sell is just as important as deciding which stocks to buy in the first place. The refusal to sell, whether it's due to unrealistic expectations, stubbornness, lack of interest or inattention, is the undoing of many an investor.

As a long-term investor, you don't want to cash in every time your stock moves up a few dollars. Commissions and taxes would cut into your gain and, besides, you'd have to decide where to put the proceeds. By the same token, you don't want to bail out in a panic in the aftermath of a market plunge.

Brokerage houses' research departments are slow to issue sell signals unless a company faces serious problems. When analysts get uneasy about a stock, they often equivocate with phrases like "weak hold." You should take that to mean, "Don't buy any more shares and if you've got a profit, seriously considering selling this stock."

Here are some clues that it is time to consider selling a profitable stock no matter what the analyst's report says.

The fundamentals change. Whether you own IBM, Consolidated Edison or an obscure company most people have never heard of, you need to follow the corporation's prospects, its earnings progression and its business success as reflected in market share, unit sales growth and profit margin. Annual reports, news stories, research updates from brokerage houses, and investment newsletters are fertile sources of such information, along with the references listed on pages 60 and 61.

If the company's fundamentals start to weaken, it's time to reconsider your investment. An example might be a fast-expanding retail chain whose sales per store, after rising for years, suddenly decline. Maybe the profit margin has slacked off after a series of consistent increases. These problems could signal that the business has peaked.

The dividend is cut. The progression and security of its dividend are important to any stock's prospects. A dividend cut or signs that the dividend is "in trouble"—meaning that analysts or creditors are quoted as saying they don't think the company can maintain its payout to shareholders—can under-

TRIPLE WITCHING HOUR

Q: *I am new to investing and was puzzled to see a recent market swoon attributed to the "Triple Witching Hour." Are these a regular happening or are they sporadic events? How can I anticipate them?*

A: Triple Witching Hours occur four times a year on Friday with the simultaneous expiration of options, index options and index futures (see Chapter 18). They often add volatility to the market, but knowing that they're coming won't help you much because the volatility moves prices both ways and it's virtually impossible to know which way the market is going in the last hour of any particular day. The best strategy is to hang on and remember that whatever happens on a given day, the fundamental strengths (or weaknesses) of the market will eventually prevail.

mine the stock price. (But see the example of Occidental Petroleum earlier in this chapter.)

You reach your target price. Many investors set specific price targets, both up and down, when they buy a stock; when the stock reaches the target, they sell. A good target is to double or triple your money, or to limit your patience with a stock to a loss of 20%. Such guidelines can prompt you to take your gains in a timely fashion and to dump losers before the damage gets too painful.

You can take the simple step of setting a "mental protective stop." Watch the stock listings and sell any stock that hits your mental stop point. You can set your sell level anywhere, perhaps arbitrarily choosing a price level that will give you double the current return on money-market funds, for example. Once you've reached your objective, take the money. If the goals you set are ultraconservative, you might miss some gains from time to time, but that's better than holding on too long and falling victim to the Wall Street maxim that says: "Bulls make money, bears make money, pigs get slaughtered."

How the Pros Decide to Sell

Over the years we have asked successful investment professionals how they decide that it's time to sell a stock. Here are some highlights of what they said.

■ *Sell in stages as the price goes up.* The chairman of a family of mutual funds: "Almost all stocks move in two-steps—two years of appreciation, two years of digestion, two more years of growth. So after a run-up in price, we sell 50% of our position, even though we may be investing for a longer term, and let the other half run."

■ *Sell when everyone else is buying.* The executive director of investments for a large pension fund: "Heavily promoted investments give me a warning signal. By the time they gain notoriety, the smart money has gotten out. You wind up holding something at the top of the market that you don't want."

■ *Sell when momentum slows.* The stock portfolio manager of a mutual fund company: "When growth slows, we sell." As an example, he cited a major shortage of liability insurance that once sent premiums soaring: "In this litigious age, people don't go without insurance. So the sales and earnings of such companies as Aetna, SAFECO, American International Group, and Chubb swelled—and continued for about a year and a half. Then growth in revenues and premiums slowed and we sold them all."

■ *Sell when the grass is greener elsewhere.* The chairman of an international group of mutual funds: "Sell when you've found something better. We sell a stock to buy one that shows better potential for appreciation. We used to sell a stock to buy another that we thought had 30% more potential. We did not reach our goal of being right two-thirds of the time, so we changed our criterion to 50%. Let's say you own a $10 stock that has an appraised value of $20. Then you find another $10 stock with a $30 value—50% better than the first one. That's when we sell the first stock."

A note of caution: Fund managers and other professional investors are by nature of their work more active traders than is appropriate for individuals to be. We present their comments because we think they can provide some insight into the professional's mind and methods, not because we think you should emulate their behavior.

HOW MUCH MONEY DID YOU MAKE?
Keep Your Eye on the Total Return

Some investors make the mistake of thinking that the change in price between the time they buy and the time they sell represents the sum total of how well or poorly their stocks perform. If a stock goes from $20 to $30, you've made $10 a share; if it goes to $15, you've lost $5 per share. That way of looking at investment results doesn't go far enough.

The quickest way to recognize the shortcomings of looking only at price changes is to imagine buying a utility stock that pays a dividend of 8%. You buy it at $20 and hold it for a year, then sell it for $22. Was your gain limited to $2 a share? Clearly not, because you collected that 8% dividend, which amounted to $1.60 per share. Assuming you owned 100 shares for a year, you pocketed $160 in dividends, plus the $200 profit from the price increase. Thus your *total return* was $360. Expressed as a percentage of your purchase price, you made 10% on the price of the shares, but your total return was 18%.

Counting dividends (whether you receive them as cash or reinvest them in additional shares) and interest as part of your investment return is really the only accurate way to figure it, whether you're dealing with stocks, bonds or mutual funds. Most compilations of investment results, including those you'll find in this book, are compilations of total returns and assume that earnings are reinvested in additional shares of the same investment and compound at the same rate.

On the other side of the equation, forgetting to take commissions and taxes into account is a common way to *over*state your profits. Commissions are discussed in Chapter 15. How taxes affect your investments is the subject of Chapter 16.

ADVANCED INVESTING I:
Timing the Market

Professional portfolio managers have so much difficulty deciding whether the stock market is poised to go up or poised to go down that at first glance it seems preposterous for individual investors to even try to guess. But the temptation is often irresistible because the payoff looks so lucrative.

In his book, *Stock Market Logic*, Norman G. Fosback, president of the Institute for Econometric Research, calculates that if you had bought a portfolio representative of the average stock on the New York Stock Exchange in 1964 and held it until 1984, you would have earned an average of 11% per year. That means $10,000 would have grown to $87,500.

If you had anticipated the three bear markets during that 20-year period, sold all stocks and held cash, then bought stocks when the next bull market started, you would have achieved a 21% average annual return and your $10,000 would have grown to nearly $490,000. If you had "sold short" (a technique by which you make money when stock prices fall) during those three bear markets, that $10,000 would have multiplied to nearly $1,400,000. If you had correctly anticipated every 5% swing in the market up or down, buying stocks on the upswings and selling them short on the downswings, you would have reaped a profit of more than $5 billion in 20 years!

Such perfect timing is impossible, of course, as Fosback points out. But the promise that good timing can spark up returns has spawned numerous investment newsletters and fills the sleep of small investors with dreams of riches. In fact, there is an entire industry devoted to the idea of perfect timing.

Meet the technicians. Examining the financial balance sheets of individual companies to determine their strengths and weaknesses is the hallmark of "fundamental" stock analysis because it looks at financial fundamentals for clues to a company's prospects for growth. Another school of thought, called "technical" analysis, looks at patterns created by the movements of the market for indications of what's going to happen next.

Technicians study past trading patterns in hopes of spotting relationships that appear ready to repeat themselves, thus creating money-making opportunities for those who know what's going to happen next. For example, many technicians believe that if the number of stock issues rising in price exceeds the number of decliners by a certain amount for a certain length of time, the market is probably headed up for a while. This advance-decline theory is also said to work on the downside.

The Dow theory, named after one of the founders of Dow Jones, is one of the most widely followed methods of technical analysis. It holds that a significant market move up or down (a bull or bear market) is underway when a change in the primary direction of the Dow Jones industrial average (which reflects price changes of 30 large-company stocks) is "confirmed" by the Dow Jones transportation index (which is composed of 20 transportation-industry stocks) moving in the same direction at the same time. Disciples of the Dow theory don't claim that it will predict a change in market direction, just that it will confirm it in time for attentive investors to take advantage of the primary trend.

Large brokerage houses have technicians on their staffs of analysts, and their reports are available on request. The best-known technicians publish their own newsletters, and the successes of a few, such as Martin Zweig and Stan Weinstein, have earned them celebrity status. (See Chapter 8 for more on investment newsletters.) Technical analysts usually try to make money on short-term moves in the market rather than on the long-term potential of a particular stock.

Looking for major market shifts. Although it is unrealistic to think that you—or anyone, for that matter—can consistently spot minor ups and downs in the market before they occur, it is often possible to anticipate the major moves. You won't be able to do it every time and you won't be able to predict the timing of the change with great precision, but the early signs of major market changes have enough characteristics in common that paying close attention to what's going on can often give you a jump on the crowd and a higher-than-usual investment return.

In the early stages of a bull market, you can increase your profit opportunities by stepping up the pace of your dollar-cost averaging plan or shifting more cash into stocks. In the early stages of a bear market, you'll want to be careful about committing new cash to stocks, and you might consider selling parts of your most profitable holdings and moving the proceeds into the kinds of cash vehicles described in Chapter 2.

How to Spot a Bull Market in Advance

Here are four signs that, according to historical standards, the market has been down far enough and long enough that the next major move should be up.

1. Stocks are cheap. Look for the Standard & Poor's 500-stock index to show a price-earnings ratio of 11 or lower coupled with a dividend yield of 5% or more. Another sign of a market ripe for an upward move is a price-to-book ratio on the S&P industrial average of around 1.4. *Barron's,* the weekly business newspaper, reports these numbers regularly.

2. Interest rates are low. This makes stocks more attractive than bonds, especially when coupled with high dividend yields. In addition, low interest rates tend to encourage borrowing, which creates economic activity, and that's good for the stock market. A sustained drop in both short- and long-term rates can usually be counted on to give the market a boost.

3. Pessimism is rampant. Talk of a new Great Depression and widespread abandonment of the stock market is often a sign that things are about to bottom out. Cash levels of mutual funds and other institutional investors are high and the opinions of market newsletter writers are low.

4. The market seems to be falling apart. This is called the selling climax: In a final burst of gloom, the market experiences breathtaking drops on huge volumes of selling. On one or more days, the Dow Jones industrial average may plunge 50, 75 or 100 points or more on New York Stock Exchange volume of several hundred million shares.

How to Spot a Bear Market in Advance

The only thing more dangerous to your investment results than unwarranted pessimism is unwarranted optimism. Bull markets, when they come, don't last forever. Yet investors are often surprised when they end.

You needn't be. Certain warning signs tend to converge as stock prices reach the top of a cycle. History never repeats itself exactly, but the following are the warning signals that have flashed in the past.

1. Stock prices are too high for company earnings. When the price-earnings ratio for the Standard & Poor's 500-stock index moves into the high teens, look out. When it hits 20 or more, trouble is almost certainly around the corner. In late 1961, the P/E of the S&P 500 hit its all-time high of 23.5, just as the market began a seven-month, 29% freefall. Other bear markets have started before the market's P/E approached this extreme. Just before the crash of 1987, it ran consistently at about 20 and had kissed the 22 level.

Another useful measure is the ratio of share price to book value. There's often an uncanny correspondence between price-to-book ratios that exceed 2, and the onset of bear markets. At the end of 1972, for instance, the figure stood at 2.3, which was followed by the bear market of 1973–74 that robbed stocks of 46% of their value. In the summer of 1987, the ratio stood at 2.9—and you know what happened in the fall.

2. Dividend yields are low. Almost without exception, yields below 3% spell the impending end of a bull market and the onset of a bear market. On the eve of the devastating 1973–74 decline, the S&P 500's yield fell to 2.7%. In the summer of 1987, it was 2.9%.

3. Interest rates are rising. Rising interest rates are the bane of bull markets. They make bonds and other fixed-income investments more attractive. They also dampen economic activity, raising the specter of recession.

4. Optimism is rampant. There will be a general feeling that the market will never go down again. Everyone you know will be in stocks.   arious experts, to their later regret, will proclaim a new era, in which the lessons of history no longer apply. One possible indicator is sentiment among investment newsletter writers. A preponderance of bulls is said to be bearish.

How to invest in a bear market. The uncertainty of the stock market and the difficulty of predicting the direction of its next move are good arguments for taking the long-term view, but some kinds of markets call for especially cautious tactics.

On the average, bear markets since 1950 have led to a 27% decline in the Standard & Poor's 500-stock index. You don't want to get caught in a crunch like that.

The onset of most of those bear markets was followed by a recession within seven to 12 months. Stock prices bottomed out and began rising before the end of each of those six recessions, usually three to eight months in advance of an economic upturn. Wouldn't it be nice to be able to protect yourself while the market is down and be in a position to ride it back up when it changes direction? There are some things you can do.

■ A bear market is no time to own stocks with high price-earnings ratios. The market will clobber them if they report disappointing earnings next time around.

■ A bear market is also a bad time to own small stocks with relatively few shareholders. Their prices could be devastated by a few big sell orders. Annual reports and stock prospectuses available from brokers should tell you how many shares of the company are in the hands of the public.

■ Ask these questions about the stocks you own in a bear market: Would the company's sales be hurt by higher unemployment? By higher energy prices? By less spending on the part of businesses? Your broker's research department can provide guidance about your holdings. But some common sense will help you rank your stocks by degree of risk in a bear-market recession. (See the definition of defensive stocks on page 58.)

Why not just sell all stocks and funds and sit out the storm? Whether you should do that depends on how much risk you're willing to take. Getting out of stocks altogether carries risk, too—of lost opportunity for profits if all your investments sit in a money-market fund when stock prices bottom out. When down markets do end, the bull reemerges with a bang. Yale Hirsch notes in *Don't Sell Stocks on Monday* that in bull markets that began between 1949 and 1982, the Dow Jones industrial average rose 38% on average in the ensuing 12 months and that those gains constituted two thirds of the entire upward moves before the next bear market started. Ironically, panicked selling of stocks when the urge to throw in the towel is almost too great to resist usually occurs at the very end of bear markets—precisely the wrong moment.

For money you want to leave in stocks, look into these possibilities:

■ *Recession-resistant companies.* Their profits can grow in just about any economic environment because they provide basic goods or services people need or want no matter what: drugmakers, food processors, grocery chains, beverage companies, tobacco sellers and hospital-management firms.

■ *Utility stocks.* Gas and electric companies do well in down markets thanks partly to their high yields, but thanks also to the fact that demand for electricity remains fairly steady because people continue to wash clothing, watch T   and turn on the lights.

■ *Dividend raisers.* Look for companies that regularly raise their dividends through fat times and lean times, using the signs of value described in earlier sections of this chapter.

■ *Value stocks.* As described earlier, these are stocks with low P/E or low price-to-book-value ratios but good prospects. Their earnings could fall in a recession but can usually be counted on to recover.

ADVANCED INVESTING II:
Companies that Own Their Markets

We'd all like to have a piece of the profits of businesses that are near-monopolies. In fact, you can. The companies won't be giants like General Motors or General Electric but more likely unglamorous companies that churn out such products as recycled plastic bottles, round cartons for premium ice cream, stamp pads, football uniforms, free-laying carpet tiles, binders used in desktop publishing, and even tennis-ball fuzz.

What sets such companies apart from the crowd is simply this: They have a lock on their lines of business. Because they make things nobody else does or make them so much better or cheaper, their positions are almost unassailable. Operating outside Wall Street's limelight, they often trade at modest price-earnings ratios. Debt is minimal or nonexistent. And because of their dominance, profits tend to rise steadily.

There's a term for such companies: "niche" stocks. True niche companies are resistant to competition—they got there first. They have the technological and marketing edge, plus a proven ability to parlay those advantages into fat profit margins. Many combine the ability to make lots of money in good times with the strength to muddle through in hard times.

Don't make the mistake of confusing a niche with a fad. Remember video-game parlors? Gasohol refiners? Condominium converters? Fads attract "me-too" competitors. So the trick is to separate the enduring from the transitory and not pay too much when you buy the stock.

What's a niche stock? There's no textbook definition, but look for these qualities:

■ *It sticks to the business it knows best.* A firm that tries to make something for everyone or spreads into too many unrelated fields becomes too tied to the business cycle to be a niche stock. Beware of companies that, having conquered one business, take on entrenched opponents in others. McDonald's doesn't deliver packages and Federal Express doesn't sell hamburgers.

■ *It has the dominant market share.* The company should be the biggest seller in its market niche. This isn't always easy to determine: Check annual reports of the company and any competitors you can think of and compare sales figures.

■ *It's tough to break into the business.* If a business is lucrative, other companies will want to jump in, so look for markets in which the financial or technical obstacles to competitors are formidable. For instance, Calgon Carbon is the leading producer of activated carbon for water purification systems. It's a lucrative business, but one that analysts estimate would take $20 million to $50 million to break into. That's some barrier.

■ *It is financially strong.* A company that takes full advantage of a secure market should show a long record of rising earnings. Also critical is a balance sheet earmarked by low debt as a percentage of total capital—or no debt at all. In short, it should meet the tests of value described earlier in this chapter.

■ *It shows a high profit margin.* A corporation that does its thing better, cheaper or faster than everyone else should get a premium price and control its costs. Compare the company's profit margins, which you can find in the annual report or get from a stockbroker, with the industry averages listed in *Value Line Investment Survey.*

■ *It has a record of stability.* A couple of decades of product leadership would be ideal. That's too much to expect from a high-technology or health-related company, where business conditions change much faster. But it's possible in such prosaic industries as packaging or chemicals.

How to find them. Your own knowledge about a product line or an industry can lead you to a niche company. So can annual reports and 10-K forms, research departments of regional brokers, investment newsletters or reference sources like *Value Line*. Mutual fund reports to shareholders can also give you some leads, especially reports from funds that specialize in finding such companies themselves.

Here are examples of niche companies analysts have recommended from time to time: (*Inclusion on the list is not a recommendation to buy that stock. Before you act, test the company's fundamentals against the criteria described earlier in the chapter.*)

Avemco (private aircraft insurance); Calgon Carbon (water-purification products); Consolidated Papers (coated paper); General Binding (specialized office supplies); Intermet (foundries); Russell (athletic clothing); Sanford (stamp pads, markers); Sealright (waterproof paper containers); Shorewood Packaging (packaging for phonograph records, tapes and compact discs); Steel of West Virginia (steel minimill); Wellman (plastics, bottle recycling).

ADVANCED INVESTING III:
When Bad Things Happen to Good Stocks

This variation on value investing entails looking for good companies whose prices have been beaten down by nonrecurring events that don't necessarily reflect on the long-term quality of the management. Sometimes a company's underlying strengths are enough to pull it through unexpected catastrophes that would sink a weaker one. And sometimes these setbacks can create once-in-a-lifetime buying opportunities.

The theory behind this approach is that the stock market is not always efficient (contrary to what a technician would say) because investors often shun otherwise solid companies plagued with temporary setbacks, such as mothballed nuclear power plants or flawed birth-control devices, that drive their stocks' prices down to bargain-basement levels. Prominent examples from the past decade or so include Union Carbide, Gerber, General Public Utilities, and Monsanto. Each came roaring back from the brink of disaster.

■ *Union Carbide.* In 1984, a leak of toxic gas at a pesticide plant in Bhopal, India, killed more than 2,000 people and injured tens of thousands more. The tragedy was a shocking blow to Connecticut-based Union Carbide, which owned 51% of the Indian plant. Within days, billions of dollars' worth of

LOST STOCK RECORDS

Q: *My daughter has lost her AT&T stock purchase records and several stock certificates. She also lost records of an assortment of the Baby Bell stocks and some AT&T stock she received after the AT&T breakup. She sold most of the Baby Bell stocks for which she had certificates, but she has no records of purchase for reporting capital gains to the IRS. Can she get this information?*

A: Ordinarily when stock certificates are lost, the company that issued them can send replacements. Your daughter should write to American Transtech, the transfer agent for AT&T and all of the Baby Bells (P.O. Box 45048, Jacksonville, FL 32232; 800-348-8288). It can provide the information she needs and arrange for replacements for the lost stock certificates. The company should also be able to inform her of any stock splits that affected her and help her estimate her costs for tax purposes. Your daughter should include her social security number and, if available, the account number, issue date and number of shares she owned.

lawsuits were filed against Union Carbide on behalf of Bhopal victims.

Union Carbide's stock price quickly fell 21%, including a drop of nearly $6 per share in a day. In Bethesda, Md., analysts at the Robert E. Torray & Co. investment firm, one of few that specializes in buying stocks hit by bad news, did their analysis, then started writing checks. Over a couple of weeks, Torray bought more than a million shares of Union Carbide at a price in the low teens—and doubled its money in less than five years.

■ *Gerber*. After a New York City woman charged that she found glass slivers in Gerber baby food in October 1984, Gerber Products' stock price dived 15% in two days to $22. Five years later, the price had risen better than threefold.

■ *General Public Utilities*. Limping along after a disaster at its Three Mile Island nuclear-power-generating plant the previous year, it shocked investors in 1980 by suspending dividends. The news, more ominous to investors than the Three Mile

Island disaster itself, drove GPU's stock price down 36% to a modern low of $3.38 per share. In early 1991, GPU's stock sold for $45 per share.

Can you do it? Buying good stocks on bad news can pay off big, but it's not for the faint-hearted and it's something to try with only a small portion of your portfolio. At the end of 1988, Kiplinger looked to see what had happened to stocks on the New York Stock Exchange that fell 25% or more in price during any one-week period in 1985, figuring that three years was long enough for a beaten-down stock to demonstrate its ability to climb back. And in fact, some companies *had* made fabulous comebacks, often because they had become takeover targets of other companies: A.H. Robins, for instance, which was bought by American Home Products, and Essex Chemical, which was bought by Dow Chemical. But half of the casualties of 1985 either barely survived or had fallen even further by the end of 1988. As a group, our portfolio of snakebit companies grew 21% during the period, while the Dow Jones industrials grew 40%.

Clearly, careful selection is the key. Finding a solid investment prospect among a list of torpedoed stocks isn't all that different from ordinary investing homework. You need to look at the underlying values of the company.

■ *Low debt load.* Using the sources listed on pages 60 and 61, look for cash flow three to four times larger than interest payments on debts. Avoid highly leveraged companies, such as s&l's, and high-flying stocks with big price-earnings ratios. Debts and high P/E's just make things worse.

■ *Substantial assets.* Look to see if the company has substantial assets that could be sold to raise cash if necessary. Saleable assets include interests in other companies, subsidiaries with well-defined markets or even plants and equipment that can be sold and leased back to the company from their new owner.

■ *Few competitors.* Don't buy companies that are highly vulnerable to foreign competition. The tougher the marketplace, the tougher it is to come back. On the domestic front, public utilities are good bets because they have a monopoly in their markets and can be expected to be around for years to come. Kansas Gas and Electric, which dropped 26% in a single week in 1985 following nuclear-plant problems, had risen in price by 87% three years later.

MISTAKES EVEN SMART INVESTORS MAKE

It's a sad fact that many people fail to live up to their investing potential because of common mistakes even smart people make. Here's our list of the six transgressions we see most often.

Acting on tips. Investors get compelling, authoritative tips from friends. You get "cold calls" from aspiring young brokers pushing companies you never heard of. You get friendly calls from your own broker about stocks you know nothing about. If you act on those suggestions without first investigating, you're begging for trouble. If your friend or broker knows this hot tip, so do a lot of other people. Assume that this information is already fully reflected in the stock's price. And if that's the case, is the stock still worth buying?

Getting sentimental. Falling in love with a stock is a common transgression of retired employees who have accumulated lots of stock in the company they worked for all those years. Children who later inherit those shares have the same strong, sentimental attachment to the firm and tend to hang on. Don't do it. Weed out the poor performers in your portfolio, wherever they came from originally.

Fooling yourself. Say your 100 shares of a $20 stock go up to $22, so you claim bragging rights to 10% profits. However, when you figure in commission, your shares really cost more like $2,050. If you sold for a $50 commission, you'd get $2,100—a 5% gain, pretax, that makes passbook savings account rates look good in comparison.

Fooling yourself this way is expensive and makes it difficult for you to choose well among competing investments. Get an accurate idea of the tax and administrative costs of your investment when figuring your gains and losses.

Failing to diversify. All your life people have warned you against putting all your eggs in one basket. You no doubt understand the concept, believe in it and are thoroughly sick of such simplistic preachments. But note this amazing fact: Many investors *still* put all their eggs in one basket. They tend to invest in clumps of things, thinking in terms of individual investments rather than in terms of industries. A carefully researched portfolio of auto-industry and airline stocks could all get beaten up at the same time by some common transportation plague such as increased fuel costs. A diverse list of stocks could all be clobbered if they aren't balanced by certificates of deposit or other investments that will protect you if stock prices fall through the floor.

Losing patience. It's normal to feel let down when nothing much happens to your stocks right away. Don't lose patience, though. Make an investment not on the basis of a stock's performance over a few months or even a year. If you selected it carefully and the fundamentals are still sound, hang in there. With a long-term outlook, you can ride out the interim slides.

Taking a flier on a penny stock. These are low-priced, not widely owned and not traded on any stock exchange. True, a $3,000 investment in a $3 stock gets you 1,000 shares. If the stock goes up a dollar, you've got a 33% profit. But the fact is, a dirt-cheap stock price is a more likely a tip-off to a troubled company than an undiscovered IBM. What's more, commissions on low-priced shares are typically quite high. These are deals you can live without.

5

SUCCESS WITH BONDS

---■---

BONDS BELONG in your investment plan for good reasons, but maybe not for the reasons you think.

■ The kinds of economic forces that depress stock prices —the early stages of a recession, for instance—tend to boost bond prices, making bonds a natural choice to diversify and hedge your stock holdings.

■ Bonds can generate impressive profits from capital gains. As we will point out, sometimes you can even calculate those gains years in advance, on the day you buy the bonds.

■ Bonds can provide a predictable stream of relatively high income you can use for living expenses or for funding other parts of your investment plan.

■ Some kinds of bonds offer valuable tax advantages and unparalleled opportunities to take advantage of the time value of money, that is, to invest a modest amount with a reasonable prospect of collecting a large amount a few years later. (The importance of the time value of money is explained in Chapter 1.)

Note that the word "safety" doesn't appear on the list. A lot of people think bonds are about the safest investment around, but such a notion can be costly. Bonds entail several kinds of risks, each of which will be dealt with in this chapter. First, though, you have to master the lingo, and the vocabulary of bonds is different from the vocabulary of stocks.

WHAT YOU NEED TO KNOW ABOUT BONDS

Bonds are IOUs issued by corporations, state and city governments and their agencies, and the federal government and its agencies. When you buy a bond, you become a creditor of the corporation or agency; it owes you the amount shown on the face of the bond, plus interest. You get a fixed amount of interest on a regular schedule—every six months, in most cases—until the bond matures after a specified number of years, at which time you are paid the bond's face value. If the issuer goes broke, bondholders have first claim on the issuer's assets, ahead of stockholders.

Bonds typically have a face value of $1,000 or $5,000, although some are larger. Investors may actually receive a bond certificate or they may not. Increasingly, bond ownership is in the form of a "book entry," meaning the issuer keeps a record of buyers' names but sends out no certificates. Treasury bonds, for instance, are issued in book-entry form.

A long-term bond typically matures in 20 to 40 years, although some bonds are issued for shorter periods. A bond due to mature in five to 10 years is called an intermediate-term bond. A bond issued for two to 10 years may be called a note. After they are issued, bonds can be freely bought and sold by individuals and institutions in what's called the secondary market.

Different kinds of bonds. Bonds share those basics, but they come in a variety of forms.

■ *Secured bonds* are backed by a lien on part of a corporation's plant, equipment or other assets. If the corporation defaults, those assets can be sold to pay off the bondholders.

■ *Debentures* are unsecured bonds, backed only by the general ability of the corporation to pay its bills. If the company goes broke, debentures can't be paid off until secured bond-

Short-Term vs. Long-Term Bonds

Q: *What are the advantages of short- and intermediate-term bonds over longer-term issues?*

A: In general, the shorter the maturity, the less the bonds are subject to price fluctuations due to interest rate changes and inflation. Bonds with maturities of 20 to 30 years usually offer the highest yields, but sometimes they pay only slightly more than you can earn on intermediate-term bonds (those with maturities of three to ten years). And sometimes those higher rates can disappear. Most long-term bonds can be redeemed early, or called, on specified dates. If interest rates fall, you can expect the issuer to refinance its debt at lower rates. In that case, bondholders would be paid off, but they'd lose the high rates they had counted on.

holders are paid. Subordinated debentures are another step down the totem pole. Investors in these don't get paid until after holders of so-called senior debentures get their money.

▌ *Zero-coupon bonds* may be secured or unsecured. They are issued at a big discount from face value because they pay all the interest at maturity, with no payments along the way. (Although buying such a bond may sound a little nutty, in fact zero-coupon bonds offer a number of potential advantages to investors, as we will see later in this chapter.)

▌ *Municipal bonds* are issued by state or city governments or their agencies and come in two principal varieties: *General obligation* bonds are backed by the full taxing authority of the government. *Revenue* bonds are backed only by the receipts from a specific source of revenue, such as a bridge or highway toll, and thus are not considered as secure as general obligation bonds. The interest paid to holders of both revenue and general obligation municipal bonds is exempt from federal income taxes and, usually, income taxes of the issuing state.

▌ *U.S. Treasury bonds,* which in maturities of a year or less are called Treasury *bills* and in maturities of under ten years may be called *notes,* are backed by the full faith and credit—and the printing presses—of the federal government.

■ *Agency securities* are issues of various U.S. government-sponsored organizations, such as the Federal National Mortgage Association and the Tennessee Valley Authority. Although they are not technically backed by the full faith and credit of the U.S. Treasury, they are widely considered to be moral obligations of the federal government, which presumably wouldn't let an agency issue fail.

■ *Convertible bonds* can be swapped for the same company's common stock at a fixed ratio—a specified amount of bonds for a specified number of shares of stock. Convertible features make some companies' bonds more attractive by offering the possibility of an equity kicker: If the price of the stock rises considerably after you buy the convertible bonds, you can profit from the rise by swapping your bonds for stock.

For example, suppose you buy five convertible bonds issued by Xerox at $1,000 each. The bonds pay 7% and each is convertible into 20 shares of Xerox stock. When you buy the bonds, Xerox is selling at $45 a share. Because break-even conversion price is $50, you've paid $5 a share for the conversion privilege. If Xerox stock climbs above $50, you can make a profit by converting your bonds to stock. If the price were to go to, say, $60, you could quickly turn your $5,000 bond investment into $6,000 worth of stock.

Because their fate is so closely tied to that of the stock price of the issuing firm, convertible bonds tend to be more closely in sync with the stock market than the bond market. There's more about convertibles later on.

■ *Callable bonds.* Some bonds can be called, meaning they can be redeemed by the issuer before they mature. A company might decide to call its bonds if, for instance, interest rates fell so far that it could issue new bonds at a lower rate and thus save money. This is obviously to the corporation's advantage, not yours. Not only would you lose your comparatively high yield, but you'd also have to figure out where to invest the unexpected payout in a climate of falling interest rates. And if the bond is called for more than you paid for it, you'd also owe tax on the difference.

UNLOCKING THE POTENTIAL OF BONDS

When a new bond is issued, the interest rate it pays is called the *coupon rate*, which is the fixed annual payment expressed as a percentage of the face value. An 8% coupon bond pays $80 a year interest on each $1,000 of face value, a 9% coupon bond pays $90 and so forth. That's what the issuer will pay—no more, no less—for the life of the bond. But it may or may not be the yield you can earn from that issue, and understanding why is the key to unlocking the real potential of bonds.

Take a new bond with a coupon interest rate of 9%, meaning it pays $90 a year for every $1,000 of face value. What happens if interest rates rise to 10% after the bond is issued? New bonds will have to pay a 10% coupon rate or no one will buy them. By the same token, you could sell your 9% bond only if you offered it at a price that produced a 10% yield for the buyer. So the price at which you could sell would be whatever $90 represents 10% of, which is $900. Thus, you lose $100 if you sell. Even if you don't sell, you suffer a paper loss because your bond is now worth $100 less than you paid for it. It is selling at a discount.

But what if interest rates were to decline? Say rates drop to 8% while you're holding your 9% bond. New bonds would be paying only 8% and you could sell your old bond for whatever $90 represents 8% of. Because $90 is 8% of $1,125, selling your 9% bond when interest rates are at 8% would produce a $125 capital gain. That $125 is called a "premium."

Actual prices are also affected by how much time is left before the bond matures and by the likelihood of the issue being called. But the underlying principle is the same, and it is the single most important thing to remember about the relationship between the market value of the bonds you hold and changes in current interest rates:

As interest rates rise, bond prices fall; as interest rates fall, bond prices rise. The further away the bond's maturity or call date, the more volatile its price tends to be.

Because of this relationship, the actual yield to an investor depends in large part on where interest rates stand the day the bond is purchased, so the vocabulary of the bond market needs more than one definition for yield. Coupon yield (the annual payment expressed as a percentage of the bond's face value) is only one way to look at a bond's payout. These are the others:

■ *Current yield* is the annual interest payment calculated as a percentage of the bond's current market price. An 8% coupon bond selling for $900 has a current yield of 8.9%, which is figured by taking the $80 in annual interest, dividing it by the $900 market price and multiplying the result by 100.

■ *Yield to maturity* includes the current yield and the capital gain or loss you can expect if you hold the bond to maturity. If you pay $900 for an 8% coupon bond with a face value of $1,000 maturing five years from the date of purchase, you will earn not only $100 a year in interest, but also an additional $100 when the bond's issuer pays off the principal. By the same token, if you buy that bond for $1,100, representing a $100 premium, you will lose $100 at maturity.

The yield to maturity can dramatically affect investment results. You can figure it out with a financial calculator, or your broker will gladly do it for you. To get a close approximation of yield to maturity, assume that the discount or premium is spread equally over the number of years left to maturity. Call that the "annually accumulated discount" and apply the following formula:

$$\text{Yield to maturity} = \frac{\begin{array}{c}\text{annually accumulated discount}\\ \text{+ annual interest payment}\end{array}}{\begin{array}{c}\text{average of face value +}\\ \text{current price}\end{array}} \times 100$$

In the case of the bond selling for $900 with a coupon yield of 8% and five years to go to maturity, the yield to maturity would be 10.5%:

$$\frac{(20 + 80)}{\dfrac{(1,000 + 900)}{2}} \times 100 = 10.5$$

If you bought the premium bond for $1,100, your current yield would be 7.3% but the yield to maturity would be only 5.7%. (To apply the formula to a premium bond, you subtract the annually accumulated premium from the annual interest payment.)

Why would you ever want to buy a premium bond? For one thing, it's possible that the low yield to maturity could be counterbalanced by the extra interest you collect prior to maturity. That assumes the current yield on the issue exceeds yields available elsewhere. Also, tax considerations could make the capital loss valuable to you a few years down the road, when it could be used to offset income from other sources.

▌ *Yield to call* is the same as yield to maturity, except it is calculated assuming that the bond will be redeemed by the issuer on the first possible call date.

The daily bond listings in most newspapers show the maturity date for each issue, the coupon yield, the current yield and the current price. You have to figure out yield to maturity yourself, get it from a broker or look it up in a standard investor's reference, such as Standard & Poor's monthly *Bond Guide,* which is available at libraries. This is what the listings might look like for a couple of bonds issued by American Telephone & Telegraph:

Bond	Current Yield	Vol	Close	Net Chg.
ATT6s00	7.5	146	80-1/4	-1
ATT7-1/803	8.4	5	84-3/8	-5/8

The first bond, listed as "ATT6s00" was issued to pay 6% on its face value (also called par value and shown as 6s in the listing) and will mature in the year 2000 (the "00" in the listing). The next column reveals that it is paying a current yield of 7.5%, which means that investors are buying it at a discount. And sure enough, the "Close" column, which shows the price of the bond at the time the market closed that day, shows that it was selling for 80¼, or 80.25% of $1,000, which is $802.50 for each $1,000 bond. The yield to maturity on this issue, taking into account the fact that you will collect $1,000 per bond in the year 2000, isn't shown. (It would be 9.09%.) The listing also doesn't show whether the bond is callable, but that is probably a moot point in this case. A company is unlikely to call in a bond on which it is paying only 6% interest. The "Vol" column shows the number of bonds that changed hands that day (146

HOW TO READ THE BOND LISTINGS

A Current yield is the annual yield you'd get if you bought the bond at that day's price. If the bond is selling at a discount from the issue price, the price shown in the column labeled "Last" will be less than 100. If the bond is selling at a premium, the price will be more than 100.

B Each number in the "Sales" column stands for $1,000 worth of bonds traded that day. Bonds are usually priced at $1,000 each.

C The first number after the name of the issuer shows the interest rate at which the bond was issued, known as the coupon rate. Read the letter "s" following the rate as a spacer to avoid confusion between the rate and the next set of numbers if there is no fraction there to serve the same purpose.

D This is the year in which the bond matures.

E The notation "cv" indicates that the issue is a convertible bond, meaning it can be exchanged for a fixed number of shares of common stock of the issuer.

F A "zr" listed before the maturity date indicates a zero-coupon bond.

for the first issue listed, only five for the second), and the "Net Chg." (meaning net change) shows that the price went down a dollar (meaning interest rates undoubtedly rose that day).

The second listing can be interpreted the same way. These are bonds issued to pay 7⅛% of face value ($71.25 per bond) each year until they mature in 2003. Volume was skimpy; only five bonds sold that day. The last price paid was $843.75, producing a current yield of 8.4%. (The yield to maturity would be 9.14%.)

HOW TO REDUCE THE RISKS IN BONDS

Interest rate changes create one of the chief risks you face as an investor in bonds: The market value of the bonds you own will decline if interest rates rise. This unalterable relationship

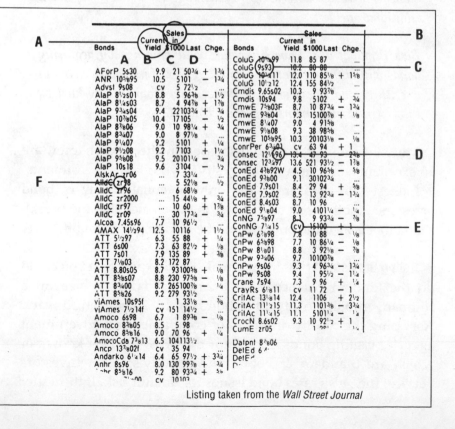

Listing taken from the *Wall Street Journal*

suggests the first risk-reducing step you can take as a bond investor.

Risk Reducer #1: *Don't buy bonds when interest rates are low or rising. Put your cash in a money-market fund or in certificates of deposit maturing in three to nine months. The ideal time to buy bonds is when interest rates have stabilized at a relatively high level or when they seem about to head down.*

That step will help reduce your market risk, as will the next two precautions:

Risk Reducer #2: *Reduce the potential volatility of your bond holdings by sticking to short- and intermediate-term issues with maturities of three to five years. They fluctuate less in price than longer-term issues and they don't require you to tie up your money for 10 or more years in exchange for a relatively small additional yield.*

Risk Reducer #3: *Diversify your bond holdings by acquiring bonds with different maturity dates. A mix of issues maturing in one, three and five years will protect you from getting hurt by interest rate movements you can't control.*

Mutual funds, which are discussed in the next chapter, are an excellent way to achieve diversity in your bond investments.

Interest rate rises aren't the only potential enemy of bond investors. Another risk to consider is the chance that the organization that issued the bonds won't be able to pay them off.

Rating the default risk. It's not realistic to expect that you could do the kind of balance-sheet analysis it takes to size up a company's ability to pay off its bonds in 10, 20 or even 30 years. Assessing the creditworthiness of companies and government agencies issuing bonds is a job for the pros, the best known of which are Standard & Poor's and Moody's. Fitch Investors Service, Inc., also rates bond issues for default risk. If the issuer earns one of the top four "investment grades" assigned by the companies—AAA, AA, A or BBB from Standard & Poor's and Fitch, and Aaa, Aa, A or Baa from Moody's—the risk of default is considered slight. Here's a detailed breakdown of the companies' rating systems for issues considered to be worthy of the investment grade designation. (Sometimes the ratings will be supplemented by a "+" or a "−" sign.)

S&P	Moody's	What it means
AAA	Aaa	The highest possible rating, indicating the agencies' highest degree of confidence in the issuer's ability to pay interest and repay the principal.
AA	Aa	A top rating, only marginally weaker than the highest.
A	A	High capacity to repay debt, but slightly more vulnerable to adverse economic developments.
BBB	Baa	The lowest investment-grade rating, indicating "adequate" capacity to pay principal and interest but more vulnerability to adverse economic developments.

Ratings below investment grade indicate that the bonds are considered either "speculative" (BB and Ba, B and B) or in real danger of default (various levels of C and, in the S&P ratings, a D, indicating that the issue is actually in default). You can consider any issue rated speculative or lower to be a "junk" bond, although brokers and mutual funds usually call them "high-yield" issues. They are very risky and best avoided unless you're willing to study the company's prospects very closely. Even then, junk bonds should never occupy more than a small sliver of your portfolio.

Bond safety ratings aren't guarantees; they are based on the informed opinions of the rating companies' analysts. At Standard & Poor's, for example, more than 400 researchers are involved in rating bonds. They spend days or even months examining the debt structure and earning power of a corporation or municipality before assigning a rating.

Check the rating of any bond you're considering purchasing. A broker can give you the rating, or you can look it up in the Moody's or S&P bond guides found in many libraries. For a mutual fund, the prospectus (See Chapter 6) will describe the lowest rating acceptable to the fund's managers, and the annual reports should list the bonds in the fund's portfolio, along with their ratings.

How ratings affect prices and yields. In general, the lower the rating, the higher the yield a bond has to offer to attract investors. For example, on the same day that a AAA-rated U.S. agency bond maturing in the year 2000 sold at a price that paid an 8.17% current yield, a Sears, Roebuck issue rated A+ and maturing in 1999 yielded buyers 9.5%. A bond rated B+ being offered by RJR Nabisco and scheduled to mature in 2001 had to pay 18.6% to find buyers and sold for about 81 cents per dollar of face value.

The agencies keep track of the issues they've rated, raising or lowering ratings when they think a change is justified. Hundreds of "fallen angels" get downgraded each year, and hundreds get upgraded. The last thing you want is to have the rating of a bond issue lowered while you're holding it in your portfolio. To guard against that, you have to pay attention to the company's prospects *after* you buy the bond.

What happened to Fort Howard Paper is a good example of the consequences of a lowered rating for bond investors. In the early 1980s, Fort Howard was considered so solid that its bonds yielded just one-quarter of a percentage point more than Treasury bonds. But in the aftermath of a leveraged buyout (LBO) of Fort Howard in 1988, its ratings plunged. (In a leveraged buyout, the buyers typically take on huge debts in the company's name to pay off the sellers.) With the company now burdened by additional debt, S&P chopped Fort Howard's credit rating from AAA to a far less reassuring BB-, then down again to B. In response, the price of Fort Howard bonds plunged and bondholders who had bought on the strength of the company's AAA rating only a few years earlier took a bath. By 1990, some Fort Howard bonds were selling for as little as 39 cents on the dollar.

Lightning also struck holders of RJR Nabisco bonds in 1988 when that company became the object of the largest LBO ever, sparking lawsuits for restitution by investors who got burned when some RJR bonds fell to under 36 cents on the dollar.

To avoid such a situation, stick with high-rated bonds. Even then, watch the financial news with this in mind: A bid to take over a company may be good for stockholders, who can sell their stock at the high takeover price. But a takeover paid for with additional debt can be disastrous for bondholders.

Risk Reducer #4: In general, don't buy any bond with a safety rating lower than A, and watch for news that may affect the rating while you own the bond.

Ratings aren't the final word on good bond buys. In fact, the market often recognizes problems with bond issues before the rating services can react. In 1989, Integrated Resources, Inc., a huge financial services firm that has since declared bankruptcy, defaulted on nearly a billion dollars' worth of debt. The default wasn't entirely without warning, but the firm's CCC rating at the time gave little notice a complete collapse was imminent.

Such a possibility underscores the importance of considering a bond's rating in the context of other information about bond issues you might buy.

■ Compare the bond's price and yield with those of bonds with identical ratings to see which is a better buy. If the issuing company seems a likely target for a takeover—it's undervalued, has well-known brand names in its stable of products or has divisions that could be sold separately—look for what's called "poison put" provisions in the bond. Essentially, poison puts guarantee that anyone holding bonds in a company that is taken over can redeem those bonds at par (face value). This protects investors and discourages takeovers at the same time.

∎ Make sure you're looking at the bonds' current credit rating. Buying on the basis of an outdated rating can be an expensive mistake.

∎ Make sure there's a market for the bond. This sounds obvious, but one thing that caused junk bonds to lose so much of their value so fast when the LBO bubble burst was the fact that there were suddenly many, many sellers and very few buyers.

IF YOU MUST FLIRT WITH JUNK BONDS . . .

On any given day, the newspaper bond listings are likely to contain some tempting propositions. How about this one, for instance: Early in 1991, you could have called any broker and bought a bond issued by Navistar, the transportation company, maturing in 2004, with a coupon yield of 9%, for $800 per $1,000 face value. That discount made its current yield 11.3% and its yield to maturity an even more impressive 11.7%.

Here's another one from the same day: An 11% coupon issue from Orion, the motion picture company, was selling at 66 ($660 for a bond with a face value of $1,000). It was due to mature in 1998. That bond was paying 16.7% in current yield, with an astonishing yield to maturity of 45.7%. (You were promised 16.7% a year for seven years, plus a $340 capital gain in 1998 for every $1,000 bond you bought in 1991.)

These deals seemed too good to be true. In fact they were real, but some quick homework with the Standard & Poor's monthly *Bond Guide* would have revealed the following: The Navistar issue is a *sinking fund debenture,* meaning it is not backed by the assets of the company (the debenture part of the name) but the company has pledged to regularly put aside money to pay it off (the sinking fund). Navistar's safety rating at the time was BBB-, which put it smack at the bottom of the medium-grade investment-quality category. Conclusion: The Navistar issue may have been worth considering by an investor willing to take the additional risk for the prospect of additional reward.

As for the Orion issue, it is also a sinking fund debenture, but it carried a rating of CCC+ at the time, putting it in the category of junk bonds. Standard & Poor's defines an issue rated CCC as having "a currently identifiable vulnerability to default." That doesn't mean the issue or the company will default, but it does spell out the risk pretty clearly.

Should you be looking for discount bonds such as these? Yes and no. Issues like the Navistar debentures could constitute a prudent risk for a small portion of your portfolio. Issues like the Orion debentures are best left alone by individual investors. They are speculations, not investments.

SHOULD YOU BUY CONVERTIBLE BONDS?

Convertible bonds combine the features of stocks and bonds in one investment. They are redeemable for a set number of shares of stock of the same company, or at a specified ratio—25 shares of stock for each $1,000 in bonds, for example. If the price of the company's stock rises, so will the price of its convertible bond, although not dollar for dollar. If the stock falls, the convertible will fall, too; but because it is a bond, its movement will also be affected by interest rates. Thus, fundamental or economic factors that are bad for stocks (recession, for instance) may be balanced by factors that are good for bonds (falling interest rates). If the stock rises high enough, you can exchange your bonds for stock and, if you wish, sell the stock and pocket the profits.

It sounds like the best of both worlds, but before you rush out to buy, consider a few more facts about convertibles. First, they are usually debentures, meaning they are not backed by the assets of the company. Second, they are usually *subordinated* debentures, meaning other, unsubordinated debts will be paid off ahead of them in case of bankruptcy. Third, default risks aside, most convertibles are callable on short notice. The issuer is unlikely to allow its stock price to climb very high above the conversion price, which limits your profit potential. Fourth, you pay a price for these hybrid securities: They pay less interest than you could get from the same company's bonds, and you can expect to pay a higher price to buy the convertible than it is worth as either a stock or a bond. That higher price is called the conversion premium or, in the

---

HOW TO RIDE THE YIELD CURVE

Whether you're buying corporate bonds or Treasuries, knowing a little bit of economic esoterica can help with your decisions about when to buy and which maturities to choose. The yield curve is a simple device used by economists to keep track of what's happening to interest rates. You can use it, too.

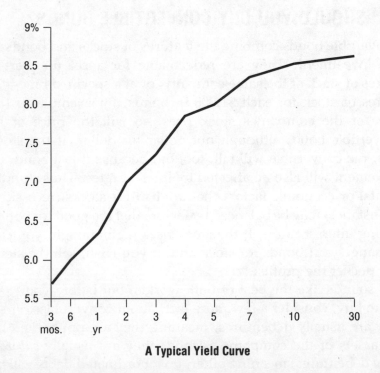

A Typical Yield Curve

parlance of Wall Street, "water." It represents the distance the stock price has to climb to reach the break-even point for converting the bond.

This doesn't mean convertible bonds aren't worth considering. It does mean that the investment decision is more complicated than the decision to buy either stock or bonds issued by the same company. As a cross between the two, convertibles demand that you be concerned not only with the ability of the company to pay its debts, but also with the anticipated direc-

---

The yield curve is nothing more than a line graph formed by plotting bond interest rates on the vertical axis against maturities on the other. Normally, the longer the maturity the higher the rate, so the line on the graph slopes upward to the right. From time to time the line will slope the other way, creating what's called an inverted yield curve.

Yield curves generally become inverted when the Federal Reserve Board pushes up short-term rates to slow down a hot economy and cool inflationary pressures. Long-term rates don't tend to change much because investors don't expect those conditions to persist for 20 or 30 years. An inverted yield curve creates opportunities for money-market investors to earn high interest, but it also creates some danger to the economy. If the Fed overreacts and raises short-term rates too high, it risks pushing the economy into a recession. The yield curve has been inverted five times since 1953, and that was followed four times by a recession within 12 to 28 months.

This sort of situation has practical implications for investors. An obvious strategy when the yield curve is inverted is to stick with short maturities, putting your cash into money-market funds, CDs or Treasury bills, where it will earn high interest.

But don't concentrate on short-term bonds exclusively. If a recession is in the offing, then long-term rates are likely to decline. That means the appearance of an inverted yield curve may represent a good opportunity to lock in those rates by using new money to "go long"—say, ten years or so. A middle course would be to dollar-cost-average out of a money-market fund into a long or intermediate bond fund, which would permit you to earn high short-term rates on your money without committing yourself too far down the road while you wait for the situation to clarify.

tion of interest rates and the price appreciation potential of the company's stock. In a climate in which interest rates are declining and prospects look good for stock prices, such as happens near the end of a recession, for example, carefully selected convertibles offer the promise of price potential and relatively small downside risk. But the interplay of interest rates, call provisions, conversion premiums and stock prices is so complex that it seems safe to assume that invididual investors get talked into buying convertibles by their brokers more often than they think of it themselves. In short, convertibles require more time and attention than most investors are willing to give them.

TREASURIES: THE SAFEST BONDS OF ALL

One way to eliminate the default risk entirely is to stick with IOUs from the U.S. Treasury. Because they are backed by the federal government, there is virtually no chance that you'll miss a payment of interest or principal or that Uncle Sam's credit rating will be lowered, no matter how many billions of dollars he is in the red. (Remember, he owns the presses that print the money.)

Risk Reducer #5: For maximum safety of principal, stick with bonds issued by the U.S. Treasury Department.

Buying Treasuries doesn't eliminate the market risk, however; once issued, their value fluctuates with interest rates, just like corporate bonds. But the risk of default is nil.

Treasuries have other attractive features as well. Interest (but not capital gains) is exempt from state and local income taxes. Because the market for them is so vast, they are easy to buy and easy to sell. Commissions tend to be modest. In fact, you can buy Treasuries direct at regularly scheduled auctions (you don't have to attend) and eliminate commission charges entirely.

All these advantages do come at a price: Treasuries tend to yield a little less than corporate bonds with comparable maturi-

HOW TO SELL T-NOTES AND T-BONDS

Q: *I have been purchasing Treasury bills and two-year Treasury notes under an account with the Federal Reserve Board Treasury Direct Bookkeeping Securities System. I hesitate to purchase intermediate- or long-term notes or bonds because I have been unable to determine how I can sell them prior to maturity. Is there a simple procedure for selling notes or bonds?*

A: You must set up an account at a bank or brokerage to hold your securities, then transfer your notes and bonds out of the Treasury Direct bookkeeping system. Your bank or brokerage can then sell the security for you for a fee—which usually runs between $25 and $50.

To transfer your notes or bonds, fill out Form PD 5179, *Security Transfer Request*, available from the Federal Reserve branch where you purchased your note or bond. Include your financial institution's routing number and handling instructions.

ties, even AAA-rated corporates. But for the peace of mind they provide, that's a small price millions of investors are happy to pay. Here's an overview of the choices in Treasury IOUs, followed by advice on the best ways to buy and sell them.

Treasury bills. These mature within a year—three- and six-month T-bills are the most common. Minimum purchase is $10,000. A key feature of T-bills that sets them apart from most other issues is that they pay the interest up front. You pay the face value of the bill minus the interest; when the bill matures, you collect the face value.

Here's how the system works: The Treasury holds regularly scheduled auctions at which investors bid for the bills. If the bids determine that the interest on that week's bills is 7%, you pay $9,300 for a $10,000 bill (assuming the maturity is a year; for shorter maturities, the payment would be adjusted accordingly). Then, when the bill matures, the Treasury sends you a check for $10,000.

The 7% interest you earn is called the "auction," or "discount," rate and it actually understates your yield. Because you're earning 7% on $10,000 but had to lay out only $9,300 to get it, you're a little ahead of the corporate-bond buyer, who would have had to ante up the entire $10,000. You can calculate the bond equivalent yield for a T-bill by figuring the interest earned on the actual cash investment. In this case, you're putting up $9,300 in exchange for $700 in interest. Thus your bond equivalent yield is 7.5%.

Treasury notes. Treasury notes, like corporate bonds, pay interest semi-annually. Notes are issued in medium-term maturities of two to ten years and are sold about once a month in minimum denominations of $1,000 for maturities of four years or more, $5,000 for shorter maturities. They can't be called.

Treasury bonds. These have maturities of more than ten years, although some can be called in early by the Treasury. Minimum purchase is $1,000.

How to buy Treasuries. The easiest way to buy a newly issued Treasury bill, note or bond is to pay a broker or bank to do it for you. You'll probably be charged $25 to $50 per transaction, which lowers your yield a little. Some institutions also levy fees for collecting interest payments on your behalf. The major advantage of having your bank or broker handle the transaction is convenience. If you want to sell the Treasury before it matures, you simply notify the bank or broker and it will be done for you.

You can save the commission by dealing directly with the government yourself. It's not terribly complicated to buy Treasuries in person or by mail at any of the country's 12 Federal Reserve banks, their 23 branches or at the Treasury Department in Washington. You can get details by writing to the Bureau of the Public Debt, Division of Customer Services, Washington, D.C. 20239, or by calling 202-287-4113 for recorded information. See pages 116 through 119 for a list of Federal Reserve banks and branches.

Whether you deal by mail or in person, you'll be required to fill out a tender, or bid, for the bill, note or bond you're buying. Most individuals submit what are known as noncompetitive bids, which means you'll get the average interest rate produced by the auction. The auction announcement states the date and time you must deliver in-person tenders. If you buy by mail, your envelope must be postmarked no later than the day before the auction and received by the date the security is issued. You can pay by check (for T-bills it must be a certified check) or with cash if you're buying in person. You can get a pretty good idea of the yield you're likely to get on newly issued Treasuries by checking newspaper tables of Treasury prices for comparable maturities in the secondary market.

How do you collect your interest? Under the Treasury Direct system, you supply on your tender form the number of your bank or money-market account, along with the name and nine-digit identification number of the financial institution you want to receive the funds (the number is on the institution's checks). The Treasury then deposits interest and principal payments directly to your account.

Treasury Direct also lets you sign up for automatic reinvestment of proceeds in new Treasury bills without filling out new forms. One possible hitch with Treasury Direct is that if you want to sell your security before it matures, you first must have it transferred to your bank or broker, so you could lose a little time.

WHAT U.S. AGENCY SECURITIES HAVE TO OFFER

Federal agency securities offer a way to step up the yield a bit over Treasuries without really increasing the risk. Agency debt isn't backed by the full faith and credit of the government, but no one believes that the government could ever let one of its agencies default. Still, because agency securities are not quite

continued on page 119

FEDERAL RESERVE BANKS AND BRANCHES

Send requests for application forms to purchase Treasury securities to the nearest Federal Reserve bank or branch or to the Treasury Department. The post office box or other address shown in parentheses should be used as the mailing address. The address not in parentheses is the street address.

BOSTON
600 Atlantic Avenue
(P.O. Box 2076)
Boston, MA 02106
(617) 973-3810

NEW YORK
33 Liberty Street
(Federal Reserve P.O. Station)
New York, NY 10045
(212) 791-6619
24-hour recording:
(212) 791-5823 (results)
(212) 791-7773 (new offerings)

Buffalo Branch
160 Delaware Avenue
(P.O. Box 961)
Buffalo, NY 14240
(716) 849-5046

PHILADELPHIA
Ten Independence Mall
(P.O. Box 90)
Philadelphia, PA 19105
(215) 574-6680

CLEVELAND
1455 East Sixth Street
(P.O. Box 6387)
Cleveland, OH 44101
(216) 579-2490

Cincinnati Branch
150 East Fourth Street
(P.O.Box 999)
Cincinnati, OH 45201
(513) 721-4787 ext. 333

Pittsburgh Branch
717 Grant Street
(P.O. Box 867)
Pittsburgh, PA 15230-0867
(412) 261-7863

RICHMOND
701 East Byrd Street
(P.O. Box 27622)
Richmond, VA 23261
(804) 643-1250

Baltimore Branch
502 S. Sharp Street
(P.O. Box 1378)
Baltimore, MD 21203
(301) 576-3300

Charlotte Branch
401 South Tryon Street
(P.O. Box 30248)
Charlotte, NC 28230
(704) 336-7100

ATLANTA
104 Marietta Street, NW
(P.O. Box 1731)
Atlanta, GA 30303
(404) 521-8657

Birmingham Branch
1801 Fifth Avenue, North
(P.O. Box 10447)
Birmingham, AL 35202
(205) 252-3141 ext. 215 or 264

Jacksonville Branch
515 Julia Street
(P.O. Box 2499)
Jacksonville, FL 32231-2499
(904) 632-4245

Miami Branch
9100 N.W. Thirty-sixth Street
(P.O. Box 520847)
Miami, FL 33152
(305) 593-9923

Nashville Branch
301 Eighth Avenue North
Nashville, TN 37203
(615) 259-4006
Instate WATTS:
1-800-342-8494

New Orleans Branch
525 St. Charles Avenue
(P.O. Box 61630)
New Orleans, LA 70161
(504) 685-1505 ext. 293

CHICAGO
230 South LaSalle Street
(P.O. Box 834)
Chicago, IL 60690
24-hour recording
(312) 786-1110

Detroit Branch
160 West Fort Street
(P.O. Box 1059)
Detroit, MI 48231
24-hour recording:
(313) 963-0087

ST. LOUIS
411 Locust Street
(P.O. Box 442)
St. Louis, MO 63166
24-hour recording:
(314) 444-8602

Little Rock Branch
325 West Capitol Avenue
(P.O. Box 1261)
Little Rock, AR 72203
(501) 372-5451 ext. 288

Louisville Branch
410 South Fifth Street
(P.O. Box 32710)
Louisville, KY 40232
(502) 568-9231 or 9236

continued

Memphis Branch
200 North Main Street
(P.O. Box 407)
Memphis, TN 38101
(901) 523-7171 ext. 225 or 641

MINNEAPOLIS
250 Marquette Avenue
Minneapolis, MN 55480
(612) 340-2075

KANSAS CITY
Attn: Securities Dept.
925 Grand Avenue
Kansas City, MO 64198
(816) 881-2783

Denver Branch
1020 16th Street
(P.O. Box 5228, Terminal Annex)
Denver, CO 80217
(303) 572-2300
24-hour recording
(303) 572-2477 (general information)

Oklahoma City Branch
226 Dean A. McGee Avenue
(P.O. Box 25129)
Oklahoma City, OK 73125
(405) 235-1721 ext. 182

Omaha Branch
2201 Farnam Street
Omaha, NE 68102
(402) 221-5636 or 5637

DALLAS
400 South Akard Street
(Securities Dept., Station K)
Dallas, TX 75222
(214) 651-6362

El Paso Branch
301 East Main Street
(P.O. Box 100)
El Paso, TX 79999
(915) 544-4730

Houston Branch
1701 San Jacinto Street
(P.O. Box 2578)
Houston, TX 77252
(713) 659-4433

San Antonio Branch
126 East Nueva Street
(P.O. Box 1471)
San Antonio, TX 78295
(512) 224-2141 ext. 303 or 305

SAN FRANCISCO
101 Market Street
(P.O. Box 7702)
San Francisco, CA 94120
(415) 974-2330

Los Angeles Branch
409 West Olympic Boulevard
(P.O. Box 2077, Terminal Annex)
Los Angeles, CA 90051
(213) 683-8546

Portland Branch
915 S.W. Stark Street
(P.O. Box 3436)
Portland, OR 97208
(503) 221-5921 or 5931

Salt Lake City
120 South State Street
(P.O. Box 30780)
Salt Lake City, UT 84130
(801) 355-3131

Seattle Branch
1015 Second Avenue
(P.O. Box 3567)
Seattle, WA 98124
(206) 442-1650

U.S. TREASURY
Mail General Inquiries To:
Bureau of the Public Debt
Washington, D.C 20239-1000

For In-Person Visits:
Bureau of the Public Debt
1300 C Street, S.W.
Washington, D.C.

Mail Tenders To:
Bureau of the Public Debt
Washington, D.C. 20239-1500

Telephone Device for the Hearing Impaired (TDD):
(202) 287-4097

---

as risk-free as Treasuries, they generally must pay a little more interest to attract investors.

The chief issuers of agency securities are the Federal Farm Credit System and the major mortgage-related agencies that include the Federal National Mortgage Association (Fannie Mae), the Government National Mortgage Association (Ginnie Mae) and the Federal Home Loan Mortgage Corporation (Freddie Mac). Maturities range from one to 40 years; minimum purchase requirements range from $1,000 to $25,000. The interest from issues of some agencies, such as the Student Loan Marketing Association and the Tennessee Valley Authority, is exempt from state and local income taxes. You purchase agency securities through brokers, and they are issued in book-entry form, like Treasuries, meaning a record is made of your ownership, but you don't actually receive the securities.

Technically, the mortgage-related agencies named above don't deal in bonds as such. They package mortgage loans they've purchased in the secondary market and sell "pass-through" or "participation" certificates to investors interested in receiving income from mortgage-backed securities. Ginnie Mae, for instance, insures pools of FHA and VA mortgages. If a borrower in the pool misses a payment, Ginnie Mae will make good if necessary, which isn't likely because the FHA and VA mortgages in the pool are backed by the government to begin with.

Pass-through and participation certificates start at $25,000, so for many people a Ginnie Mae mutual fund or unit trust is a more practical way to invest in mortgage-backed securities. The minimum for funds is usually $1,000.

Once bought, mortgage-backed securities behave a lot like bonds: their market value declines as interest rates rise, and vice versa. But they carry their own unique risk as well: As mortgage rates decline, many homeowners take advantage of the situation by refinancing. They pay off their old, high-rate mortgages, which then drop out of the pool. Investors get their principal back, but their interest payments may decline. As a result, the price of mortgage-backed securities can drop at the same time that the price of other bonds is rising.

Homeowners paying off mortgages in a pool have the same effect as a corporation calling its bonds: Investors get part of their principal back before they want it. In addition, cash flow is hard to predict. Because of this intrinsic unpredictability, Ginnie Maes and other mortgage pools generally pay a higher yield than Treasury bonds of comparable maturity. Over the years, this extra interest has attracted a lot of investors who didn't understand the risks involved. In turn, those risks have led to the creation of an instrument designed to make mortgage-backed income more predictable, the collateralized mortgage obligation.

Collateralized mortgage obligations (CMOs) are Ginnie Maes that are split into several different classes, or tranches. Investors choose a tranche according to whether they want a short-, intermediate- or long-term investment. All investors get interest income, but prepayments of principal go first to the short-term investors until they are paid off, then to the intermediate-term investors and so on. The real estate mortgage investment conduit, or REMIC, is a variation on the CMO idea that may not limit itself to Ginnie Mae mortgages. The minimum investment in CMO-type instruments is usually $1,000.

Swap EE Bonds for HH Bonds?

Q: *For over 15 years my husband and I purchased U.S. savings bonds with plans to cash them in after retirement. We're retired now, and our oldest bonds won't mature until 1997. Should we exchange the bonds for HH bonds so that we can put off paying federal tax on the accumulated interest and receive the semiannual interest payments? Or should we cash in all the bonds now, pay the tax and put the funds in a tax-free mutual fund?*

A: We wouldn't recommend either option. If you exchange your E and EE bonds for HH bonds, you put off federal taxes on the amount you roll over. But you earn only 6% interest, which is paid semiannually and is taxable in the year you receive it. If you cash in the bonds and put the money in a tax-exempt fund, paying taxes would leave you with less to invest (in the 28% bracket you'd have only $720 to invest for every $1,000 of accumulated savings bond interest). And tax-exempt interest, unlike savings bonds' tax-deferred interest, is counted as income in the formula that determines how much of your social security benefits is taxed. Instead, consider redeeming your EEs periodically over the years as you need the money. Your tax liability would be spread out more evenly than if you cashed them in all at once, and you could redeem the bonds with the lowest guaranteed interest rate first.

You'll find a more complete description of mortgage-backed securities in Chapter 10.

SAVINGS BONDS: NEW SPARK FOR AN OLD IDEA

Once thought of chiefly as a haven for scaredy-cats and a no-brainer gift for kids' birthdays and bar mitzvahs, savings bonds have been finding their way into serious investors' portfolios since the government liberalized interest rates in the early 1980s. Today, Series EE bonds offer an attractive, competitive yield, unquestioned safety and a couple of unique tax features that make them especially suited for savers with an eye on college costs or retirement some years away.

■ *Competitive interest rates.* EEs earn interest for 30 years at a floating rate. Bonds held for five or more years never earn less than 6% and usually earn more. The yield is either 6% or 85% of the average yield on five-year Treasury securities, whichever is higher. (Bonds held for less than five years earn interest on a sliding scale starting at 4.16% after six months, working gradually up to the 6% minimum in the fifth year.) The savings bond rate is adjusted twice a year, in May and November, to reflect current market rates. Since the 6% minimum was established, interest has ranged as high as 11% and has slipped under 7% at its lowest point. In mid 1991, it stood at 6.57%. You can get the current rate by dialing 1–800-US-BONDS (1-800-872-6637).

The 6% minimum applies to EE bonds issued after November 1, 1986. EEs issued on or after November 1, 1982, and before November 1, 1986, earn a minimum of 7.5% if held for at least five years.

■ *Convenient to buy.* Many people buy EE bonds via automatic payroll deduction, a virtually painless way to accumulate bonds little by little as the years go by. For others, buying a bond is as easy as making a trip to the bank. EEs come in denominations as small as $50 and as large as $10,000. You pay half the face amount and collect the accumulated interest when you redeem the bond, which you can do at any bank, with no commission charges on either side of the transaction.

■ *Safe as can be.* Savings bonds are protected against default by the full faith and credit of the U.S. government. The only way you can lose the principal is to lose the bond, and if you do lose the bond (or if it is stolen or destroyed), you can get it replaced by writing to the Bureau of the Public Debt, 200 Third St., Parkersburg, W.Va. 26106-1328.

■ *Convertible into an income stream.* Series EE bonds pay no current income—that is, you have to cash them in to get your interest. But $500 or more of EE bonds can be converted directly into Series HH bonds, which pay 6% interest in semi-annual installments.

ALTERNATIVE TO SAVINGS BONDS

Q: *I am 25 years old, single, and have just started investing. I am buying U.S. savings bonds each month through payroll deductions. Would I be better off putting my money elsewhere?*

A: Savings bonds are one of the safest, most convenient ways to invest, but someone your age, who can afford to take some risk, should consider a stock mutual fund for long-term investing with higher rewards. Many funds rival the convenience of savings bond payroll deduction by allowing you to invest a regular amount each month via automatic bank drafts. See Chapter 6.

■ *Special tax features.* This is where savings bonds earn their spurs. Interest is exempt from all state and local income taxes, and your options for paying federal income taxes are unique to savings bonds. You can either pay the tax each year as the interest accrues, or postpone paying the tax until you cash in the bond or give it to someone else, or until it matures. Or you could exchange your EE bonds for HH bonds and continue putting off the tax until you cash in the HHs (although the semi-annual interest payments are taxable) or until they reach maturity after 20 years. This is a possibility for retirees to consider, but tax savings shouldn't blind you to the fact that you may be able to earn more than 6%, after taxes, elsewhere.

■ *Special deal for college savings.* The practice of buying savings bonds to finance the kids' college education is an American institution. Parents and grandparents buy bonds in the name of the child, who can often count the interest as tax-free because the child doesn't have enough income to incur any tax. As an alternative, the child's tax bill can be deferred until he or she reaches age 14, when the so-called kiddie tax disappears (See Chapter 16). The child pays tax then, but in the lowest bracket.

If you buy Series EE bonds in your own name (not the child's), all income from them will be tax-free if the bonds are redeemed to pay college tuition or fees, as long as your income is under certain levels. See Chapters 13 and 16 for a more complete explanation.

MAKING MONEY WITH MUNICIPALS

Municipal bonds are issued by states, counties, cities and other political jurisdictions and their agencies. Agencies may be school districts, airport authorities, bridge and highway departments, sewer districts and so forth.

The main attraction of municipal bonds is well known: The interest earned from them is exempt from federal income tax and, in most cases, from income taxes of the issuing state as well. (The only exceptions are Illinois, Iowa, Oklahoma and Wisconsin, which grant limited exemptions.) One way to look at the federal tax exemption is this: The states and cities don't tax the interest from Treasury issues, so the federal government returns the favor by not taxing the interest from municipal bonds. (In fact, the exemption is based on the U.S. Constitution, which bars the feds from interfering with state revenues and vice versa.)

Because tax-exempt interest is worth having only if it exceeds the after-tax yield of taxable interest, figuring the taxable equivalent yield of a municipal bond is the first step in deciding whether to buy it. If it doesn't pass this test, there's no need to evaluate it further. Thus it is crucial to know how to perform the following calculation, although a broker will gladly do it for you:

$$\text{Taxable equivalent yield} = \frac{\text{yield from municipal bond}}{1 - \text{your federal tax bracket}}$$

Example: A municipal bond is offered at a yield of 6%. Your taxable income is $60,000 on a joint return, which in 1991 put you in the 28% bracket. To work the equation, you convert your bracket to a decimal, or .28. So the taxable equivalent yield is 6 divided by $(1 - .28) = 6 \div .72 = 8.33$. To match the 6% tax-free yield, you'd need a taxable bond paying at least 8.33%.

The calculation actually understates your taxable equivalent if your state doesn't tax municipal bond interest. In high-tax states such as California, Connecticut, Massachusetts, New York, Oregon and others, the double tax-free status of municipal bonds issued by the state can add to the allure considerably. If you live in a city or county that also levies an income tax, the triple-tax-free status of bonds issued by your own state or local jurisdiction raises the taxable equivalent yield even higher.

How to pick a muni bond. Municipals, like corporate bonds, vary in quality according to the economic and financial soundness of the project or the creditworthiness of the issuing jurisdiction. Also like corporate issues, they are rated for default risk by Standard & Poor's and Moody's, on the same scale as corporates: Bonds considered least risky get rated AAA or Aaa, and so forth as described earlier in the chapter. The higher the bond's rating, the less interest it needs to pay to attract investors, and vice versa.

In addition to its ratings by the credit agencies, a major point to check about a tax-free bond is whether it is a general obligation issue or a revenue bond. As explained earlier, a general obligation bond gets the full backing of the jurisdiction's ability to tax, but a revenue bond has the backing only of the revenues generated by the project it supports—a bridge, an airport or a sewage treatment plant, for instance. Every revenue bond project is different and needs to be analyzed on its economic merits.

Ask your broker for any reports his or her firm has generated on the project. The official statement from the issuer describes the bond, the project and the municipality in detail. If the bond is a new issue, your broker is required to give you a copy of the statement, just as he is required to give you a copy of the prospectus for a new corporate stock or bond issue. But this document, unlike a corporate prospectus, has no standardized format. And unlike corporations, municipal bond issuers are not required to provide regular financial information to bondholders, which puts the onus on you to stay current on the financial condition of the issuer of any bonds you may hold.

If you have only a few thousand dollars to commit to municipals, their $5,000 minimum face value suggests that buying into pooled arrangements such as mutual funds and unit trusts makes more sense than chasing after individual bonds. Funds and trusts offer diversified portfolios while providing liquidity and controlling commission costs. They are described in the next chapter.

Insured municipal bonds. Defaults are rare with municipal bonds, but there have been enough near misses to create an active demand for municipal bond insurance, and state and local budget woes make the idea especially timely. The American Municipal Bond Assurance Corporation (AMBAC) was the first to insure municipal bonds, starting in 1971. The Municipal Bond Insurance Association (MBIA), another major insurer of municipals, appeared three years later.

To insure its bonds, an issuer or underwriter pays a premium of 0.1% to 2% of total principal and interest. In return, the insurance company agrees to pay principal and interest to bondholders if the issuer defaults. Policies remain in effect for the life of the bond. Insured bonds get the top AAA rating from S&P, even if the bond has a lower rating based on its own creditworthiness. The insurance, because it makes a bond less risky, makes it more attractive to investors. As a result, its yield will be a little lower than a comparably rated uninsured issue.

Municipal bond insurance guarantees that your principal and interest will be paid. It doesn't protect the market value of your bond. Interest rate changes or a downgrading of the issuer's credit rating will still affect the market value of insured bonds, although if you hold the issue until maturity you won't lose a cent.

Taxable municipal bonds. Until a few years ago, all municipals were tax-free, but these days it's necessary to differentiate. The interest earned from municipal bonds issued to finance private business activities, such as shopping malls, is generally taxable on the federal level, though it may still be exempt from state and local taxes. The income from certain kinds of private activity bonds, such as those issued to finance the building of a hospital or to back certain kinds of mortgages, is still exempt. For investors in high brackets who have a lot of tax-sheltered income, however, the interest from such bonds issued after August 7, 1986, may be subject to taxation through the alternative minimum tax (AMT). The AMT taxes so-called preference income above a certain level at a flat rate of 24%. Most taxpayers are not subject to the AMT, but make sure you find out the purpose for which your bonds were issued.

HOW TO USE ZERO-COUPON BONDS

Bonds normally pay interest every six months. Zero-coupon bonds, known as "zeros," don't pay any interest at all until they mature, at which time they pay all accumulated interest at once. Zeros come in denominations as low as $1,000 and are sold at discounts from face value of 50% to 75% depending on how long you have to wait for maturity. A $1,000 zero yielding 9% and maturing in 18 years, for example, costs just $205.

Their huge discounts from face value make zeros an excellent long-term investment when you know that you'll need the money at a particular date in the future. The catch is, the IRS taxes the interest year by year as it accrues, just as if you had received it. Because it makes little sense to pay tax on income you haven't yet received, investors buy zeros mainly to put in their individual retirement accounts, which allow tax-free buildup of earnings within the account (see Chapter 14).

Outside of IRAs, zero-coupon municipal bonds can be a good way to take advantage of the time value of money by paying 50 cents or so today to collect a dollar of face value some years down the road. Tax-free zeros are relatively rare, however, so you may have trouble finding ones that mature when you'll need the money. They usually can be called early, too, making their maturity dates even less reliable.

Zeros as a college financing tool. The tax consequences of zero-coupon bonds needn't be as onerous as they first appear if the bonds are used as a part of a college financing plan for young children.

Buy the bonds in the child's name so that the income will be taxable to the child. (Your broker can set up a free or low-cost custodial account.) The first $550 of investment income a child reports each year is tax-free. For children under age 14, the next $550 is taxed at his or her own rate, probably 15%, and investment income in excess of $1,100 is taxed at the parent's rate—probably 28% or 31%.

The way the IRS requires zero-coupon bond interest to be reported works to your advantage. Again, consider a 9% zero that grows over 18 years from $205 to $1,000. You don't report one-eighteenth of the $795 difference ($44) each year. Instead you report interest as it actually accrues. The first year, a $205 investment earning 9% compounded semiannually earns about $19. The second year, your investment would be $224 ($205 + $19), and $20 of interest would accrue. (You'll get a notice each year from the issuer or your broker showing how much interest to report to the IRS.) It would take quite a few years for the income to trigger much tax, even if you buy, say, 10 bonds. Chapter 13 provides more details about using zeros as a college savings plan.

Choosing a zero. The most popular zeros are those issued directly by the U.S. Treasury and their close cousins created by brokerage firms, who strip the income from regular Treasuries and sell the bare bonds. The direct Treasury issues are called STRIPS. The brokers' versions go by names like TIGRS and CATS. Beyond the security of having the federal government

MAXIMIZING INTEREST
WHEN SELLING BONDS

Q: *I've been purchasing U.S. savings bonds through payroll deduction. When is the best time to redeem the bonds to get the most interest?*

A: You'll receive the maximum interest if you redeem your bonds on the exact date that you are credited with interest or as soon as possible after that. Series EE bonds accrue interest twice a year, but exactly when that occurs varies with the bond's redemption date. A bank can tell you your bonds' redemption dates as well as their guaranteed minimum interest rates. You can order the schedule of interest payment dates for series EE bonds for $1 from the Superintendent of Documents, U.S. Government Printing Office, Washington, D.C. 20402. You can also get a free copy of *The Best Times to Redeem or Exchange Savings Bonds,* which explains how to maximize the interest, by writing to the Department of the Treasury, U.S. Savings Bond Division, Office of Public Affairs, Washington, D.C. 20226.

behind them, STRIPS are noncallable; they can't be paid off early if interest rates decline.

Zeros issued by corporations offer slightly higher yields than government zeros of similar maturities. Pay special attention to the rating of corporate zeros; if the company goes broke, you may never get your money, or you may get only pennies on the dollar. Check for call features, too. If you consider any callable bond, be certain you understand when and at what price it can be called.

You can also buy zeros through a mutual fund. The Benham Target Maturity Trust (800-472-3389) and the Scudder Zero Coupon funds (800-225-2470) offer zero funds with several different maturity years. With these funds, you buy shares at a price that is expected to grow to $100 at the end of the target year. Although share prices can fluctuate day to day, if you hold on to your shares until the fund matures, you should earn the yield promised when you bought them.

Unless you buy shares in a fund, you'll need to use a broker to buy zeros. You may need more than one, in fact, to compare the availability and yields of bonds that fit your plans. Don't assume all STRIPS or broker-made Treasury zeros yield the same amount. Yields can vary depending on the commissions built into the price.

The search for tax-free zeros will be tougher. The supply isn't abundant and the call features can be troubling. You must find a broker willing to do the spadework to find appropriate bonds.

As an alternative, you could do your own spadework to find a mutual fund that finds the kinds of bonds you're looking for. The next chapter will show you how.

6

MUTUAL FUNDS: THE BEST INVESTMENT IDEA ANYONE EVER HAD

MUTUAL FUNDS are the hired guns of the investment business: They do the dirty work for you. A lot of people with neither the time nor the inclination to slog through reports on thousands of stocks and bonds in search of a handful of good ones turn the job over to one or more mutual funds. The funds' professional portfolio managers pool your money with that of other investors and assemble portfolios designed to achieve specific investment objectives, which are spelled out in each fund's prospectus. Thus, instead of digesting thousands of reports, you need only digest a few.

Funds can make investing easier, but it's a mistake to think they make it easy. In their quest to attract investors of every conceivable stripe, mutual funds have multiplied so rapidly that they now outnumber the 2,200-plus stocks listed on the New York Stock Exchange. The Investment Company Institute (ICI), the national association to which most funds belong, has more than 3,200 members. ICI sorts funds into no fewer than 22 different categories according to investment objectives, ranging from aggressive stock funds that buy the shares of promising but unproven new companies to conservative bond funds that restrict their investments to the municipal bonds of a single state.

In addition to this amazing range of investment portfolios, funds offer a combination of shareholder services that is impossible to find anywhere else.

WHAT FUNDS HAVE TO OFFER

Mutual funds are sponsored by management companies that hire the experts who make the investment decisions. Sometimes a manager will guide the fund to such sterling performance for so long that the manager's name becomes practically synonymous with the fund's: Peter Lynch, who retired from Fidelity Magellan fund in 1990 after 13 years at the helm, and John Neff, who has run Vanguard Windsor fund since 1964, are examples. Other funds bear the names of founders who established their credentials as stock market gurus *before* setting up publicly available mutual funds. John Templeton, Mario Gabelli and Martin Zweig fit that description. The vast majority of mutual fund portfolio managers don't share this celebrity status. They labor in relative obscurity, which is probably just fine with them.

Because they provide expert portfolio management, mutual funds are a better choice than individual stocks or bonds for beginning investors who are still unsure of their own stock- and bond-picking prowess.

Automatic diversification. Owning shares of a mutual fund gives you a small ownership interest in all the stocks, bonds, and other investments in the fund's portfolio. Whether your aim is to own a cross section of growth stocks or utility stocks, corporate bonds or gold-mining shares, you can find a fund or funds to suit you.

Because they provide instant diversification, well-selected mutual funds are a better choice than individual stocks or bonds for investors with modest amounts of money to place at risk.

Ease of purchase and sale. You can buy funds through a broker or through the mail. You can sell them the same way, or with a phone call. By law, a fund must buy back its shares when you want to sell them. The price at which fund shares are bought and sold is based on the fund's *net asset value,* or NAV, which is the market value of the fund's holdings, minus management expenses, divided by the number of fund shares outstanding. A few specialized funds calculate their NAV hourly, but for the most part the price you pay or receive will be based on the net asset value calculated at the close of trading on the day you place your order. (A major difference between "load" and "no-load" funds, which are discussed in detail later in this chapter, is that you buy and sell no-load funds at their net asset value; you buy load funds at net asset value plus a commission, but sell them back to the fund at net asset value.)

Because most mutual funds are regularly issuing new shares and buying back old ones, the number of shares is constantly changing. Thus, they are called "open-end" funds. This distinguishes them from "closed-end" funds, which issue a fixed number of shares and usually don't buy them back. Once issued, closed-end shares are bought and sold on a stock exchange or over the counter. The distinction between open-end and closed-end funds sometimes gets muddled by the fact that some open-end funds reach a point at which they don't want any additional cash to invest and declare themselves "closed" to new investors. In recent years, the Mutual Shares and Vanguard Windsor funds have decided to close in that way. They did not thereby become closed-end funds, however, because they stand ready to redeem or issue shares for their current shareholders. There's more on closed-end funds later in this chapter.

Small minimum purchases. A few funds have no minimum
continued on page 136

HOW TO READ A FUND PROSPECTUS

A mutual fund prospectus is an awkward cross between a sales pitch and a legal treatise. It is the basic information document that all fund sellers must provide to prospective investors. In it you'll find a summary of fees and expenses, instructions for buying and redeeming shares, plus descriptions of fund objectives, management and shareholder services. Much of the wording is dictated by the Securities and Exchange Commission, which is why so many prospectuses sound alike.

The prospectus shouldn't be the only thing you read about the fund, but it is among the most important. Here are some of the questions about a fund that are answered with a careful reading of the prospectus.

How do the fund's objectives match your own?
Every prospectus has a section labeled with the word "objectives." Read this section very carefully, because it reveals how the fund intends to make money and what kinds of risks it will take in the pursuit of it. Will the fund invest in high-dividend stocks? Will it look for fast profits or long-term growth? Will it take chances you'd rather not take? Pay especially close attention to the fund's guidelines concerning the quality of its investments.

How risky is the fund's strategy?
A prospectus may not have a "risks" section as such. If it does, that's a tip-off: Pay attention to it. In other prospectuses, you'll have to ferret this out. What could go wrong with the fund's plans? Studying the fund's performance can give you a sense of how well it has handled risks in the past.

How much will it cost you to invest?
Tables in every prospectus will tell you whether the fund imposes a load, or charge when you buy, reinvest or redeem shares; they'll also spell out annual operating costs. As a rule, a company that keeps its expenses at

1% or less of its assets is considered a low-cost fund; anything above 1.5% is high.

How has the fund done in the past?

A performance table shows how you would have fared had you owned shares of the fund over the last decade, assuming it has been around that long. Dividends, capital gains distributions and the share price at the beginning and end of each year are included. Also listed is the fund's portfolio turnover rate, which is a measure of how often it buys and sells securities. Generally, the higher the rate, the greater the fund's expenses. A rate exceeding 100%—meaning the fund replaced the equivalent of its entire portfolio in the period measured—is a sign of an aggressively managed fund or a fund operating in perilous markets. For instance, a bond fund would tend to log a low turnover rate in a period of steady or declining interest rates, but a high turnover when rates head up.

The performance section lists yield and total return figures. Total return includes income and changes in share price during the period being measured and assumes that such payouts are reinvested in additional shares.

How do you buy and redeem shares?

The key information here is the minimum purchase accepted and minimum subsequent purchases. In the case of a money-market fund, also check the minimum redemption amount. If you plan to use it as an interest-earning checking account, for example, you probably won't want a fund that imposes a $1,000 minimum on redemptions by check.

One thing you won't find in the prospectus is a listing of what securities the fund actually owns. You can get that information, though, in the fund's Statement of Additional Information and from its latest quarterly or annual reports. Ask for a copy when you request the prospectus, but keep in mind that portfolio holdings change often and your report is bound to be at least a little out of date.

initial investment requirement; you can buy $20 worth of shares if you want. Many will accept as little as $250 or $500 to start. A typical minimum is $1,000 to open an account, with minimum additional investments of $50 or $100. This makes mutual funds ideal vehicles for long-term accumulation programs through dollar-cost averaging (See Chapter 4). And because funds will issue fractional shares, you can invest a flat amount on a regular basis without worrying about whether you're buying whole shares. For instance, $250 will buy 15.63 shares when a fund is selling for $16 a share. If it's selling for $15.50 the next time you buy, your $250 gets you 16.13 shares.

Automatic reinvestment of earnings. Dividends paid by stocks in the fund's portfolio, interest from bonds and capital gains earned from selling securities can be automatically reinvested for you in more shares. Reinvesting earnings is a critical element in any long-term investment plan.

Automatic payment plans. If you'd like to receive regular income from your shares, funds will set up automatic payment plans for you. If dividends and interest earned aren't enough to cover your payments, the fund will sell shares to cover them.

Shareholder services. Most funds are happy to hear from their shareholders and have set up well-staffed telephone systems to handle inquiries about everything from current account balances to requests for descriptive brochures and order forms. Funds love individual retirement accounts or Keogh accounts (because they know such accounts are likely to stay there for some years) and have simplified the custodial paperwork to the point that it is virtually painless. Companies that manage a group of funds, often called a family of funds, make it easy for you to switch your money from one member of the family to another, usually with a phone call. That provides a convenient way for you to move your money from, say, a stock fund to a money-market fund.

How Loads Affect Performance

Q: *Why is the fund's load fee excluded from most perfor-mance calculations? Doesn't that distort the actual results an investor would experience?*

A: It's important to take fees into account when calculating your own gain, but in comparing funds, keep in mind that a fund's total return is a fund's total return, period. A sales fee, if any, doesn't mean that the return on your investment is lower, it means that less of your money is invested initially.

For example: You invest $10,000 in a fund with a 6% sales fee, and the fund has a 10% total return the first year you own it. The broker kept $600, so only $9,400 of your money got into the fund. You still earned 10% on the amount invested. Suppose someone else did the same thing, but a year earlier than you. He earned 10% on his *entire* investment in the second year because he didn't pay another sales fee. The point is not that fund loads should be ignored but rather, that they affect different investors in the same fund in different ways, depending on when th ey put their money in. It is very difficult to account for such differences in a ranking system based on portfolio performance.

Easy access to information. Fund prices are published in the newspaper every day, just like the prices of the stocks and bonds that funds buy and sell for their portfolios (See the sample listing on pages 140 and 141). Most funds maintain toll-free numbers to facilitate requests for information about the fund, and in fact are supposed to provide you with a prospec-tus before selling you any shares (See pages 134 and 135 for an explanation of how to read a prospectus).

Several tracking services follow funds and report their results over various periods ranging from a week to 10 years. The list of newspapers and magazines that publish compara-tive fund performance information in every single issue is long and diverse, ranging from broad-based personal finance publications such as *Kiplinger's Personal Finance Magazine,* which publishes a monthly list of top performers and an annual compilation of results for all funds, to business and investment publications such as *Forbes, Business Week, Barron's,* the *Wall Street Journal* and *Investor's Daily.* The box on pages 146 and 147 describes a number of publications that contain comprehensive listings of funds, including, in some cases, performance results.

Convenience, shareholder services and a wide choice of portfolios tailored to different investment goals make mutual funds a suitable substitute for individually selected stocks and bonds, even for experienced investors. Your own investment style should determine whether you should use funds for part or all of your portfolio.

THE COST OF MUTUAL FUND INVESTING

In return for all this expertise and convenience, mutual funds charge a variety of fees. Like cars, hotels and stockbrokers, some funds give you more for your money than others.

Sales charges. It's tempting to divide funds neatly into two camps: *load funds,* which are sold mostly through brokers and charge you a commission when you buy shares, and *no-load funds,* which are sold directly to the public via advertising and don't charge a sales commission. Unfortunately, making the distinction is not that simple anymore. The marketing of funds has become so sophisticated that before you can know what you're paying, you need to check the prospectus for front-end loads, back-end loads and other kinds of fees that can sneak up on you if you don't watch out.

■ *Front-end loads.* Of the 1,500 funds ranked by Kiplinger in 1990, more than half—816 of them—charged a front-end load, ranging from 1% to 8.5% of the amount invested. A typical load is about 4.5% to 5.75%, often charged on a sliding scale that decreases with the size of the investment. For instance, one fund charges 5.75% on purchases of less than $50,000; 4.5% for a $50,000 to $100,000 investment and so on down until the load disappears for investors with a million dollars or more. It's important to be aware that the load is calculated on the gross amount of your investment. If you invest $1,000 in a fund with a load of 5.75%, then $57.50 will be deducted as a sales charge and $942.50 will be invested in the fund's shares. Calculated as a percentage of your investment, that $57.50 actually represents a commission of 6.1% paid to the fund.

Fund-buying tip #1: *Because the sales load reduces the size of your initial investment, you earn less in a load fund over time than you would by placing the same amount of money in a no-load fund that produced the identical performance record.*

■ *Back-end loads.* Funds prefer to call these redemption fees. They are levied against the net asset value when you sell, thereby reducing your profit or adding to your loss. The Prudential family of equity funds gives investors a choice of paying 5.25% to get in, or up to 5% to get out.

Fund-buying tip #2: *If you are investing for capital gains, a fund that charges a front-end load is preferable to a fund that charges a redemption fee because the load will be based on a smaller amount. If you are investing for income, a back-end load may be preferable to a front-end load because more of your initial investment goes to work earning interest. Other things being equal, a no-load fund is preferable to either type of load.*

■ *Deferred loads.* Sometimes called contingent deferred sales fees, these are deducted from the amount of your original investment if you redeem shares before a specified time elapses after you buy them. The amount of the charge and the conditions under which you'll have to pay it are described in the prospectus. The purpose, clearly, is to discourage you from jumping in and out of the fund.

■ *Reinvestment loads.* These are the most difficult fees to justify. They take a little nick out of the interest, dividends and capital gains that are reinvested in your account. Read the prospectus carefully to determine the fund's policy on this point. In 1991, four fund groups managing a total of about 50 funds charged their investors in this way. They were First

Investors, Franklin, National, and Smith Barney.

Fund-buying tip #3: *For a long-range investment plan, don't load up with funds that levy a fee on reinvested dividends and capital gains.*

Management fees. Most of the fees described above go to the broker who sells you the fund, although some funds that sell directly to the public also charge commissions. All funds, both load and no-load, must charge a management fee to compensate the managers for their services, pay the rent, brokerage commissions on portfolio transactions, and so forth.

HOW TO READ THE MUTUAL FUND LISTINGS

Most daily newspapers publish mutual fund tables in the business pages. Here's a guide to interpreting them.

NAV is net asset value per share: what a share of the fund is worth.

Offer price is what you pay per share.

NAV Chg. is the change in the fund's NAV that day.

p next to the fund's name means that it charges a yearly 12b-1 fee. Funds may be listed as NL even if they charge this fee.

t means the fund levies both 12b-1 and redemption fees. In most cases, p and r listed together refer to a fund with a contingent deferred sales charge. Such a fund may not be listed as no-load.

NL in the pricing column means there is no up-front/sales load.

r stands for redemption charge, which may be permanent or temporary. It may start as high as 6% and decline gradually. A fund can have a redemption fee but still be called no-load.

x stands for "ex-dividend," meaning only current shareholders get the fund's next dividend payout, which is imminent. New buyers won't get it.

A typical management fee is one half to one percent of the fund's assets. It may be either a flat rate or a sliding scale that shrinks as the size of the fund's portfolio grows. Twentieth Century funds, which are no-load, charge a flat 1%, for instance. Strong Opportunity fund, which carries a 2% load, also charges 1% for management. Scudder Capital Growth, a no-load, charges .70%. Fidelity bond funds, all no-loads, charge a two-tiered fee that can be as high as .72% or as low as .30%. Clearly, a fund's policy on management fees has nothing to do with its policy on sales fees. Careful inspection of the prospectus is the best way to ferret out these fees.

Price ranges for investment companies, as quoted by the National Association of Securities Dealers. NAV stands for net asset value per share; the offering includes net asset value plus maximum sales charge, if any.

	NAV	Offer Price	NAV Chg.			NAV	Offer Price	NAV Chg.
AAL Mutual:					SocBd	15.84	16.63	+.01
CaGr p	12.58	13.21	...		SocEq	18.98	19.93	−.10
Inco p	9.69	10.17	...		TxF Lt	10.65	10.87	...
MuBd p	10.11	10.62	...		TxF Lg	15.63	16.41	...
AARP Invst:					TxF VT	15.18	15.94	...
CaGr	27.94	NL	−.10		US Gov	14.79	15.53	+.01
GiniM	15.31	NL	+.01		WshA p	12.31	12.92	+.02
GthInc	....	....	...		**Capstone Group:**			
HQ Bd	15.10	NL	...		CshFr	9.62	10.10	−.01
TxFBd	16.89	NL	−.01		Fd SW	15.70	16.48	−.12
TxFSh	15.18	NL	...		GvtInc	4.68	4.68	...
ABT Funds:					MedRs	16.28	17.09	−.03
Emrg p	10.76	11.30	−.09		PBHG	11.22	11.78	−.06
FL TF	10.37	10.89	+.01		Ray El	6.54	6.87	...
Gthln p	9.67	10.15	+.02		Trend	14.03	14.73	−.05
Utilln p	11.65	12.23	−.05		CarilCa	11.93	12.56	...
AdsnCa p	19.02	19.61	−.03		**Carneg Cappielo:**			
AEGON USA:					EmGr p	10.61	11.11	...
CapApp	4.19	4.40	+.01		Grow p	18.94	19.83	+.08
˙˙˙'˙˙	9.73	10.22	...		TRetn p	10.95	11.47	+.06
	6.05	6.35	−.02		**Carnegie Funds:**			
˙.aiu..	˙˙ 12.01		...		Govt p	9.09	9.52	...
CalMi.		˙	+.02		TEOhG	9.22	9.65	...
Eqlnc t		˙			TENHi	9.60	10.05	...
FITxF t	10.˙˙				˙˙-˙	11.72	12.81	+.01
HiInc t	6.49	o.˙.						
NtMur t	9.13	9.13	...					
NJ TF t	9.99	9.99	+.01					
NYTF	10.20	10.20	+.02		IIı..			
PA TF t	9.98	9.98	+.01		ST Bd p	...		
EclipEq	11.10	NL	+.07		SpcSit p	20.69	21.72	+.16
Emblem Fund:					**Fidelity Spartan:**			
ErnEq	11.10	11.56	+.10		CAHY r	10.15	NL	+.01
IntGv	10.33	10.76	...		CTHY t	10.64	NL	+.02
OH Reg	10.35	10.78	+.07		GNMA	9.91	9.91	...
RelEq	11.51	11.99	+.11		GovIn	10.50	NL	+.03
SI Fxd	10.13	10.55	.01		HighIn	10.63	10.63	...
EmpBld	16.97	17.72	+.02		LtdGv	9.98	NL	+.01
Enterprise Group:					LTG x	10.76	10.76	.11
CapA p	22.06	23.16	+.37		Mktln p	28.50	NL	+.35
GvSec p	11.94	12.54	ı .04		MunIn r	10.16	NL	+.01
Grlnc p	15.72	14.51	ı .12		NIHY r	10.45	NL	ı .02

Listing taken from the *Wall Street Journal*

Marketing fees. Some funds deduct the costs of advertising and marketing the fund directly from the fund's assets rather than absorbing them in the management costs. These charges, called 12b-1 fees, are typically around .25% to .30% but range as high as 1.25%. Sometimes a portion of the fee is paid to the broker who sold you the fund.

Expense ratio. The expense ratio is the cost of running the fund expressed as a percentage of the fund's assets and is the best tool you have for comparing the management costs you'll incur by investing in different funds. It includes management and 12b-1 fees, but not sales loads. The expenses are deducted from net assets and reflected in the percentage returns reported by the funds. Expense ratios can range to 2.50% or more; the higher the ratio, the less the fund has left to pay its shareholders out of earnings.

HOW TO FIND THE RIGHT FUNDS FOR YOU

In a way, worrying about management fees and expense ratios is putting the cart before the horse. The first task in choosing a mutual fund that's right for you is to narrow down the field of thousands to a few appropriate candidates. You do that by concentrating on the funds whose investment objectives and willingness to take risks match your own. After you've done that, you should compare performance records, expense ratios and shareholder services before deciding where to put your money. The resources listed on pages 146 and 147 will help you get that information.

What is the fund's investment objective? Most of the 22 categories used by the Investment Company Institute to describe funds give a pretty good clue to the kinds of investments they make: growth, aggressive growth, corporate bond and long-term municipal bond, for example. The investment objective is a crucial piece of information, and all the sources listed on pages 146 and 147 include it. A fund's goals should match yours. Later in this chapter, we suggest some funds with good long-term records to consider for various investment objectives.

What is the fund's performance record? You want two pieces of information here: the fund's performance in relation to the market as a whole, and the fund's performance in relation to other funds of its type. The industry-sponsored guides, such as the ICI's *Mutual Fund Directory*, don't include this sort of information; the independently published guides, such as the *Individual Investor's Guide to No-Load Mutual Funds*, do include it, either as part of a ranking system or in a form you can use to discern relative performance.

Compare the *total return* (price changes plus reinvested earnings) over one, three, five and ten years and consider what was going on in the market during the periods being measured. A fund that maintains a good total return in good markets and bad has earned further consideration. A good yardstick to use: Look for stock funds that consistently double your money in five years—that is, funds with a total return of 100% or more over five years. The results from bond funds will be more modest, but a five-year total return of 50% or so is a reasonable expectation.

How risky is the fund? Again, you won't find comparative information on the risk-reward relationship in the industry-sponsored guides. You'll have to look to the magazines and newsletters listed and to the data collection services. Like stocks, mutual funds have betas, which measure volatility relative to the market as a whole (see Chapter 4). But fund trackers go much further than that, producing risk ratings for bull and bear markets, and volatility groupings ranging from low to high based on standard deviations from expected results. These risk measurements are useful indicators of how much volatility to expect from a fund, but a low risk ranking is not a guarantee of safety. If the market plunges, you can be virtually certain that it will take low-risk stocks—and the funds that own them—down with it.

Of all the measures of relative risk in mutual funds, volatility rankings are probably the most common. Investment Company Data, Inc. (ICDI), which tracks fund performance for Kiplinger and other clients, measures variations in each fund's total return (price changes plus reinvested earnings) relative to other funds over the most recent five-year period. (If a fund is less than five years old, its return is measured for as many years as it is available.) The wider a fund's up and down swings over the period, the more volatile, or risky it is considered to be. ICDI assigns each fund a ranking from 1 (least volatile) to 9 (most volatile).

Bond funds typically earn a 1 because their prices don't tend to change very much. A volatility ranking of 9 is relatively rare but is awarded from time to time to very aggressive stock funds that take big risks in search of big payoffs. A ranking of 5 indicates that the fund carries an average risk.

Does the fund charge a front- or back-end load? Sales loads *do* make a difference. Consider two stock funds with nearly identical records for the five years ended December 31, 1990. Transamerica Technology rose 111.8% and Kleinwort Benson International rose 111.6%. Transamerica seems to be the winner by a whisker. But it charges a 4.75% front-end load and Kleinwort has no sales fee. Say you put $1,000 into each fund at the beginning of the period. Transamerica immediately deducts $47.50 for the commission, leaving you with $952.50 working in the fund. Five years later, that amount has grown to $2,017. Not bad. But because Kleinwort has no sales fee, your entire $1,000 goes to work there, and in five years you've got $2,116—nearly $100 more despite the fractionally inferior return.

Of course, the hope is that paying a load will help you find a superior fund you might otherwise overlook. But loads don't pay for more research or more-talented fund managers; they

12B-1 FEES

Q: *My friend says I should never invest in funds that have 12b-1 fees because they'll eat my profits. Is he right?*

A: Not necessarily. Some funds have relatively small ones, and the performance results reported by funds must take 12b-1 fees into account. In choosing a fund, look at its overall expense ratio and performance record. You'll occasionally find funds that, despite the 12b-1 fees, have expense ratios far below those of the average fund and, thus, are less costly than other funds without 12b-1 fees.

pay for the advice of the broker or financial planner who sells you the fund. In the case of low-load funds, the money goes directly to the sponsor.

It would be difficult to make a case that loads get you better management. Of the 1,000-plus stock funds followed by ICDI, more than 60% charge front-end loads or redemption fees. In a study of five-year results done by ICDI for *Kiplinger's Personal Finance Magazine*, 14 of the 25 top equity funds were load funds based on their percentage returns. But after factoring the effect of front- and back-end loads into those five-year returns, only 11 funds with sales charges remained in the top 25. The impact was more dramatic in one-year total returns. Funds with sales or redemption fees occupied 21 of the 25 top spots before charges were factored in but only 12 afterwards.

For bond funds the difference was even more striking. Load funds occupied 21 of the 25 top spots in the five-year ranking before commissions and redemption fees, and only 12 after. In one-year rankings, 21 load funds dominated the 25 top performers before loads and redemption fees, and five remained in the rankings after.

This isn't to say you should never consider investing in a load fund. Some do beat the pack consistently, just not as often as salespeople would like you to believe. A number of such funds appear in the listings you'll find later in this chapter. If your knowledge of funds is minimal, relying on a broker to recommend one or two that fit your goals makes sense. If you go this route, plan to hang on to the fund for several years, to give yourself time to earn back the sales commission.

Fund-buying tip #4: To avoid getting stuck with a losing load fund, choose one that's part of a family. Once you've paid the initial load, many fund families will let you switch to different funds with similar commission structures without paying again.

KEEPING UP WITH MUTUAL FUNDS

*Several personal finance and investment magazines rank the top-performing mutual funds on a monthly basis and rank most funds on an annual basis. Among the most popular periodicals covering funds regularly are **Business Week, Forbes, Kiplinger's Personal Finance Magazine** and **Money**. **Barron's**, the weekly financial newspaper, publishes fund rankings quarterly.*

The following publications and services provide comprehensive directories to funds, usually arranged according to investment objectives. Where indicated, these guides can also be valuable sources of information on fund performance. They are available in libraries, directly from the publisher and, in some cases, in book stores.

Donoghue's Mutual Fund Almanac
Includes one-, five- and ten-year records for most funds, plus information for contacting the funds. Updated annually. ($31.95, plus $3 shipping and handling; P.O. Box 8008, Holliston, MA 01746; 800-343-5413.)

Directory of Mutual Funds
A comprehensive guide to nearly 3,000 funds, including money-market funds, published by the Investment Company Institute, an industry association. No performance information. Updated annually. ($5.00; 1600 M St., N.W., Suite 600, Washington, DC 20036.) Another version of this guide is published by Probus Publishing Co. as *The Mutual Fund Directory*, which sells in bookstores for $18.95.

Still, by following the advice in this book, you should be able to find several no-load funds that can meet your objectives.

What is the fund's expense ratio? The expense ratio, which is discussed earlier in this chapter, shows how much of your potential earnings get eaten up by the costs of running the fund. Pay attention to this number, but don't fixate on it. The fund must subtract expenses (except for sales fees) before calculating its total return, and the total return is a much more

---

The Handbook for No-Load Fund Investors
Excellent guidance on choosing a fund, plus performance data on about 1,300 funds. Updated annually. ($45; P.O. Box 283, Hastings-on-Hudson, NY 10706.)

Individual Investor's Guide to No-Load Mutual Funds
Comprehensive information on about 500 no-load funds compiled by the American Association of Individual Investors; members get the book free. Includes performance records, risk ratings and information on portfolio holdings. Updated annually. ($24.95; 625 N. Michigan Ave., Chicago, IL 60611.)

Investor's Guide to Low-Cost Mutual Funds
Published by the Association of No-Load Funds and updated every January and July, it tracks more than 325 no-load funds and includes information on performance, fees and assets. ($5; The Mutual Fund Education Alliance, 1900 Erie St., Suite 120, Kansas City, MO 64116.)

Mutual Fund Sourcebook
A comprehensive directory of about 1,500 funds, including various ranking methods (performance, management fees, expense ratios, for example) and information about portfolio holdings. ($195; Morningstar, Inc., 53 W. Jackson Blvd., Suite 460, Chicago, IL 60604.) Morningstar also publishes *Mutual Fund Values*, a *Value-Line*-like compendium of mutual fund analysis updated every other week, which sells for $395 per year.

important number. For example, in a recent year, Financial Dynamics, a Denver-based aggressive-growth fund, delivered a total return of 23% and had an expense ratio of just under 1%. Founders Frontier, another Denver-based fund, with similar objectives, reported an expense ratio of 1.46%—half again as high as Financial Dynamics—but the Founders fund also had a total return of 44%. Expense ratios tend to affect payouts from bond funds more than stock funds, and they can make an important difference in money-market funds.

What services does the fund offer? Some funds make it easier than others to open and close accounts, get information about net asset values, switch from one fund to another within a family, and so forth. When you see a series of funds run by the same company—Dreyfus, Fidelity, Oppenheimer, Putnam, T. Rowe Price or Vanguard, for example—that's a fund family. Most families make it easy to switch from one family fund to another (they want to keep you in the family even though your objectives may change), by letting you do it over the telephone, or, in some cases, by waiving or reducing sales fees. You can get information about special privileges offered by families from prospectuses and accompanying literature.

The groupings of funds on the following pages will help you zero in on candidates for further investigation. In each category, the funds selected have excellent long-term records in their groups, although we are not recommending you buy any of them on that basis. Use the phone numbers to order prospectuses and other literature and review them carefully before investing. (Money-market funds are discussed in Chapter 3.)

Funds for Long-Term Investors
This is by far the biggest category of funds that invest in stocks and bonds. Some are more volatile than others, but all should be considered long-term investments that you anticipate holding for a minimum of three to five years.

Growth Funds. These seek long-range capital gains by investing in large, established companies whose stock prices are expected to rise faster than inflation. Growth-stock funds are best suited for investors who want steady growth over the long term but have little need for income in the meantime. Funds in this group generally carry average risk, with volatility rankings around 4 or 5 on ICDI's 9-point scale (See the discussion on page 144). Following are some growth funds that have done well over the past five years. Some funds listed as no-load may charge a redemption fee.

Fund	Minimum purchase	Load	Phone
Berger One Hundred	$ 250	none	800-333-1001
Fidelity Contra	2,500	3%	800-544-8888
IAI Regional	5,000	none	800-927-3863
IDEX	50	8.5%	800-237-3055
IDS New Dimensions	2,000	5%	800-222-9700
Janus	1,000	none	800-525-3713
Thomson Growth	1,000	4.75%	800-628-1237
20th Century Giftrust	250	none	800-345-2021

Growth and Income Funds. Like growth funds, these invest in common stocks of well-established companies. But growth and income funds also seek current dividend income. Risk ratings tend to be low to average for this group. These funds' goal is to provide long-term growth without much fluctuation in share price, even in declining markets.

Fund	Minimum purchase	Load	Phone
AIM Charter	$ 1,000	5.5%	800-347-1919
Dodge & Cox Stock	2,500	none	415-434-0311
Founder's Blue Chip	1,000	none	800-525-2440
Investment Co. of America	250	5.75%	800-421-9900
Lexington Corp. Leaders Trust	1,000	none	800-526-0057
State Bond Common Stock	250	4.75%	800-333-3952

Balanced Funds. These are among the most conservative funds you can buy. At times they may have the same mix of securities as a growth and income fund, but most keep 20% to 40% of assets in bonds or preferred stocks at all times, with stocks of well-capitalized, established companies making up most of the rest of the portfolio. Balanced funds tend to be steady performers, with no spectacular ups and downs and average risk.

Fund	Minimum purchase	Load	Phone
Axe-Houghton B	$ 1,000	5.75%	800-323-8734
Pax World	250	none	800-767-1729
Phoenix Balanced	500	4.75%	800-243-4361
Strong Investment	250	1%	800-368-3863
Vanguard STAR	500	none	800-662-7447

Income-Equity Funds. A high level of dividend income is the aim of this group, which often concentrates on utility companies. Risk is average.

Fund	Minimum purchase	Load	Phone
ABT Utility Income	$ 1,000	4.75%	800-289-2281
Fidelity Equity-Income	2,500	2%	800-544-8888
Fidelity Puritan	2,500	2%	800-544-8888
Keystone Custodian K-1	1,000	none	800-443-6619
Oppenheimer Equity Income	1,000	5.75%	800-255-2755
T. Rowe Price Equity Income	2,500	none	800-638-5660
USAA Mutual Income Stock	1,000	none	800-531-8181

Index Funds. The idea behind index funds is simple enough: It's tough to beat the market consistently, so why try? These funds don't try. Instead, they buy stocks that form the market index they seek to track—the S&P 500, the S&P 100 and the Dow Jones industrials are most popular—and hang on. Theoretically, this approach should yield a return that matches the index. In practice, portfolio managers of index funds can't resist doing some buying and selling to try to beat the index they're tracking. All come very close to achieving their goals, making index funds a conservative way to hitch a ride on the market. Risk, because it matches the market exactly, is average with these funds.

Fund	Minimum purchase	Load	Phone
Colonial U.S. Equity Index	$ 1,000	5.75%	800-225-2365
Gateway Index Plus	1,000	none	800-354-6339
Vanguard Index Trust 500	3,000	none	800-662-7447

Flexible Portfolio Funds. Unlike funds that carefully limit the kinds of investments they make, flexible funds can swing back and forth from all stocks to all bonds or all cash, or any mixture of investments, depending on where the funds' managers think is the best place to be at the time. Some of these funds are also known as asset-allocation funds. Most were started in the late 1980s and we don't believe that any of them have built a long-term record strong enough to merit mention here. Proceed with caution.

Global Equity Funds. Investments of these funds don't stop at the border. They invest around the world and at any time may have a majority of their portfolios in foreign stocks.

Global funds and the next category, international funds, can make or lose money two ways: on the prices of the stocks they buy, and on the movements of currency values compared with the U.S. dollar. Because so many of these funds are relatively new and their records short, volatility rankings often aren't reliable indicators of risk. International and global funds should be chosen with special care.

Fund	Minimum purchase	Load	Phone
Merrill Lynch Int'l Holdings B	$ 1,000	none	800-637-3863
New Perspective	250	5.75%	800-421-9900
PaineWebber Classic Atlas	1,000	4.5%	800-647-1568
SoGen International	1,000	3.75%	800-334-2143

International Equity Funds. These are global funds that invest *most* or *all* of their assets in companies located outside the United States. This category dominated the list of best-performing funds in the late 1980s.

Fund	Minimum purchase	Load	Phone
Fidelity Overseas	$ 2,500	3%	800-544-8888
G.T. Global Growth Series	500	4.75%	800-824-1580
Ivy International	1,000	none	800-235-3322
T. Rowe Price Int'l Stock	2,500	none	800-638-5660
Scudder International	1,000	none	800-225-2470
Templeton Foreign	500	8.5%	800-237-0738

Socially Conscious Funds. Environmental awareness infuses the portfolio choices of some of these funds. Others take care to avoid investing in weapons manufacturers, nuclear-energy producers, cigarette makers, and so on. Many also look for companies known for enlightened personnel and operating policies. As a group, these funds tend to deliver a return that is competitive with funds with similar investment objectives but no social or political screens on their portfolio choices.

Fund	Minimum purchase	Load	Phone
Calvert Ariel Appreciation	$ 2,000	4.75%	800-368-2748
Dreyfus Third Century	2,500	none	800-645-6561
Pax World	250	none	800-767-1729
Calvert Social Investment Eq	1,000	4.75%	800-368-2748

Funds for Income-Oriented Investors

Funds designed primarily to generate income hold mostly bonds and will fluctuate in price due more to interest rate changes than to stock market gyrations. The following categories are suitable for the bond portion of your portfolio allocation but shouldn't be viewed as opportunities for long-term growth.

Volatility rankings tend to be on the low side.

High-Quality Corporate Bonds. These stick mostly to the bonds of top-rated companies with the best prospects for paying interest and principal on time. The average maturities of their holdings will vary, although some funds specialize in short- or intermediate-term issues of two to seven years. A few concentrate on zero-coupon bonds, signaled by the words "target maturities" in the name.

Fund	Minimum purchase	Load	Phone
Benham Target Maturities	$ 1,000	none	800-472-3389
IDS Selective	2,000	5%	800-222-9700
JP Income	300	5.5%	800-458-4498
Scudder Short Term Bond	1,000	none	800-225-2470
SteinRoe Intermediate Bond	1,000	none	800-338-2550
Vanguard Investment Grade	3,000	none	800-662-7447

Global Bond Funds. These funds buy bonds issued by foreign companies as well as U.S.-headquartered firms. If the value of the currency of a country rises in relation to the dollar, funds owning bonds from that country benefit from the exchange rate, which can give their portfolios an added boost. If the dollar rises, however, the fund suffers. If you understand the dynamics of such currency movements, it is appropriate to use global funds for a portion of your portfolio. They should not serve as a substitute for U.S.-oriented bond funds but as a supplement to them.

Fund	Minimum purchase	Load	Phone
Fidelity Global Bond	$ 2,500	none	800-544-8888
Freedom Global Income	1,000	none	800-225-6258
Merrill Lynch Retirement Global Bond B	1,000	none	800-637-3863
Scudder International Bond	1,000	none	800-225-2470
T. Rowe Price Int'l Bond	2,500	none	800-638-5660

U.S. Government Bond Funds. As the name implies, these funds invest in IOUs issued by the Treasury and backed by the full faith and credit of the federal government. They may also invest in debt issued by federal agencies such as those described in Chapter 5, which don't carry the full government backing but are considered just as safe.

Fund	Minimum purchase	Load	Phone
Benham Treasury Note	$ 1,000	none	800-472-3389
Dreyfus U.S. Govt. Intermed Sec	2,500	none	800-782-6620
Fidelity Spartan Govt. Income	10,000	none	800-544-8888
Mutual of Omaha America	1,000	4.75%	800-228-9596
Prudential Govt. Intermed	1,000	none	800-648-7637
Voyager U.S. Govt. Sec	1,000	4.75%	800-553-2143

Ginnie Mae Funds. Ginnie Mae funds get their name from the acronym used for the Government National Mortgage Association. The funds load up on Ginnie Mae pass-through certificates (See Chapter 10), although they also buy other kinds of mortgage-backed securities. Their yields tend to reflect current mortgage rates. An important point to remember is that mortgage funds will be more volatile than bond funds when long-term interest rates are falling because homeowners tend to refinance, thus taking their higher-rate mortgages out of the pool.

Fund	Minimum purchase	Load	Phone
Alliance Mortgage Sec Inc	$ 250	4.75%	800-227-4618
Cardinal Govt. Obligations	1,000	4.5%	800-848-7734
Dreyfus GNMA	2,500	none	800-782-6620
Franklin U.S. Govt. Securities	100	4%	800-342-5236
Lexington GNMA Income	1,000	none	800-526-0057

Municipal Bond Funds. These funds buy tax-free bonds that are issued by state and local governments and their agencies. Some specialize in single states, but most buy from a broad range of issues around the country. The following funds stick to high-quality bonds.

Fund	Minimum purchase	Load	Phone
Financial Tax Free Income	$ 250	none	800-525-8085
Kemper Municipal Bond	1,000	4.5%	800-621-1048
Mutual of Omaha Tax Free	1,000	4.75%	800-228-9596
Nuveen Municipal Bond	1,000	4.75%	800-524-6500
SteinRoe Managed Municipals	1,000	none	800-338-2550
SAFECO Municipal Bond	1,000	none	800-426-6730
United Municipal Bond	500	4.25%	800-366-5465

Funds for Aggressive Investors

These funds swing for the fences, going for profits by investing in risky stocks or bonds that in the opinion of the funds' managers have a chance to hit it big. This is a high-risk environment suitable only for a small portion of the portfolios of experienced, knowledgeable investors.

Aggressive-Growth Funds. These seek maximum capital gains and don't care about dividends. They look for companies or industries that are down-and-out or for fledglings with good prospects but no track records. Many use options, short sales and other specialized techniques in an effort to boost return. (For an explanation of these techniques, see the glossary.)

Fund	Minimum purchase	Load	Phone
AIM Weingarten	$ 1,000	5.5%	800-347-1919
AIM Constellation	1,000	5.5%	800-347-1919
Associated Planners Stock	500	4.75%	800-338-1579
Dreyfus General Agg Growth	2,500	none	800-782-6620
Janus Venture	1,000	none	800-525-3713

High-Yield Bond Funds. "High-yield," of course, is the salesperson's name for junk. These funds come in both the corporate and municipal varieties and invest in bonds rated BBB or lower by Standard & Poor's rating service, or Baa and lower by Moody's. The yields are several points higher than those available from investment-grade bond funds, with typical holdings yielding 12% to 14%. The risks of default are higher as well. A number of junk bond funds started rethinking their position after the big shakeout of the late 1980s (See Chapter 5) and have moved at least part of their portfolios out of junk bonds and into high-quality issues. Such a fund could be a prudent risk for a small slice of your portfolio.

Fund	Minimum purchase	Load	Phone
Fidelity Aggressive Tax-Free	$ 2,500	none	800-544-8888
Financial Bond Shares Hi Yld	250	none	800-525-8085
Merrill Lynch Corp. Hi Inc. A	1,000	4%	800-637-3863
Phoenix High Yield	500	4.75%	800-243-4361
T. Rowe Price High Yield	2,500	none	800-638-5660
T. Rowe Price Tax Free Hi Yld	2,500	none	800-638-5660
Vanguard Fixed Inc. Hi Yld	3,000	none	800-662-7447

Funds for Special Purposes

If you've got a special interest in a market niche—gold, biotechnology or health care companies, for example—there's probably a fund that can accommodate you. If the overused word "hot" could properly be applied to any segment of the mutual fund business in the last decade, it would be the so-called sector funds, led by the Fidelity group, which sponsors 36 of them.

Rather than assembling a diversified portfolio spanning a number of different industries, sector funds concentrate on a single industry. Thus, their fortunes rise and fall with that industry's fortunes and their volatility rankings tend to be above average. A list of successful sector funds over the past several years reads like a list of the country's big growth businesses. Following is such a list.

Fund	Minimum purchase	Load	Phone
Fidelity Select funds	$ 1,000	3%	800-544-8888
Biotechnology			
Food & Agriculture			
Health Care			
Telecommunications			
Financial Strategic funds	250	none	800-525-8085
Health Science			
Technology			
Flag Investors Telephone	2,000	4.5%	800-767-3524
Putnam Health Sciences Trust	500	5.75%	800-354-5487
Transamerica Capital Apprec	100	4.75%	800-472-3863
Vanguard Specialized funds	3,000	none	800-662-7447
Health Care			
Energy			

HOW MUCH ARE YOU MAKING?

By consulting the performance rankings of mutual funds that appear regularly in *Kiplinger's Personal Finance Magazine* and other publications, you can get a pretty good handle on how well your fund is doing relative to other funds. But that doesn't necessarily tell you how well *you're* doing.

The mutual fund listings in newspapers report the net asset value (NAV) of fund shares. NAV is a fund's total assets divided by the number of shares outstanding. Relying on changes in the NAV of your fund would probably understate your return because the NAV doesn't tell you whether the fund has paid any dividends or distributed any capital gains over the period being measured.

Fixing on yield will also mislead you. Yields express dividends or interest as a percentage of the offering price and don't reflect how the shares themselves may have increased or decreased in value.

Total return is the best measure. What really counts is your fund's total return—the total wealth generated by your initial investment over the time period you're interested in. That includes share appreciation as well as dividends, interest and capital gains distributions from securities the fund sells at a profit. A capital gains payment actually acts to reduce the NAV because the fund pays out money that used to count as part of the value of its portfolio.

Your personal rate of return over a given period will be influenced by whether—and when—you purchased or redeemed shares, whether you took your dividends and capital gains in cash or reinvested them, and whether you paid a sales charge (See the discussion earlier in this chapter).

Your quarterly and annual reports from the fund will stress total return, and you can approximate it in the meantime by using information that's typically included on your account statement, plus what you can glean from the newspaper listings (See pages 140 and 141).

What did you do with the money? Your return will vary according to what you do with income you get from the fund, as this example will show:

You buy the Can't Miss fund, a no-load, at its net asset value of $10 a share. Six months later Can't Miss is riding high at $15 a share, at which time the fund decides to sell some stock, take some gains and distribute $5 a share to you and its other shareholders. This restores the NAV to $10 and gives you the choice of taking the $5 in cash or reinvesting it in the fund—a choice we'll return to in a minute.

Can't Miss stays on its streak. A year after you buy it, it sports an NAV of $20—a 100% increase if you don't count the capital gain distribution. But you must count it, because you received it. That $5 plus the $10 increase in the price of a share means the $10 you invested a year ago has actually grown to $25—a total return of 150%.

The way the fund itself would calculate its total return would be to assume that the $5 distribution was reinvested in Can't

INDEX FUNDS

Q: *Should I be buying index funds? I understand that they are stock funds that strive to match the performance of the S&P stock index. That seems defeatist to me. Do they have any advantages?*

A: Index funds attempt to match the performance of a given index by buying all the stocks (or a representative sampling of them) in a given index. Pure index funds are not actively managed and thus are not dragged down by management fees, brokerage commissions and other expenses. Indexing by both institutions and individuals soared in popularity in the 1980s as people realized that relatively few portfolio managers were capable of beating the Standard & Poor's 500-stock index consistently. Another thing that attracted investors was that, for most of the 1980s, the strength of the stock market was in S&P-type stocks, meaning big companies. That could change in the 1990s.

Miss shares. That happened when shares were selling for $10, giving you 1½ shares for every one you started with. Each share is worth $20 at the end of the year, making 1½ shares worth $30—a 200% return on your original $10 investment!

As you can see, total return encompasses the total wealth generated from your initial purchase, not just changes in the market price of your shares.

CLOSED-ENDS: FUNDS THAT SELL AT A DISCOUNT

As you get more familiar with mutual funds and how they work, you might want to consider investing in closed-end funds, many of which offer the opportunity to buy their assets at a discount.

Like an open-end mutual fund, a closed-end takes money from many investors and turns it over to a professional manager. But the similarities end there. In an open-end fund, shares are continually issued as people invest new cash and continually redeemed as investors withdraw money. A closed-end fund raises initial capital by issuing a fixed number of shares and no more, a procedure similar to selling a new stock issue. After the initial offering, the shares trade either on one of the stock exchanges or over the counter. You buy and sell the shares through a broker and prices are listed in the papers every day along with individual stock issues, mostly on the New York Stock Exchange.

Until the initial offering is sold out, shares tend to sell for more than they are worth because a portion of your investment (typically 7% to 8%) pays underwriting expenses and commissions to the broker who sold the fund at the initial offering. If you pay $10 per share to buy a closed-end fund's initial offering, perhaps $9.30 would go to the manager to invest. This leads to an important rule of investing in closed-end funds.

Fund-buying tip #5: Don't buy a closed-end fund at the initial offering, when you pay a premium price. Wait until the share price has fallen below its net asset value in the secondary market.

Supply and demand determine the price at which a closed-end fund trades after the initial offering is sold out, and that's where the discounts—and premiums—come from. Closed-end funds provide a nearly unique opportunity to specialize in various investment areas, from the foreign stocks of a single country to high-yielding utility bonds, and those markets tend to be volatile. When interest is strong, investors may be willing to pay a premium price for the fund. When interest is moderate, the shares tend to sell at a discount. Several influences affect prices.

▪ *Investors attitudes toward certain kinds of assets.* Discounts on many closed-end funds specializing in high-quality bonds can be expected to shrink as investors bid up the price in the face of falling interest rates, for instance.

▪ *The way some funds are structured.* A fund may trade at a wide discount because it holds large unrealized capital gains that, if distributed to investors, could result in substantial tax liabilities for them.

MINORS AND MONEY MARKETS

Q: *My grandson is 18 years old. He wanted to invest in a money-market mutual fund, but he was told that he had to be 21 years old or have a guardian. What gives?*

A: Actually, your grandson is old enough to invest in a mutual fund, unless he lives in Alabama, Nebraska or Wyoming, where the age of majority is 19. (The age is 18 in the other 47 states and in the District of Columbia.) It is illegal for minors to trade securities such as stocks, bonds or mutual fund shares, including money-market funds.

Instead, parents can authorize purchases of shares for their children and hold them in a custodial account under the Uniform Gifts to Minors Act or the Uniform Transfers to Minors Act. For a minor who wants to invest his or her own money, there are more-complicated options, such as a limited guardianship or a revocable trust, that require the minor to give over control of the money to an adult.

▌ *Investor speculation.* As excitement mounted about Western Europe's economic integration in 1992 and the promise of new business from East Bloc nations, the price of closed-end funds investing in Spain, Germany and other Western European nations rose. Had you bought $10,000 worth of Germany Fund early in 1989, the value of your holdings would have soared to $31,695 a year later. The bulk of the gain occurred because Germany Fund shares swung from a 7% discount to NAV to a heady 76% premium.

Finding the Right Fund

You choose a closed-end fund much as you would a regular mutual fund—by matching your investment goals and tolerance for risk to a fund with a compatible profile and a good investment record.

Ask the funds in which you are interested to send recent shareholder reports and, if available, offering prospectuses. Then look up the ratio of expenses to assets. A ratio greater than 1.3%—the average for open-end stock funds—indicates that operating costs may drag down the fund's return over the long run. Exceptions are single-country funds, whose investment expenses are usually above average.

Closed-end bond funds contain a trap you don't have to worry about with open-end funds: Nothing prevents a fund from dipping into capital to maintain its dividend level and investor interest, even when earnings aren't sufficient to cover the payouts. Eventually the dividend will probably be cut, just as it would by an individual company.

Look for the discounts. Swings in discounts and premiums to NAV are crucial for short-term traders, less so for long-term investors. Still, if you're looking at several funds, all other things being equal, avoid funds selling at a premium to NAV and buy the one with the largest discount to NAV. But compare a fund's discount only with those funds that have similar objectives and characteristics. Just as important, compare a fund's present discount with its historical range, and look for slightly wider-than-average discounts.

Choose income or capital gains. Closed-ends offer a unique kind of investment called the dual-purpose fund, which has two classes of shares. The income shares are entitled to all of the dividends or interest generated. The capital shares get all capital gains. Dual-purpose funds usually terminate ten to 15 years after being launched, at which time income shares are redeemed at a specific price and the owners of the capital shares divvy up the fund's remaining assets, either by liquidating the fund or by converting it to open-end status and allowing investors to sell shares at NAV. Discounts tend to disappear as a dual-purpose fund nears its termination date, creating opportunities for capital gains by long-term investors who can buy at a discount early on, hang on until termination and not worry about volatility along the way.

Here are some closed-end funds that have been around long

enough to compile decent performance records over at least three years.

Load	Type	Phone
Adams Express	U.S. stocks	800-638-2479
Counsellors Tandem	Dual purpose	800-888-6878
First Australia Prime Income	Australian bonds	908-417-7666
General American Investors	U.S. stocks	212-916-8438
Mexico Fund	Mexican stocks	800-526-3414
Scudder New Asia	Asian stocks	800-225-2470
Tri-Continental	U.S. stocks	800-221-2450

Keep track of changes. Because the possibility of changes in a fund's discount or premium adds some volatility to its price, the timing of the purchase of a closed-end fund is more important than it is for an open-end fund. Thus, if you go this route, be sure to to stay informed. Publications that provide information about closed-end funds on a regular basis include the following. They are often available in public libraries.

▪ *Frank Cappiello's Closed-End Fund Digest* (805-282-0943), a monthly newsletter. Subscription ($200 a year) includes a copy of the *Complete Guide to Closed-End Funds*.

▪ *Investor's Guide to Closed-End Funds* (305-271-1900), a monthly newsletter published by Thomas J. Herzfeld Advisors. Subscription is $325 a year (two-month trial subscription, $60). The firm also publishes the annual *Thomas J. Herzfeld Encyclopedia of Closed-End Funds* ($125).

▪ *Value Line Investment Survey* (800-634-3583) reports on 40 closed-end funds among the 1,700 firms it follows. Subscription is $525 a year (a ten-week trial costs $65).

UNIT TRUSTS: FUNDS WITH NO MANAGERS

Just as closed-end funds can step up the action for investors willing to pool their money with others, unit investment trusts, or UITs, can slow things down. Unit trusts are sold by brokerage houses, which assemble portfolios, usually of bonds or mortgage-backed securities, and sell off pieces (called units) to investors. Like a mutual fund, a unit trust offers a slice of a diversified portfolio. Unlike a fund, a UIT isn't managed. Once assembled, it is left alone to generate interest or dividends, which are distributed to investors according to how many units they hold. Eventually the bonds in the trust mature or are called, at which time the trust pays out investors' principal and dissolves.

Units usually sell for about $1,000, making UITs a very popular way to buy municipal bonds, which commonly require a minimum investment of $5,000. Commissions are usually 4% to 5%, but there are no management fees. Because the trusts hold on to their bonds instead of trading them, you can expect to get a fixed dollar return that won't change much until the portfolio begins to mature some years down the road.

As with mutual funds, there are important differences among unit trusts that you overlook at your peril. Unfortunately, you often can't get more than a few details in advance because brokerage firms try to sell them out quickly, which has the effect of encouraging you to sign up before you receive a prospectus. The broker can tell you the anticipated yield of the units, the sales charge and the credit ratings of the bonds in the portfolio.

You need to know more. Ask about the call provisions of the bonds in the portfolio. Bonds with nearby call dates create the chance that their issuers will redeem the bonds early if interest rates decline, leaving you with a new investment decision to make in the face of declining rates. You should also ask about the earliest maturity dates in the portfolio and the lowest-rated bonds. A maturity date, a called bond or a default on the part of an issuer would each serve to reduce your return from the trust. Of the three, a default in the portfolio is clearly the worst that could happen.

Check those details yourself when you receive the prospectus. If the trust isn't what you expected, if the broker

UITs vs. Mutual Funds

Q: *My broker has suggested moving funds from a tax-free mutual fund into a tax-free unit investment trust. What do you think about this idea?*

A: One of the major problems with unit trusts is that there's no central database that measures their comparative performance. But here are a few points to keep in mind and a few questions to ask your broker:

■ Why is he recommending a UIT rather than a mutual fund or (if you have enough money to make it worthwhile) direct ownership of a diversified package of municipal bonds issued by your state?

■ What are the maturities of the bonds in the UIT's portfolio? The longer the maturities the more you expose yourself to inflation/interest rate risk. If interest rates rise because inflation accelerates at some point in the future, your returns will be eroded by higher inflation, even though you won't lose any principal if you hold the trust to maturity. On the other hand, if inflation stays under control for the duration of the UIT, you've presumably locked in attractive yields for quite a while.

■ What kinds of bonds will the unit trust own? You want to own decent-quality bonds that can stand on their own merits without the help of insurance.

■ What is the front-end commission and what annual fees will you have to pay? How do those expenses compare with what you're paying in the fund?

misinformed you or you misunderstood the description, most brokerage firms will agree to cancel your order, especially if you tell the broker in advance that you need to inspect the prospectus before you can be sure.

What if you want out before the trust matures? The larger brokerage firms usually stand ready to buy back units from their customers. When that isn't the case, you can sell them through your broker, who will look for a buyer in the secondary market, at no commission charge to you.

GOOD WAYS TO INVEST IN FOREIGN STOCKS & BONDS

Y OUR INVESTMENT portfolio should consist mostly of stocks and bonds of U.S. companies. But you should devote a portion of it to foreign stocks and bonds. Chapter 2 lays out the reason why: the promise of a growing global economy. This chapter will show you how to take advantage of that growth by investing in the countries and companies that stand to benefit from it the most.

Diversification is one good reason to go global: Interest rates, inflation, unemployment and other economic forces move at different tempos in other countries than they do here. These differences can create investment market upswings in Britain, Japan, Germany and other countries at the very time that U.S. markets are on the downswing.

This point of view is contrary to the popular notion that the world's financial markets are now so closely linked that they march in lockstep toward a common fate. According to that school of thought, when the U.S. market goes up or down, the European markets will follow quickly, then the Japanese market and so on around the world in one continuous loop.

The facts, though, are quite different. Studies show that less than 10% of the movement of Japan's stock market in the 1980s could be linked to moves in the U.S. market, and only about a fourth of the change in the Morgan Stanley Europe, Australia and Far East (EAFE) index, a widely accepted gauge of foreign share performance, correlated to the action in U.S. share prices. This isn't to say no links exist, especially during financial disasters: Virtually all stock markets plunged during the crash of 1987, and extreme movements either way in one market can be expected to reverberate in other markets. But on a day-to-day basis, financial markets around the world tend to be influenced most heavily by events in their own countries.

Another compelling reason to look beyond our borders is that investors like you are making plenty of money there. For most of the decade of the 1980s, in fact, foreign stock markets far outperformed our own. From 1986 through 1990, the EAFE index generated a five-year total return of about 114%, more than twice as much as Standard & Poor's 500-stock index produced during the same period. As a result, the list of top-ranked stock mutual funds over the past several years has been dominated by global and international funds. Foreign bond funds, a more recent development, have also performed well.

No doubt the success of foreign investments in the 1980s was due in part to a decline in the value of the dollar against the world's other major currencies. A decline in the dollar boosts the U.S. value of shares denominated in foreign currencies because those currencies buy more dollars. We don't think you can count on much in the way of a similar boost in the years ahead. Besides, outguessing the currency markets isn't something amateurs can do with much success.

Can foreign investments continue to pay off without the support of a declining dollar? Yes, they can. The economies of many nations, particularly smaller ones, can reasonably be expected to grow at a much faster rate than the economy of a giant like the U.S., where billions of dollars in economic expansion add only a fraction of a percentage point to our multi-trillion-dollar gross national product. Thriving economies in smaller countries—Malaysia, Korea and Indonesia, for example—can translate into faster-rising share prices.

If you wanted to diversify your portfolio in proportion to stock values around the world, you'd put 65% of your stock holdings overseas. We recommend a more modest level: about 10% to 20% of your stock holdings in foreign shares. Here are the best ways to accomplish that.

THREE WAYS TO GO GLOBAL

Mutual funds. Because information on foreign stocks and bonds is harder to get than information on U.S. stocks, a good approach if you have limited time and money to invest is to pick a fund to do the digging for you.

Funds constitute the simplest approach to global diversification and therefore perhaps the best. As explained in Chapter 6, they give you a slice of a professionally managed diversified portfolio. They are easy to buy, easy to keep tabs on and easy to sell. Several U.S.-based mutual funds have done an impressive job of picking foreign stocks and bonds.

One distinction you'll find is between *global* funds, which invest in U.S. as well as foreign issues, and *international* funds, which put most or all of their assets in foreign stocks and bonds. You can often tell from the name of the fund which road it takes: Kemper Global Income fund and Scudder International fund, for instance. Sometimes, though, the emphasis isn't obvious from the name: Templeton Foreign fund and Vanguard World fund, for instance, are both international funds.

These distinctions are important but they are not critical. What really counts is the fund's record when it is compared with similar funds, which you can discover by consulting the references described in Chapter 6. You'll also want to learn what you can about the fund's future direction, which you can do by studying its prospectus. A number of international and global funds with excellent records are listed in Chapter 6.

Because the net asset values of global and international stock funds are affected by fluctuations in the value of the dollar as well as fluctuations in foreign stock prices, they can be quite volatile in the short run. Thus, you should count on holding such funds for at least three to five years.

Closed-end funds. These funds, which are described in detail in Chapter 6, offer to sell a certain number of shares when they start and then generally no more. After the initial offering, the shares trade on one of the exchanges or in the over-the-counter market (see Chapter 4) and are bought and sold through brokers like any other stock.

Because share prices of closed-ends are determined by demand for the shares and not by the value of the stocks in the fund's portfolio, the price investors pay is either higher (a premium) or lower (a discount) than the share's underlying net asset value. Money is gained or lost on changes in these discounts and premiums. The changes can be breathtaking, resulting in astonishing volatility for funds as they pass in and out of favor with investors.

So-called single-country funds, which concentrate exclusively on stocks of companies based in one country, are especially vulnerable to this volatility. The price of shares in the Spain Fund plunged from a premium of more than 100% (meaning investors were willing to pay twice as much as the shares were worth) all the way down to a 9% discount over the course of a year in which the fund's net asset value was rising! This sort of violent swing underscores the fact that the action in single-country funds is often created by short-term traders and speculators rather than long-term investors. This situation dictates the cardinal rule for investing in single-country funds: *Never buy a single-country fund at a premium price. Buy only when the fund is selling at a discount from net asset value. Funds selling at a premium—especially a substantial premium—should be left to the traders and speculators.*

Be sure to apply that rule when investigating the closed-end funds listed in Chapter 6 and other closed-ends that may be suggested by your broker. You can follow the prices, premiums and discounts of closed-end funds weekly in *Barron's* and every Monday in the *Wall Street Journal*. The *Value Line Investment Survey* also tracks a dozen or so single-country closed ends. But, in general, you'll sleep better at night if you confine your global portfolio to mutual funds.

American depository receipts. Usually called ADRs, these are negotiable receipts, priced in dollars, for shares of a foreign stock being held in a U.S. bank. Owning one entitles you to everything a shareholder gets, including dividends. An ADR trades like a stock, and its price reflects both changes in the value of the underlying stock and shifts in the value of the company's home currency against the dollar. An ADR may represent one foreign share or a multiple of shares.

More than 850 ADRs trade in the U.S., many on the exchanges or over the counter via the Nasdaq National Market System (see Chapter 4). But prices for most of them can be obtained only from brokers who have access to the "pink sheets." These are literally pink sheets of paper, distributed daily, with listings of thousands of non-Nasdaq, over-the-counter stocks.

Many companies' ADRs are listed only on the pink sheets because the companies are unwilling to meet the disclosure requirements of the U.S. stock markets, which are often considerably tougher than those of their own countries. Some brokerage firms follow the larger companies' ADRs, and the *Value Line Investment Survey* tracks about 50 of them.

ADRs can give you access to shares in foreign companies that are household names in America—Honda, Toyota, Volvo, Sony, Hitachi, Pioneer, Canon, Fuji, Nestle and others. ADRs can also be the route to companies you may not be familiar with but whose businesses you understand—telephone companies in Spain or Mexico, for example. But the difficulty of obtaining and interpreting financial information on such companies suggests that you're better off letting the pros do the work. *If investing in American depository receipts means acting with less information than you can get on American-based or exchanged-listed stocks, don't do it. Instead, invest through mutual funds and closed-end funds, which are better-equipped to obtain and interpret the financial information you need.*

In other words, in sizing up ADRs, you should apply the same standards you'd use to gauge a U.S. company, as described in Chapter 4. If you can't get that information, don't make the investment.

SPECIAL OPPORTUNITIES IN EUROPEAN STOCKS

Some think that what is usually called "Europe 1992" will turn out to be the deregulation movement to end all deregulation movements. Long-established trade barriers hindering cross-border commerce among 12 European countries are being abolished. Belgium, Denmark, France, Germany, Great Britain, Greece, Ireland, Italy, Luxembourg, the Netherlands, Portugal and Spain will become one big economic market. To put it in American terms, selling French dinnerware in Greece and vice versa should involve no more red tape than selling aspirin made in Indiana to a drugstore chain in California.

Actually, members of the European Common Market have traded without tariffs since 1968. But barriers remain. Trucks are often delayed at customs posts and permitted to carry goods in one direction only, returning home empty. Taxes are inconsistent from country to country. Air travel is expensive. Plus, there are anticompetitive national product standards, epitomized by the German law that requires all beer sold in Germany to be brewed to 16th-century specifications for purity.

In 1985 Europe's leaders decided that these costs of nationalism had to go. Two years later the European Community, which has broad powers to legislate what happens within its 12 member nations, adopted the Single European Act, which set the end of 1992 as the target year for free movement of goods, services and capital. The act includes 279 directives to individual nations in specific sectors, such as farming, banking, communications, transportation and taxation. Some of those directives are already in place—standards for a Europe-wide cellular-phone network and some relaxation of customs procedures, for example. Many of the policies, however, won't be working until after the deadline.

The agreement has generated bold claims for future prosperity: two million new jobs, lower consumer prices and savings in business costs thanks to greater efficiencies, equitable taxation, new competition for government contracts and less regulatory confusion.

Even if these claims are only partly true, a unified Europe will create remarkable new opportunities. Upper-tier companies equipped and prepared to compete should emerge with bigger market shares and brighter long-term prospects. Investors in those companies should prosper, too.

There's another reason to look to Europe for part of your global portfolio: its economic outlook is robust. In the late 1970s high inflation, soaring unemployment and political unrest helped create what came to be called Eurosclerosis, a general clogging of the economic arteries. But these days Europe is resurgent. Strong trade within the European Community itself diminishes its members' dependence on exports to overseas nations and increases the chance that Europe can prosper even when the U.S. economy is slow.

How can U.S. investors join in the party? By focusing on strong European companies in industries that figure to benefit most from the arrival of Europe 1992. An industry survey by UBS Phillips & Drew, a British investment bank, identifies airlines, ad agencies, makers of over-the-counter drugs, food and beverage companies, hotels and tourist industries, and trucking lines. Anticipated losers in the new competitive environment include computer-related industries and chemical and pharmaceutical companies.

Many of the most promising companies are available as ADRs, or their shares have found their way into U.S.-based mutual funds. It's not hard to spot the Europe funds because they tend to use the word in their names: Merrill Lynch Euro (800-637-3863); Financial Strategic-European (800-525-8085); G. T. Europe Growth (800-824-1580); Fidelity Europe (800-544-8888); European Emerging Companies (800-323-8734); Capstone European Plus (800-262-6631); and SLH European (212-464-8068).

Most have been around for less than five years and have no long-term performance record by which to judge them. Examine them just as you would any fund, using the criteria described in Chapter 6.

AMERICAN STOCKS WITH GLOBAL CONNECTIONS

Actually, it's not always necessary to invest in foreign companies to earn profits in foreign lands. In fact, if you restrict your quest for globalization to foreign-based companies, you'll miss a lot of good companies based right here at home.

Plenty of U.S. brands and trademarks command large, profitable and growing niches in Europe and Asia. U.S.-based companies make parts and components for almost every car built in the world, even premium-priced European and Japanese imports. U.S. firms dominate the market for indispensable tools of the information age: entertainment and TV programming, cellular phone equipment, fiber optics, computers and software.

A lot of the names are household words all over the world: Coca-Cola, Walt Disney, Ford, General Electric, IBM, McDonald's. Here are a few more, with reasons to consider adding them to your global portfolio, provided they pass muster when you check them out. They aren't necessarily timely buys right now, and all should be considered long-term investments.

▪ *Bausch & Lomb.* Sells contact lenses in more than 70 countries, and about a third of its revenues come from foreign sales.

▮ *Boeing.* This company sells more than half its airplanes to foreign airlines and typically has tens of billions of dollars in backlogged orders.

▮ *Corning.* Not just a glass company anymore, Corning may be America's joint venture king. It is involved around the world in ventures with Samsung and Mitsubishi and more than a dozen smaller firms. It also builds and operates modern factories in Eastern Europe.

▮ *H.J. Heinz Co.* A high-profit, low-cost food producer, its name is found on labels in nearly 200 countries.

▮ *Hewlett-Packard.* More than half of its sales come from 100 different markets outside the U.S.

▮ *Illinois Tool Works.* Its plants in more than 30 countries make switches, fasteners, seat assemblies and other essentials for automobiles, airplanes and computers.

▮ *Medtronic.* This Minneapolis-based manufacturer of medical instruments is best known for its heart pacemaker. It operates in more than 80 countries, generating 40% of sales and better than 20% of profits outside the U.S.

▮ *Merck & Co.* The bluest of Blue Chips, Merck makes nearly half its sales in foreign countries, with 20% in Europe.

▮ *Toys "R" Us.* It is introducing American-style discounting to consumers overseas, with 100 stores in foreign countries and hopes for opening hundreds more in the years ahead.

▮ *US West.* One of the "Baby Bell" companies created by the break-up of AT&T some years ago, US West has reached far beyond its regional borders to become a partner in cable-TV franchises in Hong Kong, Britain and France. It's building the cellular phone system in Hungary and has other international projects in the works or on the drawing board.

WHEN YOU THINK YOU NEED HELP

Y OUR STOCKBROKER is a natural person to consult before making an investment transaction, and you'll find guidance on choosing and using a broker in Chapter 15. This chapter steps back a bit from the transaction stage to the investigating and decision-making stages to examine the kind of help you can get from financial planners, investment clubs, newsletters and other sources not described elsewhere.

WHAT A FINANCIAL PLANNER CAN DO FOR YOU

The business of financial planners once consisted largely of selling life insurance, mutual funds and lifetime "plans" in looseleaf binders the size of dictionaries. So it seemed, anyway. If you want a plan, you can still get one, and it can be a valuable tool: a comprehensive overview of your current financial condition, along with recommendations for achieving your financial goals. Depending on its complexity, such a plan can cost you from several hundred to several thousand dollars.

These days, though, people are more likely to turn to a

planner for help with less sweeping problems. What to do with a lump sum received from an inheritance is a common dilemma, teeming with tax and investment decisions that need to be made in a hurry. As a result of the growing demand for this sort of ad hoc advice, many planners have begun charging for their services by the hour rather than by the plan. Their fees—sometimes $90 to $100 an hour—put them in the same league as lawyers and psychiatrists. And, as with lawyers and psychiatrists, finding a good planner is the key to getting your money's worth.

A good planner can see to it that your investments are diversified and appropriate for your goals and stage in life: growth funds for an IRA, for example, or a state municipal bond fund to generate tax-free income if your bracket warrants it. A good planner can also help you anticipate the tax consequences of your investment decisions.

Many planners are registered with the Securities and Exchange Commission as investment advisers. This means they can serve as money managers for their clients, creating and managing investment portfolios and charging a fee comparable to that charged by mutual funds. If you are going to turn your investment decisions over to a planner, it is especially important that you choose an able one, that the planner keep you informed about what's happening to your investment account, and that you not hesitate to disagree when you aren't comfortable with what's being done with your money. Even then, it is up to you to make sure that the planner stays in tune with your goals and risk tolerance.

How to pick a planner. A planner's credentials are the most obvious clue to his or her preparation for the job. The best-known credential is the Certified Financial Planner (CFP) designation from the College for Financial Planning. To earn the CFP, planners have to pass a ten-hour comprehensive exam administered by the International Board of Standards and Practices for Certified Financial Planners. The vast majority of practicing CFPs prepare for the exams by taking home-study courses from the college, which usually take a couple of years to complete. Graduate courses are available for advanced planners who have already earned the CFP.

The college's fiercest competitors for status in the business are the 30 or so colleges and universities that offer undergraduate or graduate degrees in planning or that prepare students to take the CFP exam. Among them are Baylor, Georgia State and San Diego State universities, and the University of South Carolina.

In addition to academic degrees and the CFP, other leading planning credentials indicating extensive training include the ChFC (Chartered Financial Consultant), which is awarded by the American College, in Bryn Mawr, Pa., and the APFS (Accredited Personal Financial Specialist), awarded by the American Institute of CPAs.

Where to get names of planners. Where can you find a planner? The yellow pages of the phone book are full of names, but you should start your search with a reference of some kind. Lawyers, accountants and insurance agents are good people to ask. The International Association for Financial Planning (Two Concourse Parkway, Suite 800, Atlanta, Ga. 30328; 404-395-1605.), to which about 13,000 planners belong, has a registry service you can use to get names of members in your area.

The Institute of Certified Financial Planners (7600 E. Eastman Ave., Suite 301, Denver, Colo. 80231; 800-282-7526) will give you names of qualified planners nearby.

For a directory of fee-only practitioners, write to the National Association of Personal Financial Advisors, 1130 Lake Cook Rd., Suite 105, Buffalo Grove, Ill. 60089, or call 800-366-2732. A fee-only planner earns no commissions for the mutual funds, insurance or other financial products he or she may recommend that you buy.

For names of CPAs with the APFS credential, write to the American Institute of CPAs, Personal Financial Planning Division, 1211 Avenue of the Americas, New York, N.Y. 10036.

What to ask a planner. Once you've got a list of names of planners with recognized credentials, call or visit two or three and compare their fee structure and their competence as investment advisers.

▐ *Fee structure.* Planners earn their keep in one or more of three ways. Some work on a fee-only basis, charging you by the hour or for performing a specific task. Others collect commissions on the products they sell you, such as stocks, bonds, mutual funds and insurance policies. Many planners fall in-between, charging a mixture of fees and commissions.

A planner's fee structure is no indicator of competence, although fee-only planners insist that commission-based planners have a built-in conflict of interest because they have a stake in selling you something whether you need it or not. That's something to think about. If you want to invest in a mutual fund, you can be certain that commission-based planners are going to pick a fund with a front-end sales load; otherwise, they receive no compensation for their work. A fee-only planner would probably choose a no-load fund. You might not pay the commissioned planner any more in the end than you pay the fee-based planner, but in the case of that fund load, the fee is coming out of your investment rather than directly out of your pocket. (See the discussion of loads in Chapter 6.)

▐ *Investment record.* A planner you're considering as an investment adviser should be willing to provide you with information on how other clients' portfolios have performed under the planner's management. Compare those records with the performance of the financial markets as a whole and with one another before making a choice. Pay special attention to how the planner has done in achieving the objective you'll be pursuing, whether it be investing for growth, income or a combination. Ask the planners to sketch out for you how they would deploy your financial resources and decide whether you're comfortable with the answer.

SECRETS OF SUCCESSFUL INVESTMENT CLUBS

Investment clubs are small groups of people—15 is a typical number—who get together once a month, pool their ideas and money, and invest regularly in stocks and bonds they like. Members may be friends, neighbors or coworkers who divide up the responsibility for researching potential investments using methods very much like those described in this book. Along the way they may be aided by material provided by the National Association of Investors Corp., a nonprofit alliance of more than 7,000 clubs across the U.S.

Over the years, more than half of NAIC-member clubs have regularly outperformed the Standard & Poor's 500-stock index—a record that's about as good as that of professional money managers. (Nobody knows how investment clubs have fared as a whole. NAIC members account for only about a third of all clubs.)

Forming a club that lasts isn't easy. About half of all newly formed NAIC affiliates disband within 18 months, usually because of incompatibility or policy disagreements. Still, most of the clubs that make it through the start-up phase do quite well. How do they do it?

Common traits. An examination of successful investment clubs reveals common elements in their operating methods.

■ They invest all or nearly all of their money in stocks. Comparatively few clubs get into bonds, real estate, mutual funds, precious metals or limited partnerships.

■ They research new investment ideas extensively and debate the possible risks and rewards of each before committing their money.

■ They invest regularly, regardless of what the market is doing, and for the long term, keeping close watch on the businesses they invest in.

■ They buy mostly high-quality stocks with good business records and some growth potential. Diversification among different industries is a high priority.

■ They reinvest all dividends.

■ They keep up with economic news and other developments that could affect the value of their portfolios.

In a typical investment club, each member invests $30 or so per month. At meetings, members who were assigned the previous month to check into specific stocks report their findings. If they recommend buying the stock, members vote on it and the majority rules, just as it does when stocks are sold. The clubs hold their stocks for an average of seven and a half years. Nearly all members have personal portfolios in addition to their stake in their club's portfolio and use the club as a source of investment ideas.

A chance to make money is only one of the benefits of investment club membership. Novice investors learn by doing while experienced ones add to their store of knowledge.

In addition, the clubs provide a forum for discussion and debate of investment topics in general.

Joining a club. Finding an investment club to join may be difficult. There is no known public list of clubs: NAIC doesn't publish one. Clubs limit their size, and there isn't much turnover. Many clubs have waiting lists. When openings do occur, they're often filled by friends of members. And joining an older club may require a substantial investment to get your stake in the venture on a par with that of members who have been at it for a while.

There are two possible alternatives if you can't get into an existing club. First, you could start one yourself. For $14, NAIC provides step-by-step guidelines, including a sample partnership agreement and explanatory material that can be given to prospective members. It may not be necessary to recruit all the members yourself. People who you know are interested may be able to recruit others. When you get enough prospects, schedule a meeting to talk over the details.

Second, you could consider joining NAIC as an individual. For $32 a year you get the organization's investment-oriented magazine, a helpful investment manual and other materials, plus free access to the association's information reports. Write to NAIC at 1515 E. Eleven Mile Rd., Royal Oak, Mich. 48067; 313-543-0612.

A CLUB FOR DO-IT-YOURSELFERS

If you're not the gregarious sort and would just as soon ponder your investment picks in private, the American Association of Individual Investors may be to your liking. The credo of this ubiquitous, ambitious 100,000-plus member organization is simple: As an individual, you can enjoy better investment results than most professionals—if you are willing to spend the necessary time and exert the necessary effort. The AAII has dozens of local chapters, which meet several times a year to exchange investment ideas or listen to an expert discuss an aspect of investing.

AAII preaches that individuals have an important edge over large institutions such as mutual and pension funds. Individuals, goes the theory, can move more quickly and have more choices than do those trading big blocks of securities. Similarly, it's easier for an individual to change the mix of investments in a portfolio when the investment climate changes. A mutual fund, by contrast, is often locked into a specific investment strategy.

AAII's followers are certainly individual investors, but not necessarily small ones. The average AAII member has a six-figure income and a half-million-dollar-plus investment portfolio, not including home equity. The great majority have a college degree.

AAII members are asked for as much or as little as they want to give of their time and concentration. You can choose to spend time only reading the articles in the somewhat academic *AAII Journal,* a 40-page monthly (except May and December) publication devoted to the development of overall investment strategies, not specific investment recommendations. Or you can become involved in meetings of local chapters, attend seminars, buy home-study courses or tapes, or join various subgroups, such as one on computers and investing. The common thread is education—you're not told where to put your money, but how to become an intelligent investor and make up your own mind.

Should you join? The AAII approach is not to everyone's liking. AAII loses 60% of new members at the end of the first year. But after that, only 20% of members drop out. Among those who leave, the main gripe is that the material is too demanding and takes too much time. AAII's road to riches involves hard work and persistence. Members spend an average of several hours a week tending to their portfolios. You needn't fit that profile, of course, but a novice might have a tough time keeping up.

What you get. Membership in AAII (625 N. Michigan Ave., Chicago, Ill. 60611) costs $49 per year. That gets you, among other things, the *AAII Journal,* which, in addition to hard-core stock and bond analysis, typically contains articles on investment newsletters, tax angles of investing, insurance, investment news and brief summaries of new books.

Other features of membership include:

▮ The annual *Individual Investor's Guide to No-Load Mutual Funds* (See Chapter 6), which sells for $24.95 to nonmembers.

▮ *The AAII Personal Tax and Financial Planning Guide,* a 48-page tax-planning how-to book for investors prepared for AAII by the Deloitte & Touche accounting firm.

▮ *A Lifetime Strategy for Investing in Common Stocks,* a highly readable and sensible booklet written by James Cloonan, the founder and president of AAII.

▮ Membership in one of AAII's 46 local chapters, which typically meet monthly. Specialized subgroups also exist, including one on computerized investing that has its own AAII magazine.

▌ At extra cost, members are offered home-study courses, investment videos, newsletters and books devoted to using a home computer as an investment tool, plus beginning and advanced investment seminars.

DO YOU NEED AN INVESTMENT NEWSLETTER?

Investment newsletters have occasionally been the stuff of legend. In the past, one editor's instructions to his subscribers to buy or sell everything could set off a chain reaction in the market, driving prices up or down as the herd instinct took hold. These days newsletters are quieter, just another voice among many. With high-quality investment information so widely available, it's fair to wonder which of the dozens of relatively expensive investment newsletters are really worth the price.

Fortunately, the price to test the waters isn't steep. Most newsletter publishers will send you a free sample copy or sell you a trial subscription for $25 to $50 or so. What can you expect to get? Most advisory letters fall into one of several categories:

▌ *Pure stock pickers.* Louis Navellier's *MPT Review* and Charles Allmon's *Growth Stock Outlook* and *Junior Growth Stocks* are examples of this genre. Their charts and tables outweigh their words. You get a ranking or list of stocks to buy, sell or hold, sorted by the editor's criteria. Navellier uses his own formulas to calculate a "reward-risk ratio" for hundreds of stocks. Allmon practices traditional fundamental analysis (see Chapter 4). He also tells you a little about the companies he highlights in his letters.

▌ *Market commentators.* These newsletters, including *Grant's Interest Rate Observer* and *Dessauer's Journal of Financial Markets*, offer economic or political commentary, sometimes including a model portfolio or incorporating scattered fund, stock or bond recommendations. Their material appeals particularly to economists and professional investors.

■ *Technicians.* Martin Zweig's *Zweig Forecast,* Stan Weinstein's *Professional Tape Reader* and Bob Nurock's *Advisory* use charts and traditional market data to shape an overall forecast. Others, such as Robert Prechter's *Elliott Wave Theorist,* analyze market cycles and waves, forecasting enormous marketwide movements that are thought by them to occur every generation or so.

■ *Fund followers.* Some of these publications, such as Sheldon Jacobs's *No-Load Fund Investor,* are mainly statistical performance reviews. Norman Fosback and Glen Parker's *Mutual Fund Forecaster* combines commentary on fund sales and management practices with buy and sell recommendations and performance projections for hundreds of funds. Craig Litman and Kenneth Gregory's *L/G No-Load Fund Analyst* includes model portfolios and extensive analysis on more than 50 funds.

■ *Market timers.* Will the market go up or down? When will interest rates turn? Gold? Real estate? Timers usually supplement their letters with a weekly recorded telephone message for an extra charge. Bob Brinker's *Marketimer* and James Stack's *InvesTech Market Analyst* are two that try to forecast what's next and tell you where to move your assets to take advantage of it. Some, including *InvesTech,* develop different comments for long-term investors than they do for traders.

A handful of letters—*Donoghue's Moneyletter* and *United & Babson Investment Report* among them—cross the lines to deliver a collection of commentary, business and economic news and forecasts and picks for a number of investments. Others adopt specialized approaches, such as following insider trading, which tries to divine the direction a stock will move from the pattern of buying and selling of its shares by the company's executives.

How good are they? For the past dozen years or so, Mark Hulbert, editor of *Hulbert Financial Digest* (316 Commerce St., Alexandria, Va. 22314; five-issue trial, $37.50), has been the arbiter of success among newsletters. He tracks and ranks the results of about 100 letters based on their buy and sell signals, model portfolios or specific recommendations.

Hulbert believes that there is a connection between a letter's performance over the past five or ten years and its prospects for future accuracy. He finds virtually no correlation between one year's performance and the next year's. Even less encouraging is his discovery that the letters that beat the Standard & Poor's 500-stock index from 1980 to 1985 tended to lag behind it in the second half of the decade. If you were to keep score on any newsletter's ability to forecast accurately, you'd find that, at any given time, some are right, some wrong and others too early or too late in predicting the next turn of events.

The value of a newsletter often rests as much in its clarity, educational value and common sense as it does in its stock-picking prowess (provided that its prowess isn't simply awful). Newsletters can help you by providing good explanations of investment alternatives, well-supported recommendations, unusual ideas and guidance on asset allocation.

On that basis, the following five investment newsletters, in our opinion, are at the top of the list of those that deliver your money's worth. They are readable, well-informed, timely and devoid of personality-cult hype. Prices are for a one-year subscription.

■ *Grant's Interest Rate Observer* (233 Broadway, Suite 4008, New York, N.Y. 10279; 212-608-7994; biweekly; $450). James Grant brings wit and biting opinion to the often bland world of investment commentary. Again and again he hammers away at the folly of debt-laden leveraged buyouts and their junk-bond baggage, and he did so long before others. If you want a contrarian opinion about what's harming the financial markets, Grant is tops. But he makes no buy-sell recommendations of stocks or bonds.

■ *L/G No-Load Fund Analyst* (300 Montgomery St., Suite 621, San Francisco, Cal. 94104; 415-989-8513; monthly; $149). Editors Craig Litman and Kenneth Gregory, who manage money using mutual funds, speak regularly with the managers of dozens of funds and have amassed a wealth of analytical knowledge about the industry. *Fund Analyst* offers four model portfolios. Once a year, the publication also issues comprehensive three-page reports on almost 60 stock and bond funds.

■ *Standard & Poor's Outlook* (25 Broadway, New York, N.Y. 10004; 800-221-5277; weekly; $280). A conservative voice of Wall Street, this S&P publication uses good charts and graphs to present both a strategic overview and specific investment ideas. It grades stocks with stars (five stars means it's a buy, one star a sell) and offers a straightforward and centrist view of the investment climate. No model portfolio is included, but a list of recommended five-star stocks is. Bonds get coverage, too. A typical issue delivers an investment commentary, updates of stocks on the recommended list, an in-depth look at one favored stock, a survey of an entire industry and a list of stocks that meet certain criteria, such as financial strength or earnings growth.

■ *United & Babson Investment Report* (101 Prescott St., Wellesley Hills, Mass. 02181; 617-235-0900; weekly; $238). This letter, first published from an old-line advisory firm founded by the legendary Roger W. Babson, is aimed at the educated masses. You get a little of everything. For example, an issue may touch on the federal budget, the strategic petroleum reserve, the Fed, the Japanese, and state tax revenues, as well as the stock and bond markets. Investment ideas can be both general and specific. If you're seeking a fast overview, complete with buy and sell recommendations, this letter will do nicely.

■ *Zweig Forecast* (P.O. Box 360, Bellmore, N.Y. 11710; 516-785-1300; every three weeks; $265). Ask a newsletter editor for the name of a peer he or she respects and you'll frequently hear the name Martin Zweig. His technically oriented *Forecast* is no-nonsense: brief and not beautiful to the eye. Active traders especially will like its commentary and model portfolio of big-name stocks.

PART 2

STEPPING UP THE RISK

9

INVESTING IN REAL ESTATE

—————— ∎ ——————

THE FIRST PIECE of real estate you buy should be the roof over your head. Although home prices in general won't outrun inflation as dramatically as they did in the 1970s and 1980s, they'll stay a step or two ahead in most areas. Besides, homeownership provides much more than just a place to live. Because the down payment you make is only a fraction of the home's value, you get a degree of financial leverage hard to find elsewhere. Your mortgage payments buy a little more equity each month, giving you a forced savings plan that can grow to substantial proportions as the years go by. On top of that, a home remains one of the few tax shelters still available to people of ordinary means: The mortgage interest is tax deductible and you can postpone paying tax on profits from the sale of your home, perhaps indefinitely. The box on pages 196 and 197 sums up the financial advantages of homeownership.

On the other hand, it seems clear that real estate in the 1990s won't be the path to riches that it was for so many during the '70s and '80s. Commercial real estate—offices, stores, shopping centers—is especially risky for amateur investors. We don't expect commercial properties in many areas to appreciate at all until local markets have worked through a glut of office and retail space, a process that will take at least until mid decade. In the meantime, taking advantage of driven-down prices requires deep pockets and a specialized knowledge of local business prospects that few amateurs possess. This chapter will concentrate on describing investment techniques best suited to residential real estate: single- and multi-family houses and condominium apartments.

In light of the distress in many residential markets in the early 1990s, it may seem a little odd to suggest that real estate is a reasonable way to diversify the risks in a portfolio that consists mostly of stocks and bonds. In fact, many people probably shouldn't invest in real estate. Done wrong, it can be a pain in the neck with precious little reward to show for your trouble, as we'll see. But if you're patient and willing to work hard, the payoff from direct ownership of investment real estate can be substantial even in a period of sedate price appreciation, *provided* the property meets the following criteria (several forms of *in*direct ownership of real estate are considered later in this chapter):

▌ *The property produces a positive cash flow.* That is, you can charge enough rent to more than cover what you pay out each month in principal and interest on the mortgage, operating expenses and so forth.

▌ *You actively manage the property.* This is a critical requirement that permits you to deduct the depreciation allowance (discussed later) from your other income, thus reducing your tax burden at the same time the value of your investment is growing.

▌ *Rentals are in demand in your area.* You have to pay the mortgage and maintenance costs even if you're not collecting any rent. Trouble finding tenants can be a disaster for the bottom line of your rental real estate investment.

▌ *Prospects are good for price appreciation.* A couple of positive signs: The property is in a good neighborhood or one that's on the way up, and the population of the area is growing.

▌ *You invest for the long haul.* That means you must be

prepared to hold the property for several years. In some areas, it is still possible to buy a run-down property, fix it up and sell it within a few months for a profit. But those opportunities, often overrated in the best of times, are harder to find. Real estate prices are cyclical, and you should be prepared to ride out the bad times so you can sell in the good times.

WHY REAL ESTATE IS UNIQUE

If it meets the above conditions, residential real estate can be a good addition to a diversified portfolio. Besides generating income month after month and profit potential in the long run, well-selected real estate has some unique characteristics to recommend it. It is an ideal inflation hedge, for one thing. If unforeseen events lead to a spell of high inflation such as we experienced twice in the 1970s, owners of real estate can expect to prosper. Real estate also offers leverage, valuable tax benefits, and the chance to profit from local pockets of prosperity even if the national economy is struggling.

Leverage in real estate. Leverage comes from using borrowed money to buy the property. The smaller your down payment, the more leverage you've got working for you. Without leverage, real estate investing wouldn't be worth the trouble. With it, the profits can sometimes be spectacular.

Consider Fred and Ed, two investors who buy identical three-bedroom condominium apartments in the same building on the same day. Each pays $100,000. But Fred, feeling flush from a recent inheritance, pays cash. Ed puts $20,000 down and borrows the rest. Five years later, each investor sells his apartment for $125,000. For Fred, that's a 25% return on his $100,000 in five years; he could have done better in a passbook savings account. But Ed, who had only $20,000 in the property, gets a return of 125% on his investment! (In reality the return would be a little bit less because the example doesn't take into account principal and interest payments Ed would have to make along the way. But Ed's investment would still far outperform Fred's.) That's how leverage works.

Of course, leverage can work against you, too. If the price of the condo had dropped $5,000 after five years, Fred's loss would have been 5% of his investment, but Ed's loss would have been a much more painful 25% of his original $20,000 investment. That's why having the ability to wait out bad markets is a key to making money in real estate. If you are forced to sell when the market is down, leverage can greatly magnify your losses.

Tax benefits. The costs of owning investment real estate—interest on the mortgage, operating and maintenance costs, mileage you drive to inspect the property and so forth—are deductible in the year you incur them. And real estate offers a deduction for an expense you *don't* pay—depreciation. If your income is within certain limits and you meet other tests described later (See A Rule That Limits Real Estate's Allure, page 201), you can use that depreciation deduction to shelter up to $25,000 a year of income from other sources, even your salary. You'll have to pay back at least some of the depreciation deductions when you sell the property, but it can be a valuable tax break until then.

National trends vs. local markets. The local nature of real estate markets offers another opportunity for profiting from well-selected properties. Stocks and bonds are bought and sold in a national marketplace, but real estate is strictly a local affair. Whatever the national trends, if you buy good properties in good locations, don't pay too much, and structure the deal so that rental income covers your out-of-pocket expenses, you can make nice profits in real estate over the long haul. But it will take a lot of work—much more work, in fact, than monitoring a portfolio of stocks and bonds. This chapter will describe that work in some detail. If it sounds like more than you're willing to undertake, then forget about owning real estate directly because you'll almost surely lose money doing it. Indirect owner-ship, described later in the chapter, would be a better idea.

ARE YOU CUT OUT TO BE A LANDLORD?

If you think you can make money as a landlord, you should be able to answer yes to each of the following questions:

▪ *Do you have the analytical skills and patience needed to find and buy good investment properties?* As a homebuyer, you may be willing to pay a premium for an unusual house in a desirable neighborhood. But paying a premium price can be deadly for an investor. You'll need to spend time searching for properties and analyzing their income and appreciation potential.

▪ *Can you afford to tie up thousands of dollars for three to ten years?* Lenders typically require a 20% to 30% down payment from investors buying a detached house, condo apartment, duplex or small multifamily building. And your investment will be difficult to sell on short notice.

▪ *Do you have the time and ability to manage the property?* Somebody has to find tenants, collect the rent, oversee the property, keep the books and perform necessary repairs and maintenance. You could hire a management company to do the job, but you'd still have to monitor the property manager and you'd pay 3% to 10% of your rental income for the service.

Undeterred? Then let's go shopping. As a potential landlord, you're looking for three things: the right location, the right building and the right price.

The right location. Location is synonymous with success in real estate. Good neighborhood schools, nearby stores, parks and recreational facilities are obviously important. The prop-erty should be near public transportation, so that renting is not dependent on owning a car; the street shouldn't be too steep and the house shouldn't have too many stairs because either condition could cause older renters to look elsewhere.

The right building. You want a place that's typical, not unique.

Remember, you're not going to live there; you want to rent it out. Your chances of finding a tenant are best if the place appeals to most people looking for something in that price range. The structure should be in good condition and you should have access to records that will permit you to make accurate estimates of maintenance and repair costs.

The right price. Single-family detached homes and condominium apartments are often overpriced relative to the rent they can command. That's because their prices are influenced by the value buyers place on them as homes, which includes the prospects for future price appreciation. But tenants are willing to pay only for current shelter value, which depends on such things as square footage, the number of bedrooms and distance

---

WHY A HOME IS STILL A GOOD INVESTMENT

Your home is one of the best investments you can make. Here's why:

It forces you to save.
When you pay the mortgage each month you pay both interest and principal. The principal repayments, plus any increase in home value, gradually build up your equity in the property—that's the difference between what you owe and what the home would sell for, and it's a valuable asset as years go by.

You get access to leverage.
The long-term mortgage you use to finance your home lets you tap into a great wealth builder. You increase the earning power of your money when you borrow large sums using your home as collateral for the loan, as illustrated in this chapter.

Tax law subsidizes homeownership.
You can deduct all the interest on up to $1 million you borrow to buy or build a home, plus up to $100,000 in home-equity loans. If you're in the 28% tax bracket, for every $1,000 of interest you pay on your principal residence, you get a $280 tax subsidy for homeownership. Local property taxes are also deductible in the year you pay them.

to their workplace. If you keep in mind the features that make a place good to rent, as opposed to being a good place to own, you are more likely to pay the right price.

THE NUMBERS YOU NEED

Whether you will profit from a real estate deal will depend on two things: cash and time. Your goal should be to part with as little cash as possible as slowly as possible and to recoup your investment as quickly as possible. In that direction lies your profit.

You can't rely on appreciation alone to make your investment profitable. You should also evaluate a property on its

You get access to tax-deductible interest.
Home-equity loans are among the last remaining sources of credit with tax-deductible interest.

You can postpone the tax bill when you move.
If you sell your home and buy another, you can probably defer the tax bill on your profit. To do so, you must buy a home that costs at least as much as the price you get for the one you sell. And you must buy or build *and* occupy your new home within two years—before or after—you sell the old one. Special rules apply if you sell your home while you are in the armed services or living outside the U.S.

You get a once-in-a-lifetime tax break.
You have the right to skip any tax due on up to $125,000 of the profit you ultimately get from your home or series of homes. You must be at least 55 years old when you sell your home and you must have owned and lived in it for at least three of the five years leading up to the sale. If you are married and the house is owned jointly, you qualify as long as either you or your spouse meet the requirements.

ability to produce current income and on its potential to generate higher and higher rents as time goes by. For example, you may be able to charge more for a house in a sought-after neighborhood if there are few other rental homes nearby.

How much rent can you charge? You'll need to check what comparable properties in the area are going for, of course. A rule of thumb says that the annual rent should be at least 9% of the market value of the property. On a $100,000 home, that means $9,000 a year, or $750 a month. Another common gauge is something called the gross rent multiplier, or GRM, which approaches the question from the other side. Real estate experts recommend paying no more for a property than 90 to 110 times its gross monthly rent. By that measure, a house that rents for $750 a month and sells for $100,000 has a GRM of 123, and seems priced too high for the rent it can get.

As you can see, the rule-of-thumb approach has its limitations. What you really need is a property that, when rented, will produce a positive annual cash flow, however slight. Assuming continuous occupancy, rental income should cover mortgage payments, maintenance, taxes and insurance. If rents don't cover those costs, you'll experience negative cash flow—an operating loss. Not only must you dig into your pocket every month, but you'll also be forced to rely on future appreciation to offset the loss and provide a good return on your investment. That would require a pool of prospective buyers ready to purchase your property when you are ready to sell it (and willing to pay a price higher than would be justified by rents alone), as well as readily available and reasonably priced mortgages. The best way to avoid putting yourself at the mercy of the market forces is to buy properties only if they produce a positive cash flow.

THE TAX ANGLES OF REAL ESTATE

Running a real estate investment is partly common sense, partly a matter of knowing some special tax rules. You've got two potential kinds of current and future income: rent and price appreciation. And you've got several kinds of tax-deductible expenses, led by interest on the mortgage and depreciation. The income sources are largely self-explanatory. (Later on we'll show how to include them in a calculation of your return.) The expense items require a little explanation.

Mortgage payments. Only the interest is tax deductible. If you hold the property for so many years that the interest portion of your mortgage payments shrinks into insignificance, it makes sense to seriously consider refinancing.

Rental expenses. You can deduct the out-of-pocket costs of producing rental income. In addition to mortgage interest, that includes the following expenses:

■ Property taxes.

■ Insurance premiums.

■ Management-company fees.

■ The cost of advertising to attract tenants.

■ Legal and accounting costs connected with drafting a lease or evicting a tenant.

■ Repair and maintenance expenses.

■ Utilities, if you pay them.

■ Money you pay to others to care for the property—for cleaning or gardening, for example.

■ The cost of travel necessary to care for your property. Typically this means a flat mileage deduction for driving eight miles from your home to your rental apartment to unplug a drain. The considerable expense of visiting a distant rental property, including the cost of food and a hotel room, is also deductible, provided that the principal purpose of the trip is to inspect or work on your property.

Depreciation. This is the real estate investor's good-luck charm, the deduction that can turn a losing property into a winning one. Each year you get to write off a portion of the price you paid for the property (minus the value of the land, which you can't depreciate). The current annual depreciation allowance for residential rental property is 3.64% after the first year, a rate that reduces its cost "basis" to zero in exactly 27.5 years. (Commercial properties, such as stores and office buildings, get an annual allowance of 3.17% because they are deemed by law to be fully depreciated after 31.5 years, and thus decline in value a little less each year.) If you bought the place and started renting it out when the depreciation schedule was more generous, you get to keep using that schedule.

The allowance has nothing to do with whether the property actually *is* depreciating in value. Even if its value is growing by leaps and bounds, you still get to claim depreciation. It is a crucial element in any real estate investment, especially if rental income doesn't cover expenses. The tax saving from depreciation could more than make up the difference.

For instance, say you're collecting $700 a month in rent on a condo but the mortgage payment, condo fees and other expenses amount to $800. At the end of the year you're $1,200 in the hole. That's tax-deductible, so in the 28% bracket you're actually $864 in the red—before depreciation. Say the apartment (not counting the land, which you can't depreciate), is worth $85,000. Applying the 3.64% depreciation allowance yields a tax deduction of $3,094 for the year. In the 28% tax bracket, that saves you $866. Thus, depreciation has turned your loss into a slight gain.

As alluring as that sounds, relying on depreciation to carry you while you hope for the value of the property to go up can be a short-sighted investment strategy. Uncle Sam's apparent generosity is really more like a loan than a gift: Every dollar of depreciation you claim (and you *must* claim it) serves to reduce the cost basis of your property. (The cost basis is just what it sounds like: the value of your investment.) The effect of that is to increase the taxable profit when you sell. It's even conceivable that you could sell at a loss and still owe taxes on a gain because the depreciation allowances have reduced the basis to below the selling price.

Here's an example of how depreciation can backfire on you if the value of your property fails to appreciate. Say you buy a rental house for $105,000 and hold it for five years. The building itself is worth $85,000 and you claim your depreciation allowance at the rate of $3,094 per year for five years, a total of $15,470. That reduces your cost basis for the building to $69,530. Add in the value of the land and your total basis is $89,530. You sell the house and land for $95,000. Now, that's a *loss* of $10,000, since you paid $105,000 for the place. But for tax purposes, because you depreciated the basis of the property to $89,530, you're going to owe taxes on a $5,470 capital gain. You can see that the depreciation allowance cuts both ways. The IRS giveth and the IRS taketh back.

You can *increase* the cost basis of your property by making improvements that add to its value—replacing single-pane windows with double panes, for example, or adding a Jacuzzi to the bathroom, installing central air-conditioning and adding landscaping and other enhancements that can reasonably be considered permanent improvements that raise the market value of the property.

A RULE THAT LIMITS REAL ESTATE'S ALLURE

So far, the discussion of depreciation has assumed that you qualify to use the allowance to offset income from other sources. Most people do qualify, but some don't. If you fall into the latter category, you should think long and hard before ever becoming a landlord.

Beginning in 1987, the tax laws divided income and deductions into two major categories: active and passive. (There's actually a third category, portfolio income, which crosses the lines. It is discussed in Chapter 16.) Salaries are considered active income. Income and losses from real estate are considered passive. Your ability to mix active gains or losses with passive gains or losses is restricted to some degree, and for investors in certain categories it is seriously restricted.

Normally, you simply are not permitted to use passive losses to offset active income on your tax return, a rule that would kill a major attraction of rental real estate if it weren't for a notable exception the law provides.

To qualify for the exception, you must "actively participate" in managing of the property. If you do, and your adjusted gross income is under $100,000, you can deduct as much as $25,000 of rental losses against other income, including salary. The loss allowance is phased out at the rate of 50 cents for every dollar of adjusted gross income (which is your income before subtracting itemized deductions, exemptions and rental losses) above $100,000. Thus, it's gone at $150,000.

Passive losses you can't deduct in the year incurred aren't lost completely because you can use them to offset passive income you might generate in future years. Even if you have no passive income, you can use the excess to offset any kind of income in the year you sell the property.

What does it take to actively participate in the management of your property? You'll probably qualify as long as you're involved in approving tenants, setting rents and approving repairs and capital improvements, even if you pay a management firm to handle the routine matters.

FIGURING YOUR GAIN—OR LOSS

There are several common methods of calculating your return from a rental property. Let's examine a $120,000 house as an example. You put 25% down ($30,000) and finance the rest with a 30-year, 10%, fixed-rate mortgage. The lender requires you to pay 3 points (3% of the loan amount) to get the mortgage and another 1% for settlement expenses such as loan appraisal, credit report, title insurance and attorney's fees.

Let's assume you sell the house after five years, and that the property appreciates 5% a year. For purposes of the illustration, we'll keep rents, property taxes and maintenance costs level for those five years. For simplicity's sake we'll also assume that the house stays rented the whole time, with no rent lost between tenants, that you actively manage the property yourself and that you are in the 28% tax bracket.

Before-tax cash flow. This is the simplest concept because before-tax cash flow is the cash left at the end of the year, after you have paid the mortgage, maintenance and other bills and collected all rents. Because this example covers the first year of ownership, the calculations include settlement costs.

BEFORE-TAX CASH FLOW

Purchase price	$120,000
Settlement costs	+ 3,600
Total cost	123,600
Mortgage balance	-90,000
Total cash invested	$ 33,600
Gross income	
Rent ($1,000 x 12 months)	$ 12,000
Expenses	
Mortgage payments ($790 x 12)	$ 9,480
Real estate taxes	1,500
Insurance	700
Maintenance	+ 900
Total Expenses	$ 12,580
CASH FLOW BEFORE TAX	$ (580)

(Gross income *minus* expenses)

After-tax cash flow. Hmmm. Not so hot. You're losing money. But let's see what happens when you take income taxes and depreciation into account—especially depreciation. First you have to add something back in: The principal payment on the mortgage belonged in the calculation above because it is a legitimate expense; you've got to pay it each month. But when figuring out your taxes, principal payment works the same as it does for your mortgage: It isn't deductible. So you've got to add principal payments back in as an item of income.

There's a little twist to the depreciation allowance, too. In the first and last years of ownership, you don't get the full year's worth. Regardless of the day of the month you buy or sell the place, the IRS declares it to have been "placed in service" at the middle of the month of purchase. That complicates things a bit, but for the sake of simplicity let's say you bought the place on January 1, meaning you get 11.5 months of depreciation the first year.

Cash flow before tax	$ (580)	
plus principal payments	+457	
Deductible operating loss		$(123)
Other deductible expenses		
points (amortized over 30 years:		
$2,700 ÷ 30)	$ 90	(90)
Depreciable portion of property		
Price paid (includes other		
closing costs):	$120,900	
minus value of land	-40,000	
Depreciable portion	$ 80,900	
Depreciation allowance		
$80,900 ÷ 27.5	$ 2,942	
$2,942 ÷ 12	$ 245/mo.	
$245 x 11.5 months	$ 2,818	(2,818)
Taxable income (or loss)		(3,031)
Tax saving in 28% bracket		
(Tax loss x tax rate: $3,031 x 28%)	$ 849	
Cash flow before tax		(580)
plus tax saving		849
CASH FLOW AFTER TAX		$ 269

Total return after sale. Presto! Depreciation has turned this loser into a winner—not by much, and not by enough to make this particular property worth all the trouble of ownership in the first year, but a winner nonetheless. Now let's see what happens after five years of rent collecting and 5% price appreciation per year, after which you sell the place and count up your profits.

First you've got to calculate what you net out of the sale. Assuming you're working with a broker, you'll need to subtract commissions and other sales-related costs and the balance of your mortgage.

Sales price		$ 153,154
minus sales expenses		
6% commission	$9,189	
1% other	$1,532	-10,721
Gross sales proceeds		$ 142,433
minus mortgage balance		-86,982
NET SALES PROCEEDS		$ 55,451

Of course, net sales proceeds aren't the same as your profit. To figure that, you first need to calculate your "adjusted cost basis"—that is, the amount on which your taxable gain will be figured.

Cost ($120,900 + $2,340 for points not	
yet amortized)	$123,240
minus total depreciation	
($2,818 x 2) + ($2,942 x 3)	
plus $360 (amortized points)	-14,822
ADJUSTED COST BASIS	$108,418

Now that you've got your adjusted cost basis figured out,

you can calculate how you came out on this deal after five years.

Gross sales proceeds		$142,433
minus adjusted cost		108,418
Taxable gain		$ 34,015
Tax owed (28% bracket)	$9,524	
Net sales proceeds		$ 55,451
minus tax on gain		-9,524
Net sales proceeds after tax		$ 45,927
plus annual cash flows after tax		
($269 x 5)		1,345
Total proceeds		$ 47,272
minus cash invested at start		33,600
TOTAL RETURN		$ 13,672
% return on cash invested		41%
Annual average after-tax return		8.2%

Comment on this deal: An average annual after-tax return of 8.2% is quite good, (on an annually compounded basis, you earned 7.4%). But to justify the trouble of buying, managing, keeping the books and selling a real estate investment, you'd probably want to earn a higher return than that, either through a higher positive cash flow each year or through higher annual appreciation, or both.

A BETTER WAY TO JUDGE YOUR RETURN

The return on your original investment—which is actually the return on your down payment—is important to know, but it's not really a true picture of how you're doing year after year. If you've invested in a good piece of real estate, the value of the property should be increasing as time goes by. If your income from the property fails to keep up with the increased equity, your investment return is actually declining, whether you know it or not. You can check on how you're doing by calculating what's known as your return on equity.

Knowing your return on equity allows you to play "what if?" with your real estate investments: What if you sold the property and invested the proceeds elsewhere? Could you get a better return? Inattentive real estate investors are often surprised by the answer.

Return on equity is nothing more than your annual cash flow before taxes divided by your current equity in the property. (Current equity is the market value of the place minus the balance you owe on the mortgage.) Say you buy a $100,000 rental property with a $20,000 down payment. The property produces a cash flow of $1,000 before taxes in the first year. After that, both the cash flow and the value of the property grow by 10% per year, and you pay off $400 on the mortgage each year. This table shows what your return on your $20,000 investment would look like after the first, third and fifth year of ownership:

	Year 1	Year 3	Year 5
Before-tax cash flow	$ 1,000	$ 1,210	$ 1,464
Investment	20,000	20,000	20,000
Return on investment	5%	6.05%	7.3%

Because your return on investment is increasing each year, you may conclude that you're doing just wonderfully. But in fact, as your equity was rising, your return on that equity was declining, as this table shows, assuming 10% equity and income growth per year.

	Year 1	Year 3	Year 5
Before-tax cash flow	$ 1,000	$ 1,210	$ 1,464
Property value	100,000	121,000	146,400
Loan balance	80,000	79,200	78,400
Equity	20,000	41,800	68,000
Return on equity	5%	2.9%	2.2%

Whenever equity in the property increases as fast as or faster than the income, as might happen in a market where prices were rising rapidly, return on equity will fall. Even if property values increase slowly and rents rise rapidly, return on equity is still likely to decline, although not as dramatically as in this example. What can you do about it?

One thing you can do is refinance to pull some cash out of the property and put that cash to work in an investment that promises to produce a higher rate of return. You might use it, for example, to buy another piece of property. When the return on equity from that one diminishes sufficiently, repeat the process. Using the equity built up in one property to acquire another is the classical way for small real estate investors to accumulate substantial assets over time.

THE ACCIDENTAL REAL ESTATE INVESTOR

A lot of people find themselves investing in real estate almost by accident. This happens most commonly when you can't—or don't want to—sell your residence when you move, and so decide to convert it to a rental property instead.

Converting your home to a rental property. The rules are the same as for other rental real estate except for two notable differences: First, the tax laws are much stingier when it comes to depreciation; and second, you confront the possibility of losing one of the most generous tax breaks available to home-owners.

▪ *Longer depreciation schedule.* Odds are, your home appreciated while you lived in it, but you don't get to depreciate the higher market value. Uncle Sam says that your basis in a converted residence is the lower of the house's value when you converted it to rental property or its original cost plus the value of improvements. In other words, you're almost certainly going to have to use the adjusted original cost, even if you bought the place 20 years earlier. If you rolled over the profit from a previous home into this one, your basis is further reduced by the amount of the rollover. Furthermore, if you bought your home after 1986, you must depreciate it over 27.5 years, even if more generous depreciation schedules were in effect at the time. If you purchased before then, your writeoffs may be stretched out over an even longer period, depending on rules in effect at that time.

■ *Lost rollover rights.* The second tax wildcard you're dealt when you convert your home to a rental property is the loss of your right to a tax-free rollover of profit into a new home when you sell the property. That break is available only when the home sold is your principal residence. It is possible to reestablish the place as your residence, but it takes long-range planning and the advice of an accountant or other tax expert.

INDIRECT WAYS TO INVEST IN REAL ESTATE

You don't have to own and manage your own properties to be a real estate investor. A much less bothersome route is to buy shares of publicly traded companies and mutual funds that own, develop, or manage real estate.

Real Estate Investment Trusts
A REIT (rhymes with street) is a pool of real estate projects or loans or a combination of both. You can buy shares in a hundred commonly traded REITs the same way you'd buy any stock.

REITs can be high-yielding investments because they get special tax treatment at the corporate level. The income of most companies is taxed twice—once at the corporate level and again at the shareholder level when shareholders report dividends as income. REITs are virtually exempt from corporate income taxes, provided they pay shareholders at least 95% of net income each year.

Real estate investment trusts come in three general types:

■ *Equity REITs* invest in actual real estate, such as shopping centers and office buildings. Shareholders earn dividends from tenant rents and have a shot at capital gains when properties are sold.

▮ *Mortgage REITs* put you in the loan business—you buy a piece of a real estate loan portfolio. These are volatile, high-yielding securities whose prices can suffer when interest rates (and thus investor yield expectations) rise or if mortgage rates drop and owners refinance. As a group, mortgage REITs are less attractive for long-term investors than equity REITs.

▮ *Hybrid REITs* combine equity and mortgage holdings. Finite real estate investment trusts, called FREITS, have a limited life, usually about five to 15 years, after which assets are sold and shareholders get the proceeds. Be wary of these. If a FREIT chooses its time to sell years in advance, it is betting that market conditions will be favorable at that time. If they aren't, the sales price will suffer.

In the early 1970s, high-yielding mortgage REITs heavily leveraged with debt were almost killed off entirely by a collapse in commercial real estate prices. For 24 consecutive months starting in April 1973, REITs posted negative total returns.

But during the early '80s, equity REITs quietly outperformed the S&P 500, and with fewer gyrations. Investors began returning to REITs and 33 new ones were started up in 1985 alone. Since then their performance as a group has been decidedly lackluster, although there have been a few standouts.

A few did very well in 1990–91. American Health Properties and Nationwide Health Properties posted total returns of 30% and 48%, respectively, in the 12 months ending January 31, 1991.

Future promise. The best equity REITs can plausibly promise 12% to 15% annual total returns, largely because other sources of cash for real estate have been drying up. The ranks of savings and loans, which once the largest suppliers of capital to the building industry, have dwindled and survivors face tough new loan restrictions.

An analysis by Coldwell Banker concludes that with little new construction in the pipeline, the commercial building glut will be over by the mid '90s. With time, then, existing real estate could become much more valuable, and well-run REITs should be in a position to profit from the climb.

What to look for. REITs with good performance records, such as New Plan Realty Trust (800-468-7526), Weingarten Realty Investors (800-688-8865), Federal Realty Investment Trust (800-658-8980), and Western Investment Real Estate Trust (415-929-0211), tend to share certain characteristics:

▮ *Simplicity.* They focus on a particular geographical area or type of development.

▮ *Strong cash flow.* Cash flow—net income plus amounts written off for depreciation that require no cash outlay—determine dividends. Depreciation permits REITs to pay out more than 100% of net income in dividends.

▮ *Sustainable yields.* Dividends of the strongest REITs tend to be relatively modest. Strong REITs deliver competitive total returns because their stock prices keep appreciating. Weak REITs with weak stock prices must offer a high dividend to be competitive, and often that dividend cannot be maintained.

▮ *Experienced management.* Superior performance over at least five years is one of the surest signs of a solid operation. Experience is especially crucial in buying new properties at attractive prices and in tapping capital markets correctly. Good managers can add value to what they own by improving the tenant mix, adding space, marketing and generally upgrading their holdings. Managers who own what they manage have every reason to care about results. To get the share ownership figures for the trust's officers, ask the REIT to send its latest proxy statement and 10-K form. Ten percent or more insider ownership is a plus.

▮ *Boring but essential holdings.* Among the projects that REIT analysts tend to like most are grungy old strip shopping centers. Successful REITs find ways to buy such properties at big discounts and rehab them into money-makers. Such rehabs are recession-resistant, too, especially if they're anchored by a supermarket or a big discount store. A good mix might also include a high-volume drugstore, cleaner, liquor store, discount shoe shop and electronics store.

How to buy them. The standard advice is to buy REIT shares at a discount, meaning when the share price is less than the per-share value of assets. But that's easier said than done. You can't appraise the assets yourself, and most brokers can't be of much help. A REIT may provide you with an appraisal, but it probably won't be current when you get it. And although many REITS trade at discounts, the best ones tend to sell at stubborn premiums. We suggest you buy REIT shares at discount, whenever possible. If you expect to buy and hold for five years or more, you can pay less attention to the discount.

Diversify your REIT holdings, just as you would stocks or bonds. Try to find a knowledgeable broker whose firm has at least one analyst covering several different REITs.

Stocks of Related Companies

Companies with big holdings of real estate assets include major home builders, some paper and forest product companies, railroads, oil and mining companies, certain insurance, manufacturing, and retail companies. Only through careful study of their balance sheets and financial reports will you be able to determine how their real estate holdings might affect their stock prices and whether the property has any chance of being sold at a price high enough to have a significant impact on the company's profits.

Mutual Funds

Four mutual fund families offer real estate-oriented funds. Fidelity Real Estate Investment Portfolio (800-544-8888) and United Services Real Estate (800-873-8637) concentrate on the U.S. market. Evergreen Global (800-235-0064) and Templeton Real Estate (800-237-0738) have charters that permit them to invest globally. All four may own REIT shares. All are no-load except the Templeton fund, which charges an 8.5% sales fee.

There is one closed-end real estate fund, the Real Estate Securities Income fund (212-832-3232), which trades on the American Stock Exchange.

Real Estate Limited Partnerships

We've yet to find a limited partnership we could like. They charge high fees, are illiquid and have been marked by mediocre performance and failed expectations ever since they became popular in the early 1980s. Real estate syndications have suffered from overbuilding, the bust in the Oil Patch and low inflation. For more about why we don't recommend limited partnerships, see Chapter 12.

INVESTING IN RAW LAND

Investors in raw land are taking a long shot at success. For one thing, vacant land doesn't produce any income while you're waiting for the price to go up. The methods available to finance its purchase aren't nearly as flexible as they are for property with a building on it. You can't depreciate land. All these factors make small parcels of empty land very speculative ventures you should enter into only with the expectation of a very large reward.

The biggest challenge is to pick property that winds up on the high side of the wide price swings that are the hallmark of empty land. Then there's the very real chance of being ripped off if you're foolish enough to buy land without checking it out thoroughly. The third—and fairly new—challenge is to avoid running into environmental laws that could block your plans for the property or even cost you unforeseen thousands of dollars if you must remedy an existing problem.

Price volatility. Land values tend to go up and down in sync with a region's economic fortunes. Prime farmland in central Iowa fell from a peak of $3,500 per acre in 1982–83 to about

$1,200 during the depth of the Farm Belt's troubles in 1986. Volatility is also influenced by outside factors. Much of the building frenzy in Texas—and the related run-up in land prices—was fueled by generous federal tax incentives. When tax reform removed most of those in 1986, investors fled, hastening the price collapse.

Rip-offs. Land scams are far from extinct. An outfit called Kilgore Mining Co. sold property in Arkansas to people in other parts of the country. Fast-talking telephone salespeople told investors that the company was selling some of its coal-rich acreage to raise the cash needed to strip-mine the rest of it. The pitch: an $8,000 investment would quickly skyrocket in value to around $28,000. In fact, Kilgore was selling phony titles to land it either didn't own or didn't own mineral rights to, or that had no coal on it. The perpetrators were caught, convicted and ordered to pay back nearly $3 million. But they had already spent the money.

Environmental restrictions. The law makes it risky to buy land without an environmental checkup. If you purchase a plot of wetlands, for instance, the government probably won't let you build on it without a great deal of difficulty and expense, if it lets you build at all. If land contains buried hazardous waste, you could be forced to pay thousands to have those wastes removed, even though you had nothing to do with putting them there in the first place.

■ *Wetlands.* These are loosely defined under the Clean Water Act as land that is sometimes wet or swampy or that supports certain kinds of vegetation and wildlife. No development is permitted on designated wetlands without permission from the U.S. Army Corps of Engineers. Unfortunately for some buyers, you can't always spot such property with the naked eye. In one case, unsuspecting investors bought vacation lots for $36,000 each, only to discover that they couldn't build on the lots because they are wetlands. You can get wetlands maps

DEDUCTING INVESTMENT PROPERTY LOSS

Q: *I recently sold a vacant lot at a lake property development at a substantial loss. The property was held in title with two co-owners for over 20 years. We've been told we can deduct the loss on our federal income tax return if we establish the fact that the property was an investment. How can we do that?*

A: There would be no question of your intent if you and your co-owners had drawn up a document when you bought the property saying that you never intended to build and that you would sell when the value increased. Even without such proof, you have a strong case with the Internal Revenue Service for treating it as investment property because you never built on the land and you bought the property with other people.

from the U.S. Geological Survey, Earth Science Information Centers, which has four regional offices around the country. The maps costs a couple of dollars each. Check also with county extension agents in the area.

■ *Hazardous chemicals.* Under the 1980 Superfund law, you may be on the hook for cleanup costs of contaminated soil and water, even if you had nothing to do with creating the problem. You can call the EPA's hazardous waste hotline (800-424-9346; in Virginia, 703-920-9810) for information on the EPA's list of contaminated sites, but you may have better luck asking around at the local level. Call the state's department of natural resources or environmental agency. Explain that you want to know whether your site is listed on the Comprehensive Environmental Response Compensation and Liability Information System, or CERCLIS, list. The CERCLIS list contains 32,000 sites that have been called to the attention of the EPA or state agencies for possible contamination problems.

■ *Radon.* Radon is a naturally occurring, cancer-causing gas that emanates from certain rocks, such as granite. A high level of radon requires corrective steps, adding to the cost of building. For a reading on local levels, try the local health department or call the EPA's radon hotline at 800-767-7236.

How to get a good price. You can never be sure the value of your property will grow fast enough to justify your investment. But you can get a good idea of its potential by studying the area's price trends, business and demographic projections, and development potential, as well as the local political climate.

You can get a good overview from the Real Estate Research Corp.'s annual study, *Emerging Trends in Real Estate,* available for $10 from Equitable Real Estate Investment Management Inc., 787 Seventh Ave., 46N, New York, N.Y. 10019. The National Association of Home Builders has two publications that can help you: *Land Buying Checklist* ($20) and *Financing Land Acquisition and Development* ($32). To order, call 800-223-2665 (in Washington, D.C., 202-822-0370).

When you find a location you like, check out the surrounding community. What business or civic activities are nearby, and would they draw people to the area? Is the economy diverse? What are the population projections? Local chambers of commerce, realty offices and bank loan officers are good sources for that kind of information.

How to check the property. Be sure that the property is accessible and that the costs of owning it and building on it are reasonable. An unsuspecting buyer of waterfront land in Maine was stunned to discover that to build on his new lot he would have to pump sewage 400 feet uphill through solid rock—at a cost of about $30,000. In other developments, buyers faced bills of $20,000 to $30,000 just to bring in electricity.

If you are buying from a developer who operates across state lines and is selling 100 or more lots, most of what you need to know to protect yourself can be found in the property report that is required by the Division of Interstate Land Sales Registration, or ILSRD (U.S. Department of Housing and Urban Development, Interstate Land Sales Registration Division, Room 6262, Washington, D.C. 20410; 202-708-2154).

If you're buying from an owner who isn't regulated by the agency, the ILSRD report can still serve as a useful model. Current zoning restrictions and tax assessments on the property should be the first items to investigate. The ILSR report also requires information on the following items:

▮ *Title*. Find out whether there are any liens on the land and verify who owns the oil, gas, mineral and water rights. Conduct your own title search, or hire a firm to do it for you.

▮ *Roads*. Are they public? How good is the surface? Who's responsible for maintenance? In cold areas, is snow removal feasible and affordable?

▮ *Utilities and facilities*. How will water and sewer lines, electricity, gas and phone service get to the property? How much will they cost and who will pay? Has the water quality been checked recently? Is the soil suitable for a septic system? Are there any drainage problems?

▮ *Services*. Where are the police and fire stations, school and hospital? Shopping centers? Offices where potential buyers of your property might work?

Look for unique parcels. Unless your parcel has some distinguishing feature, such as a waterfront location, be skeptical about its appreciation potential in a large resort or retirement community. In a new development, the developer's remaining inventory should be small, so the company won't be competing with you in the resale market. Better yet, buy in the resale market, in which lots are often cheaper and problems have had time to surface.

Compare local prices. Before you agree to a price, check comparable properties in the area. Developers often advertise their lots in distant big cities, where potential buyers are accustomed to high land prices.

The sad news about financing raw land. Banks willing to make loans on raw land typically require a large down payment—25% to 30% isn't unusual—and other assets for collateral. They also favor loans of five to 10 years, which raise the monthly payments. Financing offered by a developer or an individual seller may be a better bet. An owner may be willing to finance the sale and may accept a ten-year note with 5% to 10% down. A good negotiator should be able to borrow at below bank rates.

If you're buying rural land, community banks may offer more competitive rates, or you might get good terms through a local farm credit bank. Call the Farm Credit Council (202-626-8710) for the number of a local farm credit lender.

The sad news about taxes and raw land. Land deals don't have many tax advantages. Land isn't depreciable, and the deductibility of interest on a loan used to buy it may be restricted. If the land is an investment, then interest on the loan falls under the investment interest rules. That limits your deduction to the amount of taxable investment income you receive—from interest, dividends and capital gains, for example—during the year.

Even if you buy the land with an eye toward eventually building a home on it, you must treat the interest on the loan as investment interest until you begin to build. Once building begins, you can treat interest as fully deductible home mortgage interest—assuming you can move into the place as your first or second home within 24 months.

In the good news department, real estate taxes you pay on the land are fully deductible.

INVESTING IN MORTGAGES

$\mathbf{O}$WNING REAL ESTATE directly by buying and managing properties, and indirectly by buying shares of real estate investment trusts or mutual funds, offers a chance for capital gains in the future with an income stream along the way. But what if you want the income but don't want to take the risks inherent in trying for the capital gains? After all, mortgages often pay double-digit yields while bonds and other income-oriented investments are paying single digits. For investors in search of income, mortgages offer a tempting combination of relatively high interest payouts plus a high degree of safety of principal.

There are two ways to invest in mortgages: the right way and the wrong way.

The wrong way is to buy a mortgage from a lender who wants to get rid of it. Homesellers who "take back" a second mortgage from the buyer to facilitate the sale are often willing to sell it at a substantial discount so they won't have to wait several years to get their money. They may offer these secondary-market second mortgages through advertisements in newspapers, or a real estate broker may help them find investors willing to take the paper off their hands. Don't be one of them. The yields are often so dazzling—in the neighborhood of 18% to 20%—that they can blind you to the fact that your security in the property is subordinate to that of the lender on the first mortgage. In addition, you are taking the risk that a homebuyer you know little about (except that he or she needed a second mortgage in order to afford the home) will be able to pay you back. You don't need the headaches.

The right way to invest in mortgages is through vehicles known as mortgage-backed securities. Owning them is a safer way to get above-average income than owning mortgages themselves, but they are not without risks. Understanding those risks requires understanding where mortgage-backed securities come from.

MEET GINNIE, FANNIE AND FREDDIE

Most mortgage-backed securities originate with three federally connected agencies: the Government National Mortgage Association (GNMA), known as Ginnie Mae; the Federal National Mortgage Association (FNMA), known as Fannie Mae; and the Federal Home Loan Mortgage Corporation (FHLMC), known as Freddie Mac. Of the three, only Ginnie Mae is technically a full-blown federal government agency. The other two are government sponsored but are quasi-private organizations with no government guarantee backing their securities.

The role of all three agencies is essentially the same—to buy up mortgage loans from lenders such as banks and savings and loan associations, package them into multi-million-dollar pools and sell off pieces of the pools to investors. The pieces are known as participation certificates or pass-through securities and often sell in minimum denominations of $25,000. Investors who buy them get the homeowners' principal and interest payments passed along to them as income.

This payment schedule is one major difference between bonds and mortgage-backed securities: Bonds pay interest semi-annually; mortgage-backed securities pay interest *and* principal every month. The principal portion of the payment is

RISK IN RESIDENTIAL MORTGAGES

Q: *I am interested in investing $20,000 in residential real estate mortgages from a mortgage company. I've been guaranteed a minimum 16% return on my investment. How risky is this?*

A: The return that you have been guaranteed suggests that there must be a fairly high degree of risk. First mortgages carry less risk than second mortgages because the first lien has priority: If the borrower defaults, the first mortgage will be paid off with the proceeds of a default sale and whatever is left will be used to pay off the second mortgage. Perhaps the firm is making predominantly second mortgages or is lending to borrowers who have been turned down by banks and other lenders.

tax-free; the interest is fully taxable. Another difference is that although the mortgages mature in 30 years, the average life of a mortgage-backed security is thought to be about 12 years because so many homeowners move or refinance and in the process pay off their mortgages early.

The three agencies work slightly different markets. Ginnie Mae restricts its buying and packaging activities to government-insured or guaranteed FHA and VA mortgages, making the principal about as safe as it can be. Fannie Mae and Freddie Mac buy conventional mortgages, but their certificates carry an implicit government backing and for practical purposes aren't considered any riskier than Ginnie Maes.

What could go wrong? Setting aside for a minute the daunting $25,000 minimum investment, Ginnies, Fannies and Freddies appear at first glance to be the ideal combination of above-average returns and below-average risks. They are backed by the federal government, yet often yield a percentage point or two more than Treasury bonds of comparable maturity. So how could you possibly lose?

It's easy. Like any fixed-income investment, mortgage-backed securities operate under the influence of interest rates.

If rates go up, the market value of your holdings goes down because newly issued securities pay more than yours, as explained in Chapter 5. In that respect, Ginnies, Fannies and Freddies act like bonds. But when rates go down, the value of bonds goes up, and that's not necessarily the case for mortgage-backed securities. Homeowners tend to refinance to take advantage of lower rates, meaning they pay off their old mortgages. So as rates decline, the mortgage pool shrinks. You get your principal back early and must look for a place to reinvest it at a time when interest rates are low. You could move the money into newly issued mortgage-backed securities and comfort yourself with the thought that you're still earning a higher yield than you could get from other investments, but the fact remains that you were counting on an even *higher* payout.

What can you do? How can you protect yourself against such an unexpected turn of events? You have three choices.

▌ *Mutual funds.* You can cushion some of the blow—and sidestep the $25,000 minimum—by investing in one or more of the dozens of mutual funds that buy Ginnie Mae, Freddie Mac and Fannie Mae pass-throughs and participation certificates and parcel out shares in them for a typical minimum investment of $1,000 or less. The principal portion of the mortgage payment is automatically reinvested in the fund and the interest is passed along to shareholders each month.

Because a fund holds mortgages with a variety of maturities, it is somewhat insulated from the effects of interest rate movements. However, a fund may pack its portfolio with high-yielding certificates in an effort to attract investors. If it has paid a premium for those certificates—meaning it paid more than face value to get the higher yield, as described in Chapter 5—it will be forced to write off that premium if the mortgages get paid off early. When that happens, the net asset value of the fund declines and its investors lose money.

A mortgage fund that is yielding significantly more than most other funds of its type or that is yielding more than a percentage point or two above the current rate being charged by lenders for new 30-year mortgages most likely paid a premium price for some of the mortgages in its portfolio. If so, the yield differential will not last. Those mortgages are most likely to be refinanced by homeowners, which could cause the fund to lose value and will certainly depress its yield. Such funds are especially vulnerable when interest rates are declining and should be approached with caution. If you avoid such funds and invest for the long run—three to five years, at least—a mortgage mutual fund can be a reliable way to earn high yields with virtually no risk of default. For a list of such funds with good performance records, see Chapter 6.

∎ *Collateralized mortgage obligations.* Called CMOs, these mortgage-backed securities—along with their cousins, REMICS (real estate mortgage investment conduits)—were devised by brokerage firms in the mid 1980s to solve two problems: the erratic cash flow from Ginnie Maes and their kin due to the unpredictability of principal paybacks, and the high $25,000 minimum investment that priced many investors out of the market.

A CMO takes the cash flows from a lot of mortgage-backed securities and splits them into groups of bonds with different maturities—three years, five years and ten years, for example. The minimum denomination is $1,000. Most maturity classes receive interest from the mortgages, but principal repayments go first to the class (called a tranche) with the shortest maturity. When those bonds are retired, principal is channeled to the bonds with the next shortest maturity and so forth until all classes have been retired when all the mortgages in the pool have been paid off.

Despite the creation of CMOs with as many as a dozen different tranches, investors aren't shielded entirely from the prepayment risk inherent in mortgage-backed securities. Principal payback may actually come sooner or later than the date specified for the tranche. And because the CMO is returning principal throughout its life—not just at the end, like a bond—you get nothing back at maturity. Imagine your surprise if you've spent the principal, thinking it was all interest.

Uncertainties like that make investors demand a higher yield from a CMO than they would from, say, a U.S. Treasury note or bond with the same maturity. As a result, CMOs typically yield about a percentage point more than Treasuries, sometimes higher.

A few more things to know about CMOs:

■ They don't necessarily contain government-backed mortgages. The issuer could also be a bank or even a homebuilder. The underlying collateral may be conventional, uninsured mortgages with the backing not of the government but of the financial services company, such as a brokerage firm, that packaged the deal. The safest CMOs, however, contain Ginnie Maes, Fannie Maes and Freddie Macs.

■ Count on holding them until maturity. Although there is a secondary market for CMOs, their steady erosion of value caused by the payback of principal make them a poor trading vehicle for small investors.

■ *Stock in the issuers.* Both Fannie Mae and Freddie Mac sell common stock to the public on the New York Stock Exchange. (Ginnie Mae, which is a government agency, does not sell stock.) They make money by collecting fees for the pass-through and participation securities they package from mortgages they buy from thrifts and other lenders, and from interest on such mortgages they hold for their own portfolios.

Although these stocks are classified as part of the banking industry, which is characterized by generally sedate stock price movements, they tend to be volatile, with higher highs and lower lows than the market as a whole. Investing in them offers reasonable prospects for avoiding the vagaries of interest rate swings and early principal payouts while tapping into future profits from the anticipated long-term strength of the secondary mortgage market. But it is not a good way to invest for income. Yield on these issues averages less than 3%. If it's income you want, you'll have to stick with the mortgage-backed securities themselves, with all their uncertainties.

THE OVERSELLING OF PRECIOUS METALS & COLLECTIBLES

T HE LIFE SPAN of a gold bug is yet to be determined, but the world may be close to finding out.

▌ Since gold prices peaked at $850 an ounce in 1980, the metal has failed miserably to live up to its ancient reputation as an inflation hedge. Its price in the summer of 1991 was actually *lower* than it had been ten years earlier—a decade in which prices rose by nearly 50%. If you had bought gold in 1982 at the decade's low price of $325, in nine years your investment would have grown to roughly $365—an annual appreciation rate of less than 2% during a period when the Standard & Poor's 500-stock index delivered better than 10% per year.

▌ Gold's bragging rights as the world-champion hedge against disaster are also being seriously challenged. In the face of financial and geopolitical catastrophes ranging from the worst stock market crash in history to a multi-national war in the Middle East, gold mostly slumbered—meandering between $400 and $500 an ounce and spiking only briefly and weakly when the news was at its worst.

In the aftermath of such a disappointing decade for gold, has the time come to reject both claims and conclude that gold *won't* protect you against inflation and disaster? Or should you keep the faith, anticipating that the link is only temporarily broken? The risk of the first choice is that you could be wrong and your portfolio battered some day by unforeseen events. The risk of the second choice is that you forfeit other opportunities to make your money grow.

For most people, our advice is simple: Forget the gold and invest your money elsewhere. Even the most fervent believers in the metal's right to a place in your portfolio don't recommend making it more than 5% to 10% of your assets. At that level, you'd need substantial assets before a little gold would make much difference even if some unforeseeable event caused gold's price to double or triple.

If you do have a substantial investment portfolio—say several hundred thousand dollars—the choice isn't as clear. The ups and downs of supply and demand for gold can create opportunities to profit even if neither disaster nor hyperinflation occurs in your lifetime. But buying and selling to take advantage of price changes would require paying close attention to market forces. Forgetting for a moment the irony of doing such a thing (gold investors often insist that a major attraction of gold is that you don't *have* to pay attention to the markets), it's important to know how gold and other so-called hard, or tangible, assets differ from stocks and bonds and other financial assets.

THE WHYS AND WAYS OF GOLD

Gold will always have value because it is useful, durable and rare. If all the gold ever mined were gathered in one place, it would form a solid block only about the size of a 10-story office building. Because gold is virtually indestructible, metal mined 5,000 years ago could theoretically still be found somewhere in the world, or orbiting around it. Commercial uses for gold range from the everyday, such as in jewelry and camcorder parts, to the exotic, such as the components of satellites. Gold is also remarkably malleable: An ounce of it can be stretched into a wire 50 miles long.

The world has long recognized these intrinsic qualities of gold, and it still does. People manage to bribe their way out of locked-up countries by crossing the palms of officials with gold, the universal currency. And in times of crisis, many people still seek refuge in gold. In October 1987, the month the stock market crashed, the U.S. Mint sold 198,000 ounces of American Eagle coins compared with 63,500 ounces the month before.

Ways You Can Invest

Gold comes in shapes and sizes ranging from 400-ounce bricks to tiny wafers weighing only a gram.

Coins. The most popular form of ownership is bullion coins: American Eagles, Australian Kangaroo Nuggets, British Britannias, Canadian Maple Leafs and Chinese Pandas weighing from ⅟₂₀ of an ounce up to an ounce, with a couple of sizes in between. (South African Krugerrands have been illegal for Americans to import, although existing supplies could still be bought and sold.) Coins sell for about 3% to 6% more than the value of their gold content on the day of the transaction. So, for example, if gold costs $385, you'd pay about $408 for a one-ounce gold bullion coin at a dealer, bank or a brokerage house.

If you own gold, you need a way to store it securely—say, in a safe-deposit box—and you should also buy insurance for your holdings. Some dealers simplify the logistics of ownership by sponsoring "certificate" plans, under which they store the gold for you and issue a certificate entitling you to delivery of the metal if you want it. You can also find statement accounts at some dealers. These leave the gold in the dealer's name, with you as the "book entry" owner, something like stock held in street name (See Chapter 15). The chief advantage of this form of ownership is convenience: You can buy and sell your gold over the phone and not worry about storage. You pay commissions on purchases and sales and a small charge for storage and insurance.

Mining stocks and mutual funds. Stocks of companies that mine gold make wonderful conversation pieces because they have such interesting names: American Barrick, Battle Mountain, Placer Dome, Echo Bay, Golden Knight. Whether they make wonderful investments is another question.

Gold-mining stocks are affected by overall trends on Wall Street and by corporate decisions both good and bad that may have little to do with the price of gold itself. A company that institutes low-cost mining methods, strikes a rich lode or astutely hedges its sales through the futures market can experience solid earnings. A poorly managed company will surely sink no matter what happens to gold prices, but a well-managed company should soar if prices explode. The major full-service brokerage firms (See Chapter 15) follow gold-mining stocks and will be happy to offer their recommendations.

Gold-oriented mutual funds buy the shares of domestic and foreign companies that mine, explore for, process or sell gold. Some also own a bit of bullion. The funds are easy to find because almost all have the word "gold" in their names. The rewards for investing in them are a lot harder to find. They are highly risky and only rarely in the past decade have investors earned returns commensurate with those risks. Total returns of 20% to 30% in a single year occur from time to time. Returns in the *minus* double-digits are more common.

The best of the bunch over five years to the end of 1990 were Oppenheimer Gold & Special Minerals (800-255-2755; 5.75% load) and Franklin Gold Fund (800-342-5236; 4% load). They turned in total returns for the period of 151% and 100%, respectively. But their returns for the the last three of those five years were barely positive in one case and negative in the other, and their returns for 1990 were worse than *minus* 10%. Tread very carefully in gold funds.

You can also invest in gold via options or futures contracts—notoriously arcane devices that attempt to anticipate price changes of the metal (see Chapter 12). Leave this game to the mining companies.

SHOULD YOU INVEST IN GOLD AT ALL?

To review the argument for gold: In normal times, your stocks, bonds and cash equivalents deliver a balanced overall return while gold does little or nothing. In bad times, however, gold is supposed to prosper when other investments do poorly because it offers a refuge from the storm. So having gold in your portfolio provides a measure of protection, even though you may hope that you never need it.

The problem is, gold isn't necessarily acting that way anymore, as we saw a couple of pages ago. Why not? Three factors have been at work in the past several years—factors that can reasonably be expected to affect prices in the future as well.

Supply and demand. Record amounts of gold have come onto the market in recent years, much of it the result of modern mining techniques that can economically sift 50 tons of low-ore rock for an ounce of the yellow metal. Sustained high mine output is forecast over the next several years, a development that should serve to keep prices in check.

Trading techniques. Gold-mining companies have become aggressive and sophisticated gold-market speculators, locking in their prices on the futures markets in a way that satisfies crisis-mentality demand that might otherwise drive prices much higher. Such trading programs, experts say, have helped confine gold prices to the narrow trading band of the past several years.

Investment alternatives. Today, investors can avoid—or profit from—world crises by quickly moving their money into the most stable currencies, either directly or through international and global mutual funds or specialized currency funds.

In addition, there are less exotic ways to hedge against inflation or global uncertainty. You could buy a U.S. Treasury bill and roll it over automatically every three months or buy shares in a short-term T-bill mutual fund. Either gives you safety of principal plus relatively high current return and the opportunity to profit from the rising interest rates that would surely accompany a surge in inflation.

AN EVEN WEAKER CASE FOR SILVER

You can buy a stake in silver much the same way as you do in gold—in bars and coins of various sizes, via certificate programs and by investing in companies that mine the metal. Perhaps because you perform these transactions across the very same counters where gold is bought and sold, many investors think of gold and silver as birds of a feather. They're not. Precious-metals merchants used to encourage such mistaken linkage by speaking of the ratio of gold prices to silver prices as if there were some magical relationship between the two that eventually would be restored. Don't count on it.

Silver is a commodity whose price is determined by demand that springs mostly from industrial usage. Photographic film is the biggest source of demand, followed by jewelry and silverware, followed by electronics. Although photography's share of silver usage has climbed in recent years because of the greater silver demands of color film, demographic shifts and personal taste have combined to shrink the market for silverware. Also, as the price of silver rises, industrial users find ways to use less of it, either by substituting something else or stepping up efforts to reuse minute amounts that they would otherwise discard. Meanwhile, the output from silver mines has grown steadily in recent decades, outstripping demand in every year since 1979. That, plus the disillusionment that set in among investors when a handful of rich investors appeared to have driven prices up artificially in 1980, has dampened enthusiasm for silver as an inflation hedge.

Because silver is primarily an industrial metal, the demand for it is subject to the fluctuations of economic conditions. It does have intrinsic value, but because of its relatively ample supply compared with gold, investors have refused to assign it as treasured a place in their portfolios. The one time they tried—in 1980, when the price soared to its all-time high of $40 an ounce—the plunge that followed scared many investors away for good. Those who stuck around and bought more silver during the 1980s paid an average price of $11.25 an ounce, according to the Silver Institute. At the dawn of the 1990s, the price was languishing at less than half that level and there was a surplus of supply over demand.

Clearly, the opportunity to make money in silver, if such an opportunity exists, belongs to those with great patience.

WHY COLLECTIBLES AREN'T INVESTMENTS

One of the most misused words in the marketing of luxury goods, whether new or antique, is "investment." Purrs the TV commercial for an expensive automobile: "It's not a car, it's an investment." "Invest in a fine fur," says the furrier. The same claims are made for art, antiques and other collectibles. Collectors of everything from baseball cards and limited-edition plates to Chinese ceramics and rare stamps are led to believe they are making an investment.

High-quality tangible goods—a fine car, jewelry, hand-crafted furniture, a beautiful painting—have their own rewards of ownership, but inflation-adjusted appreciation usually isn't one of them. The best that can be said for most good collectibles is that they depreciate more slowly than lesser examples of their type. You wouldn't consider slow depreciation, or even just a holding of value, to be satisfactory in financial investments, would you? If a stockbroker tried to convince you to buy shares of XYZ Corp. because the shares would probably decline in value, but not much, you would laugh in his face.

As we have stated in different ways throughout the book, an investment is something you buy with a reasonable expectation of current income, future profit or both. An investment should exhibit some or all of the following characteristics:

■ *Liquidity.* You can convert it to cash fairly quickly, if you have to. This requires a large, well-organized market of buyers and sellers who are easy to contact.

■ *Low transaction costs.* You can sell it easily for something close to retail value; that is, you pay a low sales commission. Sellers of homes have to pay about 6% of the sales price as commission, stockbrokers normally charge commissions between 1% and 5%.

■ *Low cost of ownership.* Ideally, you shouldn't have to put more money into your investment after the initial purchase for storage and insurance.

■ *Current income.* You probably want at least a little income, as interest, dividends or rent, while you're waiting for the asset to rise in value.

■ *A track record of appreciation.* There's no guarantee that anything you buy will rise in value—stocks and bonds included—but a real investment has a track record of at least holding its value against inflation, and ideally exceeding inflation.

Tangible assets, whatever their quality of craftsmanship or rarity, fail those litmus tests of a true investment.

The biggest problem of collectibles as investments is liquidity. They are *very* difficult to sell at all, let alone for a price approaching or exceeding what you paid for them. You can't just pick up the phone and get a price quote for your rare porcelain doll or Federal-period sofa, let alone sell it in the same call, as you can with stocks and mutual funds. Unless you are an advanced collector who knows other collectors who will pay you retail (or close to it) on short notice, you must sell your goods to the same dealers you bought from originally, or wait for the next auction of your specialty and take your chances.

STOMPING ON THE STAMP MARKET

Q: *Can you tell me what happened to the market in rare, investment-grade postage stamps? Several years ago it was going great, but today you don't hear anything about it.*

A: Following years of speculation during which stamp prices climbed, the stamp market went bust in 1982–83. It has returned to being a collector's—rather than an investor's—market, and all but the rarest stamps are appreciating slowly. To determine your collection's value, have it appraised by a dealer who specializes in the type of stamps you collect.

For a printout of dealers in your area who are members of the American Stamp Dealers Association as well as information on appraisals, send a self-addressed, stamped envelope to the association at 3 School St., Glen Cove, N.Y. 11542; 516-759-7000. You can also check your library for the current *Scott Standard Postage Stamp Catalog* or the *Scott Specialized Catalog of United States Stamps*, both of which list current retail prices for stamps.

Transaction costs are very high for collectibles. To cover their business expenses—financing inventory, advertising, travel, rent, exhibiting at shows—dealers try for at least a 100% mark-up. To put it another way, they will usually pay a collector only 50% of the price they'll try to get when they resell an item. As a collector, you are usually buying at retail and selling at wholesale, so the retail price has to *double* before you can get back just your original cash outlay, which will have been eroded by inflation in the meantime. (Some dealers will guarantee in writing to "buy back" at full price anything they sold—but not in cash, only as a credit against the purchase of something else in their inventory.)

Selling at auction will enable you to keep more of the sale price: the high bid minus a commission of 10% to 25%. But you never know what might be bid for your item on the day of the auction; the price could be disappointingly low. Before the auction you may be able to set a "reserve"—a price below which your item won't be auctioned off—but if no one offers at least the reserve price, you have to take it back and try to sell it some other day, or some other way.

During your ownership of a collectible, you're getting no income from tying up your money. And you have costs of ownership, too—appraisals, insurance, maintenance, storage, security. There is also the problem of authenticity, a result of the tendency of unscrupulous people to alter antiques and produce convincing fakes whenever the price of some category of collectible begins to soar.

Profits and patience. We all hear and read stories about fabulous profits in art, coins, antiques and other collectibles, but the stories tend to spotlight unusual windfalls that don't mirror the broad market experience. The gains are typically one of two kinds: a quick profit in a hot market, which is high-risk speculation, not investing; or the opposite, strong appreciation achieved after many years of patient ownership, during which the collector received no income and took a chance on changing fads and tastes. And the big profits are rung up by the finest examples of their type, rare items that usually cost a lot of money in the first place.

So-called investment indexes of collectibles—stamps, furniture, coins, Old Master paintings and the like—are not trustworthy and are in no sense comparable to indexes of stock and bond performances. They are based on a small number of transactions of top-quality items that are not identical to each other (as shares of stock are), so they are not particularly useful for judging the value of other, vaguely similar goods.

In the 1970s and early 1980s, high-quality collectibles enjoyed strong collector demand, and many items did experience a sharp rise in their retail price (which, as we've noted, is usually much higher than what the owner can realize by selling). But this boom has blinded many collectors to the historical fact of long periods in which most of the same items languished, out of style and flat in value.

Booms and busts. There have been booms and busts in every kind of collectible—furniture, jewelry, baseball cards, rare photographs, Tiffany lamps, you name it. One of the earliest antiques manias was during the 1920s, when rich collectors paid astronomical prices for fine pieces of 18th-century American furniture. Then prices fell and flattened through the following three decades, before beginning to recover in the '60s and taking off like skyrockets in the '70s and '80s.

On an inflation-adjusted basis, the record prices paid for some antiques in the late '20s were not even approached until the million-dollar barrier was broken with the sale of fine Philadelphia tea table in 1986. At the legendary auction of the Reifsnyder collection in 1929, for example, a superb Philadelphia Chippendale highboy sold for $44,000, a great fortune at a time when the annual earnings of the typical American worker were just $1,400. If that magnificent chest of drawers came on the market today, it might well sell for more than $3 million, a price achieved by only two other pieces of American furniture, sold at auction in 1989 and 1990. But even at such a fabulous price, the highboy would have earned just 7% a year compounded since 1929, an investment return that was easily exceeded by the 10% average annual return on quality stocks over the past 60 years. Of course, a collector who might have bought that highboy at a much lower price during the dark days of the '40s or '50s, when antiques were out of favor, would have achieved a much higher annual rate of return.

During the 1920s, newspaper publisher William Randolph Hearst avidly collected Staffordshire dinnerware with transfer-printed scenes of America. In 1925 he paid $1,100 for a beautiful dark-blue-and-white platter with a view of New York City on it, made around 1830. At the dispersal of his collection in 1938, the same platter sold for $370—quite a slide in value in 13 years. If that $370 platter had managed to double in value every 10 years (roughly a 7% compounded annual rate of appreciation) it would be worth more than $12,000 today. But platters of this type can be bought for about $5,000 today. That's still a good deal of money for a piece of china, but proportionately much less than its price many years before. In short, that lovely piece of English ceramics wasn't such a hot investment, underperforming a passbook savings account.

The odds are very good that art, antiques and collectibles being bought at record-high prices today will not enjoy in the 1990s the real rate of return of carefully selected financial assets. Having said that, let's not forget that collecting is wonderful fun, and that high-quality tangibles are a joy to own. They can be a decent store of value, too, when compared not with financial assets but with other utilitarian and decorative goods.

Antique furniture, for example, is the only kind of household goods that give you current utility plus some degree of retained value. Knowledgeable collectors with a fine eye for quality have a reasonable chance of making a little money, too. They buy for love, not profit, which means they are guided in their purchases by their own tastes, not the fads of hot markets. If the things they love were shunned by other collectors at the time of purchase, they were able to buy low, giving them the opportunity to sell high a few years later—assuming that other collectors had come around to their tastes in the meantime. This has been the experience of many trail-blazing collectors of such things as folk art, '60s "muscle cars," Victorian furniture and other categories that once were ignored.

In *that* direction, not in the direction of the crowd, lies the best hope for actually making money in collectibles. Good luck, but don't include collectibles in your long-range plans for financial security. That would be confusing a hobby with an investment strategy.

CHAPTER

12

MORE INVESTMENTS
YOU CAN LIVE WITHOUT

THERE'S AN OLD saying on Wall Street that stocks and bonds aren't bought, they're sold. Brokerage firm managers like to use that expression during pep talks with their brokers, usually followed by some form of the following: "You can't wait for the customers to walk in the door; you've got to get out there and find them."

Fair enough. Brokers have a long list of good investment products to sell, without which there would be no need for books like this one. When it comes to stocks and bonds and such, the question is not *whether* you should invest, the question is *which investments* you should choose. This chapter is about investments that, in our opinion, flunk the "whether" question. For reasons of high cost, lack of liquidity, the size of the risk involved or the amount of effort required compared with the potential reward, we think you're better off without them.

LIMITED PARTNERSHIPS

The idea sounds appealing enough. Like mutual funds, limited partnerships pool large sums of money from the smaller contributions of many limited partners who otherwise could not afford to buy office buildings or other high-priced investments. The general partner, which is usually a company, may contribute only a token amount of capital to the deal but supplies the expertise the partnership needs to acquire, manage and ultimately dispose of the assets. LPs get their name because the liability of the limited partners is limited to the amount of money they invest. (You can be forgiven for wondering what's so great about *that*.)

The 1980s were tough on the kinds of investments limited partnerships often acquire: real estate, oil and gas operations, and certain commodities. But we believe the real turkey of this tale is the limited partnership vehicle itself, especially the so-called public programs sold in quantities as small as $1,000 to investors of fairly modest means. ("Private" deals, which aren't as stringently regulated by federal and state governments, are often no great shakes, either. But because they require that investors have a much higher net worth or income, they at least wind up in the portfolios of people who can afford to take the risks and pay the fees.)

The fact is that limited partnerships for individual investors with relatively modest assets don't make much economic sense anymore. Their major benefit—the ability to pass losses directly through to limited partners in need of a means to shelter other kinds of income—was eliminated by the tax overhaul of 1986.

Undaunted, LP packagers tout their offerings as the ideal way for small investors to own hard assets directly, free from the influence of stock market movements that might affect the values of similar assets owned by, say, a mutual fund.

Partnerships do get one tax break that mutual funds don't enjoy: Profits—if there are any—are passed directly to the limited partners. Their ability to thus avoid double taxation of earnings (owners of stock pay taxes on dividends that have already been reduced by the corporate income taxes paid by the company) is the major plus for partnerships. But it's tough to make enough money from a limited partnership to compensate you for their risks and other shortcomings. Here's why:

▪ *High fees.* You're in the hole from the moment you buy. LPs are sold as units, and a unit usually costs $500 to $1,000. Most deals require a minimum purchase of five units. From this, there are deductions for brokerage commissions (usually 7% to 10%), costs of organizing and offering the deal, and fees to the syndicator for acquiring the properties. Altogether, the front-end costs on real estate partnerships, the biggest category in the industry, usually amount to 15% to 20% of your capital. In leveraged real estate deals, front-end charges can consume 25% or more of your initial investment. On top of the front-end fees, the general partner or its affiliates take cuts during the operation and liquidation phases of limited partnerships, too. Finally, add the fat commissions salespeople get—up to $500 on a $5,000 investment.

▪ *Difficulty getting out.* Getting into a partnership is easy. Getting out isn't. If you do jump ship, chances are you'll take a financial bath. Unlike stocks and bonds, LPs aren't traded on competitive exchanges, and the deals aren't usually scheduled to mature for seven to 10 years. There is something of a secondary market for partnership units, where limited partners often get 50 cents or so on the dollar from buyers who demand big discounts to make up for all the front-end fees.

▪ *Tax headaches.* You can use depreciation to shelter some income from the partnership, and dollar-for-dollar tax credits are available for investors in low-income-housing and historic-rehabilitation programs. But the chance to use losses from LPs to offset salary and other income is pretty much gone.

What you're left with are all the headaches when the time comes to file tax returns. You get a Schedule K-1 from the general partner for every LP in which you've invested. The K-1 may contain more than 70 items dealing with the limited partners' share of income, losses, deductions, credits and other items that must be copied onto various IRS tax forms—among them Schedule E (for declaring supplemental income) and Form 8582 (covering passive income and losses).

To make matters worse, if your share of the partnership's reported earnings is substantial, you might have to pay income taxes in the states in which the LP does business.

■ *Blind offerings.* Investors in new LPs rarely know what specific assets the program will acquire. Many investors in real estate LPs established in the early and mid 1980s were blindsided by the propensity of the general partners to buy properties in Texas and other parts of the Oil Patch.

■ *Better deals elsewhere.* The typical all-cash real estate LP being offered today can be expected to generate initial cash distributions of 6% to 8%. Granted, those distributions may rise if rents increase, and there's potential for capital gains in the appreciation of the property. But it's hard to see why you should put your money in an illiquid partnership when essentially riskless Treasury notes and CDs can produce comparable returns.

One class of LP avoids many of the drawbacks cited here—the master limited partnership, or MLP. Because they are traded like stocks, MLPs are easy to buy and sell. Some of them generate very high yields (Red Lion Hotels and Inns LP paid a dividend of 14.5% in 1990, and Borden Chemicals and Plastics LP paid 24.5%). The tax headaches you take on can be every bit as severe as they are with regular LPs, unless you put your MLPs in a tax-sheltered retirement account. Investigate before you invest, using the standards discussed in Chapter 4.

Movie limited partnerships. This type of investment deserves special mention.

Probably the best known are the series of Silver Screen limited partnerships that financed the production of such hits as *Who Framed Roger Rabbit?* and *Dead Poets Society* and have used such stars as Paul Newman, Bette Midler and Benji the dog. However, several years after Silver Screen's blockbuster success, the limited partners were still waiting to collect any profits. Movie industry accountants and lawyers have devised an accounting system made in Hollywood and worthy of an

Academy Award for special effects. Profits seem to disappear before they get to you.

PUT AND CALL OPTIONS

Puts and calls have the effect of turning investors into traders. If you think the price of a stock is going to go down in the near future, you can buy a "put" on that stock, which gives you the right to sell 100 shares near the current price. If you think the price is going up, you can buy a "call," which gives you the right to buy it near the current price. You can also be a seller of puts and calls if you want to be on the other side of the transaction.

Stock options conjure up visions of high rollers and craps tables, but any stockbroker worthy of the name can explain how engaging in something called "writing covered calls" is a safe and conservative way to wring extra yield out of your stock portfolio. Your broker could be right, but that doesn't mean you should do it.

The technique entails selling a call option on a stock you own. A call option gives the buyer the right to buy the underlying stock ("call" it away) from you at a specified price, known as the strike price, within a specified time, which may be a few days after the transaction or as much three years.

Say you own 100 shares of IBM and the stock's price is $110. In February you sell to another investor (through your broker) the right to buy your 100 shares for, say, $120 before the end of June. You have written a covered call.

Why would you want to do such a thing? Because you collect extra income, a premium, for selling the option. Premiums vary with the price of the underlying stock and the proximity of the strike price to the actual price; two or three dollars per share is about average, in 100-share minimums. For your covered call on IBM, you collect about $400, which you keep no matter what happens to the price of the stock.

The technique works beautifully if the stock price remains

unchanged or at least stays under the strike price. In that case the option expires worthless and you wind up with more income from your stocks than you would have collected otherwise. If the price rises a lot—which is what the call buyer was betting on—the buyer will certainly exercise the option, denying you the benefit of any gain above the strike price. If the stock plunges, you can comfort yourself with the premium you collected.

Chances are good that the covered calls you write will expire worthless. So what's wrong with the technique?

▮ First, the risks may be modest, but the amount of your time and energy involved is not. Writing covered calls is hardly worth the trouble unless you do it regularly, with the aim of making 10% to 15% on your holdings. That entails a lot of bookkeeping and a lot of calendar watching. What's more, if someone is willing to buy your covered call, that investor presumably has reason to think the price of your stock is going to go up more than you think it's going to go up. You'd better take the time to find out why.

▮ Second, commissions on options are proportionately higher than on other kinds of transactions because of the relatively modest sums involved. At a full-service broker, commissions can range from 4% of your premium to 10% or more, depending on the size of the transaction.

▮ Third, writing a covered call means putting 100 shares of your carefully selected stock at risk of being snatched out of your portfolio on the basis of a temporary spike in the price. That kind of speculation is inconsistent with a long-term investment program, and that *is the main argument against writing covered calls.*

You can also buy and sell puts and calls on the major stock market indexes, specialized indexes and even foreign currencies. For investment managers responsible for hedging tens of millions of dollars worth of stocks and armed with lightning-fast computers, dealing in such options leads to what's called program trading (See Chapter 17). For individual investors, it leads to lunacy.

COMMODITIES FUTURES

The idea of speculating on the future price of soy beans, corn, cocoa, crude oil and other commodities may strike you as so absurd that it is hardly worthy of comment. But an amazing number of investors who wouldn't dream of getting involved in something so arcane allow themselves to get talked into paying someone else to do the speculating for them. But first things first.

What you trade in the futures markets is not a product but a standard agreement to buy or sell a product at some later date—usually within six months or so—at the price set when the contract is purchased. You need to put up as little as 2% to 10% of the value of the underlying commodity contract to get in on the action. This sort of leverage can lead to fantastic profits if prices move the right way: Say you buy a futures contract that commits you to take delivery of 100 ounces of gold at $400 an ounce on a specified date six months from now. That's $40,000 worth of gold, but the margin is 5%, so you pay only $2,000 for the contract. If the price goes to $440 an ounce—10% above your contract price—you make a profit of $40 an ounce when the contract is fulfilled. On 100 ounces, that's a $4,000 return on your $2,000 investment. You've doubled your money on a 10% increase in the price of gold.

The dark side, of course, lies in the direction of a price decline. Unlike an option, which gives you the right to buy or sell the underlying stock, a futures contract is an *obligation* to buy or sell the underlying commodity. (In practice that rarely happens because investors can offset a contract to buy at a particular price with a contract to sell at about the same time at the same price. That way, only money changes hands, saving commodities investors from having to cope with unwanted truckloads of live cattle or pork bellies.)

Nevertheless, if the price moves against you, you can't just let the contract expire, as you could with an option. You'll have to deliver on the contract and cover your leveraged losses. Suppose that in the example above the price had sunk 10%

instead of rising. Your contract would obligate you to pay $40,000 for 100 ounces of gold worth only $36,000. In that case, you'd be buying at $40,000 and selling at $36,000 (unless you wanted to take delivery of the gold, which would be your choice). Because you could close the deal via contracts with a 5% margin, your loss would be the $2,000 you originally invested in the $40,000 contract to buy, plus the $1,800 you'd have to spend to offset it with the $36,000 contract to sell.

To review: Your original futures contract cost $2,000 and it's a total loss. You must cover that obligation with a second contract, which costs you $1,800 (5% of $36,000). Actual loss on your $2,000 investment: $3,800. That's the dark side of leveraged speculating in commodities futures. Unless you're a farmer, a food processor or a manufacturer who needs to lock in the price of a physical commodity to protect your business, this particular speculation is best left alone.

Commodity funds. Commodity funds offer the same potential advantages as mutual funds: professional management, the ability to diversify and, often, access to up-to-date information and high-quality research. Funds are usually limited partnerships, in which money put up by individuals is used by a professional trader to speculate in futures. The organizer, a company or individual, becomes the general partner, overseeing operations and hiring the trading adviser, or manager. The other investors are limited partners; their responsibility for losses is limited to the amount they invest. Partnership units usually cost $1,000, and investors as a rule must buy at least two to five units. They are bought and sold through brokers.

There is surely something to be said for professional management, and some commodity funds have delivered truly breathtaking returns. Commissions are typically lower than they are for real estate partnerships, but management fees may be higher. What you gain in professional management, however, you lose in liquidity. There is virtually no secondary market for these investments; units usually can be redeemed

COMPLAINING ABOUT A BROKER

Q: *I invested in some penny stocks that have fallen in value more than 70% since I purchased them less than a year ago. How can I find out whether my broker has engaged in illegal activity, and what can I do about it?*

A: If you suspect that your broker is not on the up-and-up and you would like to file a complaint, you have several options. You can alert your state's division of securities regulation or, on the national level, contact the National Association of Securities Dealers (NASD), which regulates individual brokers. Send your complaint to NASD, Compliance Dept., 1735 K St., N.W., Washington, D.C. 20006.

NASD investigates all customer complaints and censures members if rules have been violated. It does not recover monetary damages, but it does provide arbitration facilities for customers with disputes involving $5,000 or less. This is a quick and inexpensive alternative to court proceedings, and NASD member brokers are required to participate.

If you want, you can file a complaint with the Securities and Exchange Commission, Office of Consumer Affairs, 450 Fifth St., N.W., Mail Stop 2–6, Washington, D.C. 20549. The SEC's Office of Consumer Affairs also offers a free publication for investors, *Beware of Penny Stock Fraud*, available at the same address.

only by selling them back to the general partner. Because fund values can fluctuate sharply, when you get into a fund and when you get out can play the key role in whether or not you end up a winner.

Hybrid funds. Some brokerage firms offer the chance to take a toe-in-the-water approach to the commodities markets through hybrid instruments that combine a commodities investment with a safe one. Such hybrids may promise you your money back if you stay the course, plus a shot at making big money in the commodities market.

Say that you invest $10,000. A hybrid fund may take $6,000 of that to buy U.S. Treasury zero-coupon bonds that return

$10,000 in five years at maturity. This means that you're fairly well assured of getting your original investment back if you hold your shares for five years. Your remaining $4,000 goes to a smart commodities manager who may just get you a nice additional profit.

The problem with these funds is that they are expensive. One popular offering collects a fee of 6% per year on total net assets—even on funds just sitting there, invested in Treasury zeros. As noted in the fine print in the prospectus, that's equivalent to a 15% annual fee on the $4,000 you have invested in commodities. You could do a lot better on your own by finding a less risky speculation and buying your own T- zero.

STOCK-INDEXED CDs

Several years ago Chase Manhattan Bank unveiled a truly novel certificate of deposit, a CD whose yield would be linked to stock market returns. Called the Market Index Investment, it took two forms. One offered either a guaranteed yield of 4% or up to 40% of the percentage gain in the Standard & Poor's 500-stock index, whichever was greater. If the S&P gained 30% during the year you held the CD, your yield would be an impressive 12%. If the market crashed, you'd still be 4% richer. The other version offered up to 75% of the S&P's gain but no guaranteed payoff. For CDs of less than a year, lesser shares of the S&P's gains would apply.

Its appeal at first glance was irresistible: You could share in the run-up of stock prices without risking a penny of principal. The worst that could happen was that you would get only your principal back. Several other institutions developed similar offerings. Then, in October 1987, the market *did* crash, and that seemed to put an end to the Market Index Investment idea. Most other banks quietly dropped their versions, but when the market started showing signs of strength again, interest reportedly returned.

An examination of the results from this sort of investment

provides the best argument for leaving it alone. Say you bought one in April 1987, about the time they became available, and held onto it through the market crash of that year, through the subsequent recovery and until the summer of 1989. Let's say further that you chose the 75% share of the S&P's gains with no guaranteed minimum return. What would you have earned?

A $1,000 initial investment in a 12-month Market Indexed Investment (MII) rolled over each April would have grown to $1,112. That works out to an annual rate of return of 5%. What would have happened had you invested in successive three-month MIIs instead? Again, not a lot—you'd have a nest egg worth $1,152 and an annual rate of return of 6.8%.

Suppose you had put your $1,000 into garden-variety CDs those same 27 months? Based on average yields available, your investment would be worth $1,164; that's a 7% annual rate of return. Meanwhile, say you put another $1,000 in Vanguard's Index Trust 500 Portfolio fund, which mirrors results of the S&P 500. That would have grown to $1,274, or an 11.4% annualized yield. What's more, you could have postponed the taxes on almost half of your gains until you sold the shares; with your hybrid certificate of deposit, you would have paid taxes each and every year.

CONTRACTUAL MUTUAL FUNDS

The major differences between contractual funds and the rest of the mutual fund universe are these:

■ You agree up front to invest a fixed sum of money each month for ten to 15 years. There's some leeway—you can make several contributions in advance or skip payments for up to a year without having your plan terminated. Despite the word contractual, the obligation to invest is not legally enforceable.

■ You plunge into a fee structure that swallows as much as half of your first year's investment. Over the life of a contract, as much as 13% of the money you put in goes not to buy shares but to compensate the broker, financial planner or insurance agent who sold you on the idea, or to the operators of the fund. As a group, these are the costliest mutual funds.

▮ You may have 45 days to change your mind. After that, if you want out of the fund before the contract is up, you may lose as much as 40% of what you've invested. Sales charges are bunched in the first year of your investment plan. And after the first 18 months these charges are totally nonrefundable to the investor.

Fidelity Destiny I, whose $2.5 billion in assets makes it the largest of this breed of fund, shows contractual plans in their best light because it has done an excellent job of managing its assets. But investors in Destiny had fewer dollars working for them in the early years than they would have in practically any other fund, meaning Destiny's performance had to outstrip similar noncontractual funds just to stay even. It did quite well. Other firms selling contractual plans with similar fees have had considerably less success. They are:

▮ First Investors, of New York City, which markets five contractual funds: Global, Government, High Yield, Income, and Insured Tax Exempt.

▮ Summit Investors, part of the Houston-based AIM family of funds.

▮ Security Action, which was begun in 1982 by a Topeka, Kansas, firm.

Contractual plans justify the enormous front-loaded charges by saying that they are an inducement for people to stick with a plan because the longer you stay with it, the more you amortize the initial fees. But a commitment to invest regularly is one thing, and a commitment to stick with one fund for as long as 15 years is quite another. Your goals in life may change—you marry, become a parent or need to tap your investments for, say, the down payment on a home. Your fund can change, too. Portfolio managers come and go: Both Summit and Security Action changed managers in 1988, and both adopted more-aggressive investment policies.

The irrefutable argument advanced by contractual funds for putting money in them is that regular, long-term investing is smart. You benefit from dollar-cost averaging—by investing the same amount of money each month, you buy more shares when the price is down and fewer when it is up, and that usually means your average cost per share is lower than it would be otherwise. Also, by taking the long-term approach and reinvesting your gains, you benefit from compounding—the shares you bought with dividends last month generate more dividends the next time, and so on.

But you can invest small amounts regularly for long periods in any of hundreds of mutual funds, and you can do it a lot cheaper than in contractuals. The alternatives for building wealth slowly and steadily are almost innumerable. The contractual fund seems suited for that very small percentage of people who feel so lacking in willpower that they can save only with a gun to their head.

PENNY STOCKS

Despite the name, an issue needn't cost mere pennies to qualify as a penny stock. The North American Securities Administrators Association (NASAA) defines penny stocks as certain issues selling from a penny to $5 a share. The Securities and Exchange Commission defines a penny stock as any stock traded over the counter that sells for less than $5 a share. Of course, many substantial and legitimate stocks sell for low prices. But too many of them are fraught with risk.

A lot of investors figure that it's bound to be easier to score big with a minipriced issue than with a high-priced one. It stands to reason that even in a powerful bull market it will take several years for IBM, at $125 a share, or Colgate-Palmolive, at $75, to double or triple in price. But a $5 stock? Better yet, a $1.25 stock? They have been known to double in less than a week. Any list of top percentage gainers—for a day, a month or a year—is likely to be dominated by stocks selling in or near single digits. By the same token, the biggest percentage losers also tend to be low-priced stocks.

Another attraction is that cheap issues allow investors to buy 100-share lots with small outlays. Buying "even lots" like that can be psychologically soothing and, in many cases, can give you a break on commissions.

Some investors even believe that cheapness is an indication of good value. That belief completely misconstrues what makes for bargains—stocks that are priced low in relation to earnings per share, cash flow per share, book value per share and other basic measures described in Chapter 4. All else being equal, a $1 stock of a company that earns 10 cents a share is no better value than the $100 stock of a company that earns $10 a share.

The big risks in little stocks. Companies with low share prices are usually small, young or both. Such companies simply have a harder time making a go of it than larger, more established concerns.

■ *Because many of these stocks are not actively traded, the spread between bid and asked price—meaning the broker's commission—is likely to be high in relation to the stock prices.* If you pay $5.50 a share for a stock with a bid price of $5 and an asked price of $5.50, the stock must rise 10% just for you to break even—and that doesn't include additional commissions beyond the spread. A spread of 12½ or 25 cents for a $70 stock is inconsequential.

■ *Low-priced stocks are more volatile.* Think about it: The minimum move for a stock is one-eighth of a point up or down, called a "tick." That means a $2 stock moves 6% on each tick.

■ *Companies with very low share prices are often in severe financial trouble.* In other words, low-priced stocks often deserve to be cheap.

Scams in penny stocks. Penny-stock swindles are estimated to bilk U.S. investors out of $2 billion a year. NASAA figures that fraud, combined with the high risks that accompany investing in tiny firms, makes the odds of breaking even, let alone making money, about one in ten.

Among the most common practices in the netherworld of penny stocks are inflated markups by brokers who buy shares for a nickel and sell them for a dime—a commission of 100%. NASAA also found instances of manipulation of share prices by brokers and their cohorts, and of high-pressure sales spiels targeting unsophisticated customers for whom such risky investments are unsuitable.

Avoiding the scams. Don't buy anything on the basis of an unsolicited phone call from a broker affiliated with an unfamiliar firm who promises big and fast profits from a low-priced stock. As one regulator had put it: Why should someone you've never even heard of want to make you the deal of a lifetime?

Be extra vigilant before investing in a low-priced stock that's not listed on an exchange or on the computerized Nasdaq market. Prices for thousands of these non-Nasdaq over-the-counter issues can be found only on the "pink sheets"—printed lists that are updated just once daily and are generally available only to brokers. Pink-sheet penny stocks are especially ripe for abuse because investors cannot get up-to-the-moment price quotes easily and because the companies don't have to issue regular financial reports, as do Nasdaq- and exchange-listed companies.

The SEC has a "cold-calling" rule designed to protect investors from high-pressure sales tactics involving pink-sheet stocks. Before a broker unfamiliar to you can sell you penny stocks over the phone, you must sign a suitability statement, plus a purchase agreement the first three times you buy shares covered by the rule. For a copy of the rule, write to the Securities and Exchange Commission, Publications, 450 Fifth St., N.W., Mail Stop C-11, Washington, D.C. 20549. To order by phone, call 202-272-7460.

If you have ever been tempted to buy a penny stock over the phone, try this: Send for the SEC rules. Then, the next time a penny stockbroker calls, starting reading the rules aloud. You won't have to hang up; the broker will hang up on *you*.

PART 3

COMMON INVESTMENT GOALS: HOW TO ACHIEVE THEM

13

INVESTING TO PAY FOR COLLEGE

▪

AT THE BEGINNING of any discussion of college costs and how to meet them, it is obligatory to recite the figures. In this way parents can grasp the breathtaking magnitude of the task confronting them. Ready? Here goes.

The average cost of four years of tuition, room and board at a private college or university has long since topped $50,000. Optimistic assumptions about the pace of future increases would put that price tag at $67,000 in five years, $90,000 in ten years and $120,000 in 15 years. The picture is less depressing at public colleges, where the tab is running at somewhat less than half those levels. The figures assume a 6% annual increase in college costs.

The idea of saving and investing enough money to handle bills like that puts many parents into a deep funk. But you probably won't have to come up with all of it—in fact, the vast majority of parents don't. A survey by the U.S. Department of Education found that parents pay the full cost less than 10% of the time. Most students' college bills are paid from a combination of sources that includes students' own savings and earnings, plus financial aid. It would be unwise to expect financial aid to bail you out, however. The bigger your income and other assets, the smaller your chances of qualifying for college aid programs, most of which are based on need.

If you can save half the cost of college, you can probably cover the rest through home-equity or other loans and your son's or daughter's savings from working during the high school and college years. Still, even half the cost is a very big number, and the sooner you start accumulating it the better. You can draw on many of the investment products and techniques described in this book. This chapter will suggest ways to construct a college savings plan that takes advantage of a number of options that have been created with college in mind or that fit especially well into a college savings and investment program.

If your child's freshman year is close at hand, you should try to minimize the risks in your plan by sticking mostly with money-market funds and certificates of deposit timed to mature when the bills fall due. If you have three or four years to go, short-term bond mutual funds and balanced stock-and-bond funds can be used to jack up the return without increasing the risk very much. If college is more than five years away, your choices are wider. In addition to portfolios of stocks and bonds and mutual funds that you assemble yourself, you can find plenty of customized college savings plans offered by banks, brokerages and mutual funds. Keep in mind that the word "college" on the label doesn't necessarily make a plan superior for the purpose. To have the best chance to succeed, your plan should have these characteristics:

■ *It should be easy and economical to contribute to on a regular basis.* Mutual funds with high front-end loads and high minimum investments would not be suitable for a college savings plan, nor would limited partnerships or real estate (except home-equity build-up, which you can draw on for loans with tax-deductible interest). No-load mutual funds and savings bonds would be more appropriate.

■ *It should include a balanced mix of long- and short-term investments.* This is a common-sense rule for *all* investment plans because it acknowledges that the interplay of stock market prices and interest rates makes some financial markets a better place to be than others at any given time. Having a variety of time horizons in your plan helps to smooth out the ups and downs and minimize the risks.

■ *It should be aimed at a specific goal.* You don't know exactly how much college is going to cost, but the numbers recited above give you a pretty good idea. Pick a goal—$25,000? $50,000?—and a time frame—10 years? 15 years? A specific goal and time let you make reasonable estimates of how much you need to put aside each month to achieve the goal, based on assumptions about investment return.

You can use the tables in Chapter 17 for this purpose. They show how fast different levels of regular contributions will grow at various rates of return. They can also provide a useful reality check for your expectations.

For example, say your child is 10 years away from freshman year. You've managed to save $5,000 and you can set aside $100 a month. How much would you have to earn on the money to have $50,000 in 10 years? Take a peek and you'll see that the earnings would be off the chart. If fact, you'd have to earn better than 16% per year—a possibility, but not a probability, and a figure that high would require taking large risks. To reach your goal, you've got to step up your contributions. Doubling them to $200 a month would cut the necessary return to about 8%. If you were to invest $150 a month, you'd need to earn about 12% to reach your goal.

The time you have left before the college bills start to arrive and the amount of money you can set aside on a regular basis should influence the kinds of investment choices you make. If you have 10 years or more to raise the money, you can afford to take more risks than if college is only two or three years away. At some point you may conclude that you can't possibly accumulate enough money to pay all the bills for college while funding your retirement plan and tending to other investment goals at the same time. In fact, most people can't do it, and that is why scholarships, loans and grants play such an important part in the college plans of many families.

But don't throw in the towel yet. One or more of the plans described on the following pages may make the difference.

SAVINGS BONDS FOR COLLEGE

U.S. savings bonds are about as safe and convenient as investments come. As described in Chapter 5, all savings bond interest is exempt from state and local income taxes, and you can defer the federal tax on the earnings until you cash them in, creating a tax-sheltered plan that's hard to beat. Interest rates are competitive: Bonds have earned better than 7% in recent years and are guaranteed never to pay less than 6% if you hold them for at least five years.

When used for college savings, bonds get even better: Interest on Series EE bonds purchased by parents in 1990 or later and redeemed to pay college tuition and fees for their children can escape federal income tax entirely if you meet certain tests. (Bonds purchased before 1990 don't qualify.)

The rules are actually fairly simple. The bonds must be purchased in the parent's name, not the child's. You must buy them after your 24th birthday or your spouse's 24th birthday and redeem them in the year you pay qualifying tuition and fees for the child attending a college, university, technical institute or vocational school. It is not a requirement that the child be born yet when you purchase the bonds, just that you pay your child's qualifying expenses in the year the bonds are redeemed.

The tax break gets phased out starting at adjusted gross incomes above $63,000 on a joint return; it disappears at about $94,000. The take-back is in proportion to the amount your income exceeds the low end of the range. A couple making, say, $80,000 is about halfway between the low and high ends and thus could escape taxes on about half the interest. For a single parent, the tax saving is phased out starting at about $42,000 and disappears entirely at about $58,000.

Those were the income ceilings in effect in 1991. They are indexed to inflation, so for a medium- or long-term savings plan, current levels aren't very meaningful. Assuming 4% annual inflation, the beginning of the phase-out zones will rise to about $76,000 for couples in 1996, $93,000 in 2001 and $113,000 in 2006. By then, the upper level of the zone will be nearly $170,000 on a joint return, making EE bonds an attractive college savings plan even for parents with very high incomes.

You don't have to keep burdensome records to prove your eligibility for the tax forgiveness when the time comes. But you should keep those earmarked bonds separate from others you might own. Record the serial numbers, face amounts, and issue and redemption dates. When you redeem the bonds, record the total proceeds—interest *and* principal—along with the name of the institution to which you paid tuition and fees (room and board doesn't count). If your bond interest exceeds the qualifying expenses, you escape taxes on the portion of the interest accounted for by the expenses.

You can buy savings bonds with no sales fees at most financial institutions, such as banks, or through your employer, with no transaction cost, in face-value denominations of $50; $75; $100; $200; $500; $1,000; $5,000; and $10,000. (The $50 and $75 denominations are not available through payroll savings plans.) You pay half the bond's face amount and can collect the face value within 12 years at the most, depending on interest rates along the way. You continue to earn interest for 30 years. For more details, see Chapter 5.

ZERO-COUPON BONDS

Zero-coupon bonds are so named because they don't pay any interest at all until maturity, although you do owe tax on the "imputed" interest year by year.

Zeros are described in detail in Chapter 5. As a college savings tool, they can be employed to best advantage in a long-range plan, although they can be useful in the relatively short range, as well. Zeros sell at a discount from face value; the further away from maturity, the steeper the discount. A $1,000 zero yielding 9% and maturing in five years would sell for $650. A bond with the same denomination earning the same rate and maturing in 10 years would cost $425. With a maturity of 18 years, the bond costs just $205.

If parents—or grandparents, uncles or aunts—socked a total of about $13,000 worth of such bonds into a newborn's account, it would grow to $60,000 by the time the college bills started to arrive. Along the way, the market value of the zeros will be more volatile than that of conventional bonds, but by buying zeros that mature during your child's college years you can safely ignore their ups and downs in the meantime.

Tax angles. Zeros don't pay interest each year, but the Internal Revenue Service wants you to act like they do. As the interest accrues, it must be reported to the IRS and the person receiving the interest owes tax on it. The situation gets muddled by what's called the "kiddie tax," which forces children under age 14 to pay tax on this kind of income above a certain amount at their parent's tax rate.

Properly handled, though, much of the income can be tax-free or be taxed in the child's low bracket. To hold the tax bill to the minimum, buy zero-coupon bonds in the child's name so that the income will be taxable to the child. Your broker can set up a free or low-cost custodial account.

The first $550 of investment income received by a child is tax-free. (That's the tax-free level in 1991. The amount is indexed to inflation and will rise as the years go by.) For children under age 14, the next $550 is taxed at his or her own rate, probably 15%, and investment income in excess of $1,100 is taxed at the parent's rate—probably 28% or 31%.

The way the IRS says zero-coupon bond interest must be

reported works to your advantage. Again, consider a 9% zero that grows for 18 years from $205 to $1,000. You don't simply report one-eighteenth of the difference, $44, each year. Instead you report interest as it actually accrues. The first year, a $205 investment earning 9% compounded semiannually earns about $19. The second year, your principal would be $224 ($205 + $19), and $20 of interest would accrue. The third year you'd earn $23, and so forth. (You'll get a notice each year from the issuer or your broker showing how much interest to report.)

Because the interest builds up much more quickly as the bonds near maturity—and after the child is 14—most of the interest earned on the bonds dodges the kiddie tax.

What if you bought your child 60 of those bonds, so you'd have $60,000 when they matured in 18 years? Here's the tax status of the $47,700 of interest that accrues over the years, assuming the child has no other investment income, and allowing for no increase in the $550 per year tax-free allowance:

▮ *Tax-free:* $9,900 ($550 a year).

▮ *Taxed at child's rate:* $27,220 ($550 for each of the first 13 years; all of the income after that).

▮ *Taxed at parents' rate:* $10,580 (interest in excess of $1,100 for each of the first 13 years; none after that).

You can see that paying the tax as you go isn't so bad when financing college with zeros bought in a child's name. The first $550 of interest income each year is tax-free to the child, assuming he or she doesn't have other investment income. By reporting the interest each year, you get to use that break 18 times; if the interest were reported all at once, you'd enjoy it only once, and it would stop at $550.

Treasury zeros. For safety of principal while you're waiting for the bonds to mature, stick to zeros issued by the U.S. Treasury.

Issued in face values of $1,000, Treasuries are exempt from state and local tax. They usually pay a little more than savings bonds. On the other hand, Treasury zeros—called stripped Treasuries in the *Wall Street Journal*'s daily price quotations—

aren't as convenient to buy in small lots, and whether your broker will be willing to take the trouble to hunt them down for an accumulation plan will depend on your relationship with the broker. You cannot buy zeros directly from the Treasury. Besides a broker, your only other alternative is a zero-coupon mutual fund.

The biggest such fund is Benham Target Maturity Trust (800-472-3389), which offers Treasury zeros maturing every five years through 2020. The Scudder fund family (800-225-2470) manages zero-coupon Treasury funds maturing in 1995 and 2000 and will no doubt add other maturities as the years go by. Neither Benham nor Scudder charges a sales fee, both require small minimum investments ($1,000 initially, $100 subsequently) and both have accumulation plans that allow you to purchase shares automatically each month via a bank draft.

Tax-free zeros. Interest from municipal bonds is free of federal tax and usually escapes income taxes in the states where they are issued. One problem is their relative scarcity, a situation that has abated to a degree in recent years but still exists. Many municipal issues can be called, or redeemed, before maturity by the issuer if rates go down.

You buy muni zeros through a broker, at discounts to face amounts of $5,000. To minimize risk, limit your choice of zero-coupon munis to those rated AAA or AA. It's not always easy to find such bonds maturing when you want them to, especially from your home state.

Special college zero muni bonds. A growing number of states offer tax-exempt zero-coupon bonds as college savings vehicles, and they are very popular among their states' residents. The bonds are a safe way to set aside money for college and earn an attractive tax-exempt yield. If you're in the 28% tax bracket, 7% tax-free is as good as 9.72% taxable. And because such bonds can also be exempt from state taxes, your taxable equivalent yield on a long-term bond could easily break into double digits.

Illinois, the first state to sell college savings bonds, got its inspiration from Michigan's tuition prepayment plan, which allows parents to pay tuition at state schools in advance in exchange for a guarantee that the investment will keep up with rising college costs. The Michigan plan became less attractive when the IRS ruled that the earnings on prepayments are not exempt from federal tax (see the discussion later in this chapter). The Illinois legislature responded with a zero-coupon, general obligation bond issue packaged to appeal to small investors saving for college, and a couple of dozen states have followed suit. Although some issuing states have sold the bonds only once, others do so annually or semiannually.

These states issue zero-coupon municipal bonds designed especially for college-savings programs: Arkansas, California, Connecticut, Delaware, Hawaii, Illinois, Indiana, Iowa, Kansas, Maryland, Missouri, New Hampshire, North Carolina, North Dakota, Oregon, Rhode Island, South Dakota, Tennessee, Texas, Vermont, Virginia, Washington and Wisconsin.

As this book went to press, four additional states, Colorado, Louisiana, Ohio and West Virginia, had authorized such bonds but had not yet issued any.

Details of the plans vary, but the states offer many features that make college bonds attractive.

■ *A range of maturities.* You can buy college bonds that mature in one year, or in as many as 30 years. Face values at maturity are usually $1,000 or $5,000 but can be less.

■ *Low risk.* Most of the college bonds are general obligation bonds, which carry high safety ratings because they're backed by the taxing power of the state. And they're generally noncallable, so the state can't pay off the bond early if interest rates fall. Noncallable, general obligation bonds are hard to find. If you buy revenue bonds, which finance a specific municipal project such as a hospital or road, it's important to check Moody's or Standard & Poor's bond rating and to ask your broker for the yield or call date as well as the yield to maturity.

■ *Enhanced value.* You can use the proceeds from these bonds for any purpose, but several states add incentives if you use the money to pay for an in-state college education. Illinois, for example, adds 0.4% to the annual yield. Indiana and Rhode Island exclude the full value of both principal and interest on the bonds from the computations that determine whether you're eligible for state financial aid.

How to buy them. Like other municipal bonds, these are sold through brokers, not directly to investors by the states. It's probably easiest to buy a college savings bond when it's first issued. Most states advertise new issues in the local media. Connecticut, Iowa and New Hampshire have even sent fliers home with public school students to promote new issues.

The bonds often sell out quickly. In Illinois, brokers and banks take orders for a week, then fill as many as they can. On long maturities, sometimes five of every six orders can't be filled because demand is so high. You can buy the bonds on the secondary market, although your broker may have to hunt for a bond with the maturity you want and may not be interested in finding bonds with less than a $5,000 face value.

You can also buy out-of-state bonds, but the bonds will be double-tax-exempt only if you live in the District of Columbia or in one of the 12 states that don't tax income from out-of-state municipal bonds. In other states you may have to pay taxes on the "phantom" interest that accumulates annually, even though you don't collect the interest until the bond matures.

STATE COLLEGE SAVINGS PLANS

What could be more appealing than the chance to pay tuition at today's rates in exchange for the guarantee that your child's actual tuition, no matter how far off or how large, will be covered by the government of your state? Such guaranteed tuition plans are offered in Florida, Michigan, Ohio and Wyoming. The money generally covers tuition at any public college or university in the state. If your child goes out of state or decides to skip college, you get a refund according to a state-approved formula.

The main drawback to prepayment plans is that they limit your child's choices. If he or she decides to go to school in another state, the return on your investment will fall far below what you would have gotten in bonds or a stock fund, for example.

Say you join the Michigan plan, where in a recent year it cost $6,756 to prepay four years at any state university in Michigan for your newborn child. But if your child chooses Harvard over the University of Michigan at Ann Arbor, your refund is not Ann Arbor's tuition but the average tuition of all public, postsecondary schools in Michigan. If your child doesn't go to college at all, your refund is the lowest tuition at any Michigan postsecondary school.

Most states are shying away from prepayment plans partly because of the risks the states are taking: They don't know any more than you do what a college education will cost in 10 or 15 years. Most private colleges have also given up on the idea.

There are also tax complications. The IRS has ruled that Michigan residents need not pay taxes on imputed interest while the tuition money is accumulating. But during the child's four years of college, parents must pay taxes at the child's rate on the difference between the original investment and its end value.

LIFE INSURANCE AS COLLEGE SAVINGS

Should you use a form of permanent life insurance as a college savings vehicle? One possible advantage is that earnings in such policies build up tax-deferred. But it's hard to assess how much college money a policy will provide in comparison with other saving alternatives. Commissions hold down your returns the first several years. Perhaps the biggest advantages of life insurance are that it forces you to save regularly and that the policy proceeds will cover your child's college costs if you die.

∎ Universal life policies are, in effect, money-market funds tied to a term insurance benefit within a tax shelter. You can withdraw some earnings to help pay for college and also borrow on the cash value of the policy, typically at a lower rate than a bank loan. But to avoid paying taxes on all the interest, you must keep the policy in force.

■ Variable life, by contrast, gives you term insurance coverage and deposits part of your premium in your choice from a list of mutual funds, including stock-oriented funds, and other investments. As with universal life, earnings grow untaxed until you withdraw the money. Because you're not limited to money market rates, variable life policies offer a shot at higher returns —in exchange for your willingness to take on bigger risks.

Universal or variable life insurance is worth considering for college savings *if you need the insurance* and if your time horizon is long enough to allow you to amortize the commission costs of the policy and, in the case of variable insurance, average out the investment markets' ups and downs. This means that an insurance-based college savings or investment plan makes most sense if your future freshman hasn't yet celebrated his or her 10th birthday.

TWO PLANS FOR PUTTING IT ALL TOGETHER

Each of the following suggested college savings plans is relatively simple and straightforward, and each sets an ambitious goal: accumulating the future cost of four years of private college for an infant. Paying the estimated $150,000 four-year price will require a nest egg of $130,000 by the freshman year.

Both plans start with a base of $1,000. The first plan, a mix of stock and bond-oriented mutual funds, assumes steady contributions of $200 a month. That's less than the contribution eventually demanded by the second plan, which relies entirely on savings bonds in the early years. The absolute safety and tax advantages of savings bonds provide their appeal, but the trade-off is a lower rate of return. For that plan, then, monthly contributions start at $150 a month and grow in steps to $450 a month in the 13th year, $575 a month by the time the child is 18 years old.

Most likely your child isn't an infant, but that doesn't mean you can't use either of these plans. In both, the critical juncture is age 13, when college is five years away. In Plan One, that's the time to throttle back on risk and start preserving gains via bonds and money-market funds. In Plan Two, age 13 is critical because savings bonds need to be held for at least five years in order to qualify for the floating maximum and guaranteed minimum interest rates.

Thus, in both a risk-oriented portfolio and a safety-oriented portfolio—whether they are the ones suggested here or others of your own choosing—five years from the freshman year is the critical juncture for assessing where you are and how your plan is doing. If it's lagging behind, you have two choices: You can step up your contribution or you can take bigger risks in hopes of a bigger payoff. The closer you get to the freshman year, the less sense it makes to choose the second option.

Plan One: Mutual Funds

With 18 years to go, you can afford to take some risks. Look for funds with good long-term records (10-year average annual total return of 15% or better), no up-front sales fees, plus low minimum and subsequent investment requirements. Some suggestions to get you started: CGM Mutual fund (800-345-4048); Lindner fund (314-727-5305); T. Rowe Price International Stock fund (800-638-5660); Twentieth Century Select Investors fund (800-345-2021).

Rather than anticipate that your funds will continue to return 15%, count on something more modest, say, 12%. You improve your odds by opening $1,000 accounts with two funds rather than putting all your chips in one. Each month thereafter, buy $100 in additional shares in each fund. At a 12% compounded rate of return, your holdings will total $80,000 when your newborn is in the 8th grade at age 13. (Your after-tax return will depend on your bracket and on the pattern of the earnings over the years. For simplicity, these examples ignore taxes. You won't be able to do that.)

With five years to go before college, start hedging your risks. At some point when the stock market is trending up rather than down, sell your shares in the equity funds and purchase shares in two well-run, no-load bond funds. From these, expect an annual total return of 8%. Keep sending $100 a month to each fund for more shares. Suggested funds (you can find more using the resources listed in Chapter 6): Dreyfus A Bonds Plus (800-782-6620); IAI Bond (800-927-3863); T. Rowe Price New Income (800-638-5660); Vanguard Fixed Income-Investment Grade (800-662-7447).

When your child turns 18, your $80,000 stake from the stock funds should be worth $130,000 in bond fund shares. Now sell the bond fund shares and consolidate the proceeds in a money-market fund. The $130,000, earning 6% to 7% money-market rates, should get you to graduation day.

If a public college or university is on the horizon, you can more than pay the projected $59,000 cost in 18 years by saving $100 a month by this method. (If you have less time than that, you'll have to step up the pace accordingly.) At $100 a month, the equity fund shares, growing at a 12% annual rate, will be worth $44,000 in 13 years. Five years later, the bond fund shares, compounding at 8%, will reach $72,000, giving you more than you'll need over the next four years to pay those bills each September and January. Then the money-market fund takes over.

As mentioned, earnings are taxed all along. But the tax bill starts low, and because you're investing a fixed sum over a span of years in which your earning power can reasonably be expected to grow, the increases in your income can go toward satisfying the tax bill. If the taxes and the risks in this plan worry you, the next plan may be more to your liking.

Plan Two: Savings Bonds

Start by investing $1,000 in EE bonds at a bank. Then, through payroll deduction where you work or through your bank, invest another $150 in bonds each month. Increase the amount you save by $25 a month each year of the plan. Assuming an average interest rate of 7.75%, EE bonds will build a $75,000 nest egg in 13 years. If rates are lower, you'll have to adjust your contribution over the years or settle for a smaller nest egg. Because there's an interest-rate penalty if EE bonds are redeemed within five years of purchase, stop buying bonds when your child is 13 but don't redeem any for another five years.

Instead, pick a money-market fund or a short-term bond fund and direct your monthly savings that way—still adding $25 a month annually to the amount you set aside. Assuming an 8% yield, your five years of deposits will grow to $38,000 by the time today's newborn is 18. By then, the savings bonds will be worth $110,000. Your college fund will hold almost $150,000. As with Plan One, you'll need to save only about half as much if your child is headed for a public school.

The key to minimizing taxes in a plan such as this is knowing the rules, as explained earlier in this chapter.

SHOULD YOU SAVE IN THE CHILD'S NAME?

Putting your college savings in a child's name can save on taxes as the years go by, but there are some potential drawbacks.

Income generated by a so-called custodial account set up under the Uniform Transfers to Minors Act (or the Uniform Gifts to Minors Act in some states), is tax-free up to $550 a year, an amount that is indexed to inflation and thus will increase over the years. The next $550 is taxed at the child's rate, probably 15%. Anything above that is taxed at your rate until the child reaches age 14. You and your spouse can put up to $10,000 each into such an account without triggering any gift or estate taxes. These trusts are easy to set up. You can get a standard form from your bank or broker and you'll pay no legal fees.

At 8% interest, an account containing $13,500 would generate $1,080 in the first year, only $530 of which would be taxable to the child, assuming he or she had no other income. If the account were in your name, you'd owe tax on the entire amount. If you're in the 28% bracket and the child is in the 15% bracket, that's the difference between a tax bill of $79.50 and one of $302.40. Because of compounding within the account, the tax difference wouldn't stay the same over the years, but you can see that the savings can be substantial. But before you rush off to set up such an account, note the following.

■ *Assets in the child's name could hurt your chances for financial aid.* If you apply, the standard methodology used by colleges counts 35% of the child's assets as available to pay for college, but only 5% or so of parents' assets. Thus, $10,000 in the child's name will count as $3,500; the same amount in the parents' name would count as only about $500 available for college.

■ *You have no access to the money.* If you need the money in a custodial account before your child turns 18 (or 21, depending on state law), you may be able to borrow from the account, but only if the money is used for the child's benefit.

■ *You have no control over how the money is used.* Once your child reaches the age of majority, he or she can use the money for anything. It doesn't have to be used for college.

Trusts. If you have at least $50,000 to put in a child's name, it could be worth the administrative costs to set up a minor's trust, called a 2503(c), or a similar kind of trust called a Crummey Trust.

You'll have to pay legal fees of several hundred dollars and file an annual tax return, but the first $5,200 or so of income earned by a properly established trust of this type is taxed at only 15%, even if the child is under 14. In a minor's trust, your child must have access to the assets at 21, when the trust terminates. A Crummey Trust can last beyond 21 but allows your child to withdraw contributions in the year that they're made. Consult a lawyer if you're interested in setting up something like that.

CHAPTER

14

INVESTING FOR RETIREMENT

T HE DREAM of a secure and comfortable retirement is the motivating force behind many investment plans—maybe even most of them. The politicians in Congress know this very well, and over the years have showered retirement-minded savers with valuable tax shelters in which to store their dollars: individual retirement accounts, Keogh plans, 401(k) plans and more. Wall Street has responded with a vast collection of investment packages tailor-made to fit into those shelters. As a result, the key to a successful investment plan for your retirement lies not only in choosing the right investments, but also in choosing the right place to keep them. This chapter will examine those places and help you choose the ones best suited to your circumstances.

Retirement planning is a complex, fluid thing subject to adjustment as your circumstances change. But the basics don't change. A financially secure retirement is the result of understanding and managing the interplay of its four essential elements: how much money you'll need when you get there; where the money will come from; how much time you have; and how much risk you're prepared to take to achieve your goal. Together, those four elements will determine what you do and how you do it.

HOW MUCH INCOME WILL YOU NEED?

A useful rule of thumb holds that you'll need 70% to 80% of your preretirement income to maintain a similar life style in retirement. Assume the higher percentage for planning purposes. Thus, if you're making $50,000 a year on the day you retire, figure you'll need $40,000 afterward. If retirement is some years down the road, it's reasonable to expect that your income will grow and inflation will devour a good deal of its purchasing power in the meantime.

It's possible to anticipate both contingencies by consulting the table on the next page. Say retirement is 20 years away. To estimate your preretirement income at that time, assume you'll get raises of 5% a year between now and then. (Figure 7% if you can count on promotions in the years ahead.) The multiplier in the table at the point where 5% and 20 years intersect is 2.65. That means today's $50,000 salary will be $132,500 ($50,000 × 2.65) in 20 years. If you're shooting for 80%, your target retirement income goal is about $106,000 a year.

WHERE WILL THE MONEY COME FROM?

Where will you get that kind of money—especially if an early retirement is part of your dream? Luckily, you probably won't have to provide all of it yourself. In fact, before you can devise an investment plan to achieve the goal of a comfortable retirement, you need to calculate the portion of retirement income your own investments must provide. And to do that, you need a pretty good estimate of what you can reasonably expect from pension plans and social security.

A trip to your company's personnel or benefits office should provide you with the answers you need about future pension payments. A phone call to the Social Security Administration

(800-234-5772) will get you a form called the *Request for Earnings and Benefit Estimate Statement*. After you've filled it out and returned it, you should get an estimate of your future benefits within a month or so. Use your estimates in the worksheet on page 275.

One of the obstacles to retiring before age 62 is that you can't count on all your long-term savings and investments to kick in with income right from the start. The worksheet reflects the fact that employer pension benefits are rarely available before age 55, that social security benefits can't start before age 62 and that IRA funds are generally tied up until age 59½.

WHAT MONEY WILL BE WORTH IN THE FUTURE

This table shows how much your current savings and investments will be worth in the future, assuming various annual rates of return. It also can be used to calculate how inflation will affect your living expenses. Say you plan to retire in 20 years and expect your investments to grow 10% a year between now and then. Find 20 years on the left-hand scale and 10% on the horizontal scale across the top. The place where those two columns intersect shows a multiplier of 6.73. That tells you that $1,000 in your retirement account today will grow to $6,730 in 20 years, assuming a 10% annual return (6.73 x $1,000 = $6,730).

But in 20 years you'll need more than $1,000 to have the purchasing power of $1,000 today. How much more? First make an assumption about inflation — 4% is a reasonable estimate for the next 20 years. Where the 4% column intersects with 20 years, the multiplier is 2.19. That means that you'll need $2,190 in 20 years to match the purchasing power of $1,000 today. (For a wider range of interest rates, see the tables in Chapter 17.)

Year	4%	5%	6%	7%	8%	9%	10%	11%	12%
10	1.48	1.63	1.79	1.97	2.16	2.37	2.59	2.84	3.11
15	1.80	2.08	2.40	2.76	3.17	3.64	4.18	4.78	5.47
20	2.19	2.65	3.21	3.87	4.66	5.60	6.73	8.06	9.65
25	2.67	3.39	4.29	5.43	6.85	8.62	10.82	13.59	17.00

How to use the worksheet. The first step in using the worksheet is to state your goal: 80% of preretirement income. In the "Anticipated Resources" section, multiplying each of your various assets by .08 assumes you will be able to earn 8% a year on those assets and lets you see whether you can live on the investment income without depleting your capital. (The 8% assumption about earnings reflects the fact that once you are retired, you'll want to keep your money in low-risk investments that produce a high level of income.) Odds are that you'll have to dip into capital on some sort of regular basis. You can use the "How Much Money You'll Need" table on page 349 in Chapter 17 to test various pay-down schedules.

Now begin to plug in your numbers.

■ *Savings and investments.* Begin with what you have in your retirement fund today and use a future value multiplier from the table on page 273 to see what it will be worth in the future. If you have $50,000 now, plan to retire in 15 years and expect your savings and investments to yield 6% a year after taxes, multiply $50,000 by 2.40—the figure where the 15 years and 6% columns intersect. That's $120,000. If that nest egg generates 8% a year, you can count on it for $9,600 toward your retirement needs.

■ *Equity in your home.* This line assumes that you will use your home equity as a source of income—by selling your home and renting or "buying down" to a smaller place and investing the freed-up equity to generate income. (We show home equity becoming available at 55 because that's the earliest you can take up to $125,000 of profit tax-free.) Begin with the current value of your house and apply a future value multiplier from the table on page 273 to estimate its value when you'll sell it. If you don't have a feel for where values are headed where you live, use 5%. Subtract any mortgage you'll still have outstanding at that time and deduct 28% of any profit above $125,000. The result is the maximum amount that can go on line 2. Multiply it by 8% to see how much annual income you can expect if you choose to use this source of income in retirement.

▮ *Individual retirement accounts.* Consider IRA money tied up until you reach 59½. For this line, apply a future value multiplier from the table to the current value of your IRAs.

▮ *Keogh accounts.* You can tap a Keogh without penalty starting at age 59½, with the same exceptions as you get in an IRA. Complete this line the same as line 3.

▮ *401(k) and profit-sharing plans.* Money in 401(k) and other profit-sharing plans can be withdrawn without tax penalty as early as age 55 if you leave the job. If you roll over a distribution into an IRA—to avoid paying all the tax at once—the money would be controlled by the IRA rules described later in this chapter.

▮ *Employer pension benefits.* Defined benefit plans rarely provide benefits before age 55. Your personnel office should be able to estimate what you can expect when you plan to retire. You can probably count on your benefits increasing for each year past age 55 that you delay retirement, provided you stay with the same employer. If you leave that company, your pension will almost certainly be frozen at the level you had

WHERE WILL THE MONEY COME FROM?

A: YOUR GOAL: Current income x Multiplier from Table, page 273 x 0.80 = $_____

B: ANTICIPATED RESOURCES AT CRUCIAL AGES

Resource	Current Value x Multiplier from Table, page 273	50-54	Age 55-59	60-62	62+
1. INVESTMENTS	$_____ x 0.08 = $_____	$_____	$_____	$_____	
2. EQUITY IN HOME	$_____ x 0.08 =	xxxxxx	_____	_____	_____
3. IRAS	$_____ x 0.08 =	xxxxxx	xxxxxx	_____	_____
4. KEOGHS	$_____ x 0.08 =	xxxxxx	xxxxxx	_____	_____
5. OTHER RESOURCES	$_____ x 0.08 =	xxxxxx	_____	_____	_____
6. PENSIONS		xxxxxx	_____	_____	_____
7. SOCIAL SECURITY		xxxxxx	xxxxxx	xxxxxx	_____
B. TOTALS		$_____	$_____	$_____	$_____
SHORTFALL (A minus B)		$_____	$_____	$_____	$_____

earned before leaving. If you have a defined-contribution pension plan, the value of your account would probably keep growing after you left because you or the company would keep it invested.

■ *Social security benefits.* Social security retirement benefits can't begin until age 62, and at that age checks are reduced to 80% of what you'd get if you waited until 65 to start collecting. The age for receiving full benefits and the reduction for early retirement will increase gradually beginning in the year 2000. The Social Security Administration (800-234-5772) can give you an estimate of what to expect.

Facing up to a shortfall. The worksheet almost certainly delivers bad news: A shortfall that paints retirement as a swan dive into poverty. But take heart. In a sense, the worksheet is stacked against you because it is based only on the growth of what you've accumulated so far and does not take into account any future savings.

HOW MUCH YOU'LL NEED TO GET $100 A MONTH

This table shows the amount of money you'll need to yield $100 a month for the period indicated in the left-hand column, assuming various rates of return on the money. Other amounts can be figured as multiples of $100. For instance, say you need to draw $750 a month for 10 years from an amount of capital yielding 8%. First find where the 10-year and 8% columns intersect. That amount—$8,242—will yield $100 a month. Multiplying it by 7.5 shows that you'd need $61,815 earning 8% in order to collect $750 a month for 10 years. At the end of the period, the fund will be depleted. (For a wider range of interest rates, see the tables in Chapter 17.)

Years	8%	9%	10%	11%	12%
10	$ 8,242	$ 7,894	$ 7,567	$ 7,260	$ 6,970
15	10,464	9,860	9,306	8,798	8,332
20	11,955	11,114	10,362	9,688	9,082
25	12,956	11,916	11,005	10,203	9,495

Say you're hoping to retire in 20 years and face an annual shortfall of $24,000, or $2,000 a month. Use the table on page 276 to calculate the size of the nest egg you'll need to generate that much income for a given length of time. If you'll need the extra $2,000 a month for 30 years, for example, your additional nest egg must total $272,560, if you assume it will be earning 8% a year after you retire. That means you'll have to invest enough over the next 20 years to have an additional $272,560 when you retire.

(A mathematical footnote: $272,560 may not seem to be enough to generate an income of $2,000 a month if it earns 8%, because 8% of $272,560 is only $21,804, which amounts to $1,817 per month. The apparent discrepancy is explained by two factors: First, the unexpended portion of the nest egg continues to earn interest, so drawing out $2,000 per month in effect depletes the fund by something less than $2,000. Second, the schedule assumes that you will exhaust the fund in 30 years, so it's okay to nick the principal a little each month.)

TIME AND RISK FACTORS

The table on page 278 shows how much extra you need to start saving each month to accumulate your retirement fund. Assuming a 10% annual yield, you can see that $100 a month invested over 20 years will build a nest egg of $76,570. (Ten dollars a month invested for 20 years at 10% = $7,657 × 10 = $76,570.) Dividing the amount you need—$272,560—by that figure gives you 3.6. Multiply that by 100 and you can see that you need to sock away $360 a month over the next 20 years to meet your goal, assuming a conservative 10% return per year.

Fortunately, that's not necessarily an *extra* $360 a month. Part of it may be covered by money you are already putting away in IRAs and other plans, plus future contributions by your employer to a job-related account. Also, the amount you need to come up with yourself probably drops as the years go

HOW $10 A MONTH WILL GROW

This table shows how much you'll have at the end of the period indicated if you save or invest $10 a month, assuming various annual rates of return. Results for other amounts can be calculated as multiples of $10. (For a more comprehensive version of this table, see Chapter 17.)

Year	8%	9%	10%	11	12%
10	$ 1,842	$ 1,950	$ 2,066	$ 2,190	$ 2,323
15	3,483	3,812	4,179	4,589	5,046
20	5,929	6,729	7,657	8,736	9,991
25	9,574	11,295	13,379	15,906	18,976

by and other retirement income kicks in. If you needed the extra $2,000 a month for five years instead of 30—to tide you over for the years between an early retirement at 50 and age 55, perhaps—the monthly savings required over 20 years would drop from $360 to $129.

What kinds of investments offer the best hope of achieving your retirement goals? As described in Chapter 1, a core portfolio of stocks, bonds and mutual funds is ideal for a long-term goal such as retirement. Other chapters in this book describe how the investments differ and how to go about selecting the best according to the time you have and your risk tolerance. In general, the more time you have, the more risk you can take.

20 years to go. With 20 years or so to go, for instance, an aggressive-growth mutual fund such as the ones listed in Chapter 6 would be appropriate for a portion of a portfolio dominated by growth stocks (or funds that specialized in them); zero-coupon bonds (especially zeros sheltered in IRAs and other retirement plans described below); well-selected real estate (provided it meets the criteria spelled out in Chapter 9) and other long-term investments.

10 years to go. With 10 years left, there's still plenty of time to recover from market reversals, but it's also time to think more conservatively. Market peaks present opportunities to move money out of risky aggressive stocks and into dividend-paying growth stocks with reinvestment plans (See Chapter 4). You can give your mutual fund portfolio a less risky profile by moving into growth-and-income, equity-income and balanced funds. At this point in your life, consider keeping about 25% of your portfolio in cash, meaning money-market funds, certificates of deposit with staggered maturities, and Treasury bills.

5 years to go. When you get to within five years of retirement, it's important to be conservative, but it's also important to remain diversified. Hang onto some growth stocks or growth-stock funds, especially those that pay good dividends. If interest rates look high, load up on bonds; if rates decline, you'll have the choice of selling them at a profit (See Chapter 5) or keeping them for the high income they provide. If you own rental real estate that has appreciated in value, look for opportunities to take the gain so you can move the money into a more liquid investment that will produce more income in retirement.

The investor's Catch-22. This discussion of investing for retirement underscores what might be called the investors's Catch 22: The more time you have to achieve your goal, the more risk you can take in pursuit of it—but, as a glance at the table of investment returns will show, the more years you have to go, the less risk you need to take to make your money grow. As you get closer to retirement, you may need to increase your risk in hopes of achieving the higher return you need to accumulate the necessary funds. But that's exactly the time when you should be reducing risk to conserve the capital you have.

What's an investor to do? The choices aren't easy, but they are clear: You could devote a small portion of your portfolio to a high-risk venture or two you would normally shun (a very volatile, aggressive stock mutual fund, for instance, as described in Chapter 6; or an option-writing strategy, as described in Chapter 12), while you kept the rest of your assets in a super-safe place (Treasury bills, for instance). That might produce the big score you need to close the gap. You could —and should—consider working for a few more years, to collect the salary, increase your pension benefit and give your less-risky investments more time to grow. You could plan to work part-time in retirement. Probably you'll decide on some combination of strategies, cursing yourself for not starting a serious investment plan years earlier than you did.

Whatever you decide, when it comes to choosing where to put your money, investing for retirement is no different from investing for any goal, no matter how much time you have to reach it: You should stick with familiar investments appropriate for your time horizon and risk tolerance. The remainder of this chapter will explore the kinds of repositories for those investments that have been created especially with retirement in mind.

INDIVIDUAL RETIREMENT ACCOUNTS

You can put up to $2,000 of your earnings into an individual retirement account every year and owe no taxes on the earnings until you take the money out. What's more, if neither you nor your spouse is covered by a pension plan at work or if you meet certain income tests explained below, you can deduct all or part of the IRA contribution from your taxable income. If one or the other of you is covered, you must meet the same income test to qualify for the deduction. If your spouse doesn't have a job, you can open a second IRA (called a spousal IRA) and put a total of up to $2,250 of annual earnings in the two accounts.

The deduction is nothing to sneeze at, but even without it, the real power of the IRA lies in the tax-deferred status of its earnings, which turbocharges the compounding process enough to make an individual retirement account something

ROLLING OVER PROFIT-SHARING MONEY

Q: *I'm getting a lump-sum distribution from a profit-sharing plan that I'd like to roll over into an IRA. I already have one IRA. Can I set up a separate one for the roll-over money?*

A: Yes, you can start a new IRA with your rollover. In fact, you can split the rollover and start several new IRAs. It is advisable to keep your rollover IRA separate from other IRA funds if there is any chance that you will get another job that offers a retirement plan. You may be allowed to roll the money into the new employer's plan, a right you lose if you mix it with any other IRA money.

you should have even if you can't deduct the contributions. If you make a series of $2,000 IRA contributions earning 10% per year compounded annually over a 20-year period, your $40,000 in contributions will grow to nearly $115,000. If you are in the 28% tax bracket and the annual earnings were taxed as they would be outside of the IRA, your account would grow to only about $92,000. If you could deduct your IRA contributions, you'd have $115,000 *plus* tax savings along the way of more than $11,000, giving the deductible IRA a total advantage of some $34,000 over an investment earning exactly the same return outside the tax shelter of the IRA.

Investment options. IRAs are sponsored by banks, s&l's, credit unions, mutual funds, insurance companies and brokerage firms. They offer almost every investment you can think of, except gems, precious metals or collectibles, which the law prohibits from being used in IRAs. (Exceptions are the American Eagle gold and silver bullion coins, but see Chapter 11 for our opinion of gold and silver as investments. Besides, since precious metals don't pay interest that can compound, the tax shelter of an IRA is largely wasted on them.)

Through what's called a self-directed IRA, you can assemble your own portfolio of investments rather than limiting yourself to certificates of deposit and plans offered by mutual funds. Self-directed IRAs, which you set up through a broker, let you decide what and when to buy and sell. You can move in and out of individual stocks and bonds and other investments at will. Self-directed IRAs are suitable only for active investors who have the time and inclination to stay on top of the investment markets.

Contribution schedules and deadlines. Nothing in the rules says you have to make your IRA contribution all at once. If you want, you can dollar-cost average into your IRA to the tune of $166 per month. IRAs can be opened any time before the April 15 deadline for filing your federal tax return, but it is normally to your advantage to make contributions as early in the year as possible to take maximum advantage of the tax-free build-up.

There's a 6% penalty for putting too much into your IRA in a given year, and you continue to pay the penalty each year until you withdraw the excess money or reduce your contribution in a subsequent year to account for the overage.

Income test. The rules allow a full tax deduction of up to the annual $2,000 contribution limit for single people with incomes of up to $25,000. The deduction is reduced by $10 for every $50 of adjusted gross income above that amount until the deduction is gone at $35,000 of income. For married couples filing a joint return, each can take a full $2,000 deduction for IRA contributions if their total adjusted gross income is $40,000 or less, with the $10-for-$50 takeback provision wiping out the deduction by the time they reach $50,000. (Actually, the minimum deduction stays at $200 when income is between $9,000 and $10,000 over the threshold, rather than dwindling gradually down to zero.)

If neither you nor your spouse is covered by a pension plan at work, the income limits don't apply. Each of you can earn as much as you like and deduct your entire $2,000 IRA contribution. The definition of pension plans includes programs you might not immediately identify as such, like profit-sharing plans, 401(k)s, 403(b)s (See page 293) and stock bonus plans. If either you or your spouse is covered by a pension plan, you're both considered to be covered and must contend with the income test to determine eligibility to deduct IRA contributions.

Withdrawal rules. Unless you become disabled, any money you withdraw from an IRA before you reach age 59½ is subject to a 10% penalty tax, plus regular income tax. (Actually, you can begin tapping an IRA at any age without penalty if you withdraw the money in approximately equal annual amounts designed to exhaust the account during the course of your life expectancy. But that generally doesn't yield much income at younger ages.) You are required to begin withdrawing the money no later than April 1 in the year following the year you reach age 70½. Thus, if you reach age 70½ in 1995, you must begin withdrawing your IRA money by April 1, 1996. When you do withdraw the money, all of it will be taxed as ordinary income if you took the deduction when you put it in; only the earnings will be taxed when you make qualified withdrawals from an IRA built from nondeductible contributions.

How the IRS knows what's going on. By law, IRA investments must be made through a custodian or trustee. This gives the government a way to monitor compliance with the rules by designating a company to handle the paperwork and report the account's status to you and the IRS each year. Financial institutions and others who sponsor IRAs have standard custodial or trustee arrangements. You can sign as many of these as you like with as many different companies as you like.

Changing investments and sponsors. What if it turns out that the IRA investment you thought would soar like an eagle flounders about like a turkey? Move it. You don't have to keep your money in the same IRA from the time you open the account until you reach age 59½. You can move the money under a couple of different provisions of the laws governing IRAs.

■ *Direct transfer.* You can transfer your account directly from one IRA sponsor to another—from a bank IRA, for example, to one sponsored by a mutual fund, or from one mutual fund to another. As long as you never actually take possession of the money, you can do this as many times as you like. In fact, mutual funds to which you are moving the money will be happy to handle the paperwork for you.

■ *Rollover.* A rollover occurs if you actually take possession of the money during a transfer, as you might if you were to close an account with a mutual fund, for example, collect the money and then put it in a bank-sponsored IRA. This you can do only once a year, and after you withdraw funds from an IRA, you have 60 days to roll it over into another account. Money that isn't contributed to a new IRA within 60 days counts as a premature distribution, meaning that it is fully taxable as ordinary income *and* it activates the 10% penalty.

Special rules when you retire. Not only will the government penalize you if you dip into your retirement fund early, but there's also a stiff penalty if you don't withdraw the money fast enough later on. Between the time you reach age 59½ and the year you turn 70½ you can withdraw as much or as little as you want from your IRA. Shortly after you reach 70½, you'll have to hew to a minimum withdrawal schedule that is designed to make sure you make a serious effort to deplete the account in your lifetime or that of you and your spouse. The IRS is determined to get its tax on the money before you die: If you don't withdraw as much as you should each year, you'll owe a 50% penalty tax on the shortfall.

Note: As this book was going to press, Congress was considering changing the age at which mandatory IRA withdrawals must begin from age 70½ to 70.

CLOSING OUT AN IRA

Q: *I am approaching age 70 and would like to convert my mandatory IRA withdrawals directly into securities or another non-IRA account—in other words, I don't want to convert them to cash to satisfy the withdrawal requirements, but I want to reinvest them. Is this allowable and can a brokerage firm do this for me?*

A: Yes on both accounts. You do not have to take physical possession of your IRA withdrawals in order to satisfy the requirement that you withdraw a minimum amount starting at age 70½, and your broker can direct the funds into securities or another non-IRA account. The money from your IRA is taxed as ordinary income regardless of whether the withdrawals are spent, converted into securities or deposited into other accounts.

For a free guide to the tax rule governing IRAs, call the IRS at 800-TAX-FORM and ask for publication number 590, *Individual Retirement Arrangements.*

DEFERRED ANNUITIES

Deferred annuities are usually sold by insurance companies. You pay them in a lump sum or on a regular schedule. They invest the money for you, often in a mutual fund of your choice. The money grows untaxed until you withdraw it, usually in a series of payments scheduled to provide you with an income stream over a specified length of time, often your lifetime.

Deferred annuities are often compared favorably with IRAs, and for good reasons.

■ Like an IRA, a deferred annuity offers the kind of tax shelter that should be music to the ears of long-term investors: Earnings aren't taxed until you take the money out.

■ Like an IRA, a deferred annuity carries tax penalties if you want to withdraw the money before reaching age 59½.

■ *Un*like an IRA, annuities impose no annual limit on contributions. This last point makes deferred annuities a good alternative if you don't qualify to deduct your IRA contributions (See page 282). If you do qualify to deduct IRA contributions, your money should go there first. A deferred annuity can be used to supplement your IRA if you have more than $2,000 to save each year toward your retirement.

Think of a deferred annuity as a personal pension plan with a measure of lifetime income protection. You make one big payment or a series of regular payments to an insurance company. After deducting its fee, the company puts your money in an investment vehicle of your choice, which grows as the years go by. When the annuity matures, instead of paying you a lump sum, the company pays you a steady income—for life or some other period you select.

A variable annuity gives you a choice of investment options —mainly different kinds of mutual funds sponsored by the insurance company.

A fixed annuity directs your money to the insurance company's general accounts, where it earns interest at whatever rate the company pays.

Both types of annuities work about the same when it comes time to take the money out. The insurance company pays you a monthly income, usually for the rest of your life, based on three factors: the amount of money in your account; your life expectancy; and the interest the company figures it can earn on the unpaid portion of your account while you're alive. If the company miscalculates and the investment account expires before you do, the company is on the hook to continue the payments until you die. (Actually, you can choose from a variety of payout plans, including some that pay a guaranteed income for your life and that of your spouse as well.)

There is a catch or two. The penalties if you want out of a tax-deferred annuity early are more severe than those that are connected with an IRA. In addition to the 10% tax penalty slapped on every penny withdrawn before age 59½, you may face early-withdrawal charges imposed by the insurance company. And if you change your mind about wanting an income stream and withdraw the cash in a lump sum, you will be taxed more heavily: Part of monthly annuity payments are considered a tax-free return of capital. A lump-sum payout is fully taxed.

A tax-deferred annuity is a tool for assuring a stream of retirement income, not a means for accumulating a lump sum you can draw on sometime down the road.

Getting the money out. When it comes time to turn your deferred annuity into an income stream, you don't have to stick with the same insurance company that sold you the annuity in the first place. You can look for an insurer offering a higher monthly income and roll the deferred annuity into it, tax-free. Once you do annuitize—that is, once you agree to a payout plan—the decision is irrevocable; you can't change your mind later on.

Some plans permit you to withdraw part of your account —often up to 10% a year—before or instead of annuitizing. You may prefer this option because it doesn't lock you into a payment schedule. Also, systematic withdrawals that don't exhaust the account allow you to leave something to your heirs. The drawback is that you may lose the return-of-capital tax benefit. Everything that you take out will be taxed as investment earnings until nothing is remaining in the account but your contributions.

What if you die before you start collecting payments from your deferred annuity? Most companies will pay to your designated beneficiary a death benefit equal to the account value at the time of your death. If your investments were running at a loss, some companies will pay the full amount of your contributions. Any investment earnings are taxable to the recipient unless he or she annuitizes the money within 60 days.

What you pay to get in. Deferred annuities usually charge a variety of fees spread out over time. Here's what a widely sold plan charged in mid 1991:

▮ A flat $30 annual contract maintenance fee.

▮ A 1.3% annual deduction from the assets of the annuity for mortality and expense risk and administration.

▮ Asset management fees ranging from about 0.50% for the company's own common stock fund to 1.5% for a portfolio managed by an outside mutual fund company.

▮ A back-end load that starts at 7% if you withdraw money in the first year and diminishes to zero after seven years. (Some annuities impose back-end charges for as long as 20 years, so this is a provision you need to check very carefully.)

Because investors tend to divide their assets among both inside- and outside-managed funds, an average management fee in this plan would work out to about 1%, making the annual expense around 2.3% plus $30. That's a typical expense ratio for a deferred variable annuity.

Variations on the theme. Probably the most heavily promoted deferred annuity plan is one called the *flexible-premium deferred variable annuity*. It gives you a range of investment choices and the freedom to invest your money at your own pace.

There are a number of mutual fund companies, including Benham, Colonial, Fidelity, Franklin, Neuberger & Berman, Oppenheimer, Twentieth Century, Wellington, and Scudder, that manage special funds open to holders of variable annuities. Depending on the company selling the annuity, you may have a choice of more than a dozen funds or only a few. Because all variable annuities involve mutual funds, they are legally securities and must be sold by prospectus.

Another popular plan is the *single-premium deferred annuity*, which differs from the flexible-premium variety in that it is purchased with one lump sum. The *deferred fixed annuity*, which has been around since the turn of the century, offers no mutual funds. Instead, you earn interest at a rate declared by the insurer each month or quarter. You might have some money

---

VARIABLE LIFE INSURANCE

Q: *I am 38 years old and am considering investing via variable life insurance. Should I do it?*

A: If you need the insurance and have the discipline to stick with the plan, variable life could make sense. It lets you invest part of your cash value in stocks and other securities, offering the possibility of higher tax-deferred yields than straight life, which pays a set rate based on fixed-income securities. Both the total death benefit and the cash value of a variable policy rise and fall with the results of the investment accounts. A minimum death benefit generally is guaranteed, but the cash value is not—so you take some risk.

Variable life is sold by prospectus, which will tell you how a company's investments have performed as well as give projected returns based on various investment options. Most insurers offer mutual funds in which to invest your premiums.

One major attraction of variable life is that, like an IRA, the investment earnings are tax-deferred (as long as you keep them inside the policy). When you evaluate the performance of the investment earnings against investments outside a policy, remember that part of the first year's premium is consumed by administrative costs and the agent's commission. Thus it will take some time to accumulate much cash value.

---

earning 7%, some 8% and some 9%, just as if you owned a Treasury portfolio of staggered maturities.

How to find a good one. Which annuity sellers have the best investment records? Variable Annuity Research & Data Service (VARDS), of Miami, tracks the total returns of almost 500 annuity funds. Nearly every variable annuity VARDS follows has some funds that consistently beat the mutual fund averages for the same class of investment and trail it for others. Ask your agent for the VARDS reports on the funds available to you in an annuity you're considering and apply the kinds of considerations described in Chapter 6. The monthly S&P *Stock Guide,* described in Chapter 4 and available in many public libraries, follows a number of annuity funds. Morningstar, Inc., which also tracks mutual funds (See Chapter 6), publishes monthly performance reports on several hundred variable annuities. The report, which costs $95 a year (for subscription information call 312-427-1985), may be available at a local library.

What if the insurance company goes broke? From time to time an insurance company may declare a conspicuously high rate on a fixed annuity, such as 10% when the average is 8%, in an effort to attract business. Banks do the same thing when they offer to pay an unusually high rate on a certificate of deposit. The difference is that bank accounts are insured but the assets of insurance companies issuing annuities are not.

Mutual funds sold through variable annuities must sequester their holdings in accounts separate from the insurance company, which provides some measure of protection. But the guarantees of fixed annuities depend on the health of the insurance company. Thus a supposedly conservative fixed annuity can actually be dicier than a variable annuity if the company isn't rock solid.

In 1983 Baldwin-United, the parent of six insurance companies that sold high-yielding fixed annuities through Wall Street brokerages, went bankrupt, owing 165,000 fixed-annuity holders billions of dollars. Baldwin collapsed when regulators discovered that the company's underlying assets weren't earning enough to meet its ambitious guarantees. Ultimately the brokerages and other insurance companies partially rescued Baldwin's customers, making good on principal and crediting about 7% interest.

There have been more conspicuous collapses of insurance companies since the Baldwin-United affair: Executive Life, First Capital, and Mutual Benefit bit the dust in the late 1980s and early 1990s, leaving state regulators picking up the pieces, Congress holding hearings and annuity customers worrying about whether they would get paid what they were promised.

All of this serves to underscore a crucial point: In sizing up an annuity, bear in mind that it's the soundness of the company, not the last half-point of interest, that matters most. Do business only with insurers whose claims-paying abilities are rated high by the rating services.

Chief among the services, at least in terms of the number of companies it follows, is the A.M. Best Co. It ranks insurers on a scale of A+ to C- and considers A+ and A the top two ratings.

Best offers a 900-number service through which, for a charge of $2.50 per minute, you can receive information on a specific insurance company. The "Bestline" number is 900-420-0400. You'll need a tone-dialing phone and the Best I.D. number for the company you're asking about. Those numbers are available by calling 908-439-2200.

Weiss Research is a Florida-based rating company that for $15 each will give you oral reports over the phone on companies it follows. Call 800-289-9222.

Three other companies follow the insurance industry. They are Moody's Investors Service, 99 Church St., New York, N.Y. 10007 (212-553-0377); Standard & Poor's, 25 Broadway, New York, N.Y. 10004 (212-208-1527); and Duff & Phelps, 55 East Monroe St., Suite 3600, Chicago, Ill. 60603 (312-368-3157). Each of those companies will give you a single rating over the phone at no cost. Most larger libraries will have Moody's or S&P ratings in their reference section. Full-service insurance agents should also have at least the Best guide available.

KEOGH PLANS

If you are self-employed, either full or part-time, some of your retirement investments belong in a Keogh plan. You're eligible even if you're already participating in a company pension plan and are actively contributing to an IRA.

You can invest your Keogh money in just about anything you like. Most people choose stocks, bonds and mutual funds.

Contributions to a Keogh plan are deductible from your taxable income in the year in which they're made. Earnings accumulate tax-free until you take them out at retirement. The most popular version of a Keogh—called a money-purchase defined-contribution plan—permits annual contributions of 25% of earned income, up to a maximum of $30,000. (To arrive at the definition of earned income for Keogh contributions, you must first deduct the contributions, which has the effect of lowering the effective limit to 20% of precontribution income.)

A profit-sharing defined-contribution Keogh has smaller annual percentage limitations on contributions but is more flexible and thus favored by part-timers whose self-employment income may be too sporadic to permit them to set up a regular schedule of contributions. The maximum deductible contribution is 15% of earnings per year, up to a maximum deduction of $30,000, which is reduced to an effective rate of only about 13% for the same reason the effective limit on defined-contribution Keoghs works out to 20%.

A "defined benefit" Keogh, which is designed to produce a predetermined amount of retirement income, permits you to exceed the $30,000 maximum. With a defined-benefit plan you decide, within certain limits, how much you would like to receive in annual retirement income, and then hire an actuary to design a program to accumulate enough money to pay that defined benefit when the time comes for you to retire.

As with an IRA, withdrawals from a Keogh before you turn 59½ will usually trigger a 10% penalty. As with an IRA, you can get around that penalty by scheduling payouts to deplete the fund over your expected lifetime. And, as with an IRA, you must start drawing down the fund shortly after you reach age 70½. You can take the money out in a lump sum, in installments, or in annuity payments, and it is taxed accordingly. The payouts must be scheduled to deplete the fund over the period of your life expectancy at age 70½.

For an IRS guide to the intricacies of Keogh plans and related retirement tax shelters, call 800-TAX-FORM and ask for IRS

DIFFERENCES IN KEOGHS

Q: *How does a profit-sharing Keogh differ from a plain vanilla Keogh, which has a higher contribution limit—25% of net self-employment income, or actually 20% of income before the contribution?*

A: The key difference between the profit-sharing Keogh—with its 15% of net income contribution cap—and the purchase-money defined-contribution plan—with the 25% cap—is that with the latter, you are *required* to make a fixed-percentage-of-income contribution each year. With the profit-sharing plan you can put in as much or as little of your profit as you like—up to the ceiling. Thus, although you get a lower ceiling, you also get more flexibility. Many people combine the two types of Keoghs to give themselves flexibility and the maximum-possible contribution.

---

publication number 560, *Self-Employed Retirement Plans*. It's free.

Simplified Employee Pensions

A relative of both the Keogh plan and the individual retirement account, the simplified employee pension, or SEP, also lets you set aside self-employment income in a tax-sheltered account. The annual contribution limit is about 13% of income, up to $30,000—the same as for profit-sharing Keoghs. The rules are similar to those governing IRAs, but there are no income limits restricting the deductibility of contributions. What's more, the annual reporting requirements aren't as stringent as they are for Keoghs. Because of their similarity to IRAs, these plans are usually called SEP-IRAs or Super IRAs. The IRS publication mentioned above explains the rules.

401(k) PLANS

If your employer offers one, a 401(k) salary reduction option (or its cousin, the 403(b) plan offered to public school teachers and employees of nonprofit organizations) is an excellent vehicle for retirement savings. Money you earmark—usually 2% to 15% of your annual salary, depending on your employer's plan, up to an inflation-indexed annual maximum of about $8,500 in 1991—goes into the account tax-free, and earnings are tax-deferred. You can get your money if you quit as early as age 55 without incurring a 10% tax penalty. A bonus: Many employers match employee contributions 50 cents on the dollar, or even dollar for dollar, up to a certain amount.

The employer may offer a variety of options for investing your salary set-asides, usually giving you a choice of stock in the company itself, a stock, bond or money-market fund, or something called a guaranteed investment contract, or GIC. If you have such a choice, size up the company stock using the criteria described in Chapter 4. Be tough. After all, you already depend on the company for your livelihood. Do you want to depend on it for your investment results as well?

Stock and bond and money-market mutual funds offered by the company 401(k) plan can be evaluated according to the standards described in the appropriate chapters in this book. But most plan participants select the guaranteed investment contract.

Guaranteed Investment Contracts (GICs)

Nearly three-fourths of all 401(k) plans offer these as an investment option and they attract $6 of every $10 these plans invest. The plans buy GICs from insurance companies, which guarantee up front what the rate of return will be for the term of the GIC, which is between one and seven years. Today, some $200 billion is invested in GICs and similar investment products.

How they work. Your plan manager takes the money designated for GICs and shops among insurance companies that offer them, looking for attractive interest rates and maturities. To spread risk, fund managers may sign contracts with as many as 20 issuers and blend the different rates of return at

LIMITS ON EMPLOYER 401(K) CONTRIBUTIONS

Q: *Last year my husband's employer informed him that because his salary was over $50,000, under federal tax law limits he could no longer save 14% on a before-tax basis in his 401(k) plan. It was adjusted to 8% before tax and 6% after tax. Is his employer correct?*

A: To prevent highly paid employees from reaping a disproportionate share of the tax benefits delivered by a 401(k), there are rules that can lower the amounts that "highly compensated" employees may contribute on a pre-tax basis. There are several complicated tests for determining who is highly compensated—and one test does tag employees who make more than a certain amount and are in the top 20% of a firm's wage earners.

Your husband can still contribute 14% of salary to his 401(k)—if he first pays taxes on 6% of it. When he later withdraws money from the plan, he won't owe any tax on the money he contributed on an after-tax basis.

various maturities to arrive at the yield on your investment.

The insurance companies in turn invest GIC money in a variety of places—government bonds, corporate bonds, private placements of stock, high-yield junk bonds and mortgages. They keep a portion of the income from these investments as a fee and pass the rest on as your guaranteed yield. The yield is usually competitive with CDs and between one-half and one-and-a-half percentage points more than yields from Treasury notes of comparable maturities. When the term of the GIC contract is up, your pension fund gets back the principal and either reinvests it in another GIC or returns it to employees retiring or cashing out of the plan.

Are they safe? GICs have delivered what their name implies: a guaranteed return. You know going in what you'll get coming out. The major risk is that a GIC is only as good as the insurance company that issues it. Concern for insurance companies' creditworthiness has prompted pension fund managers to take another look at their GIC investments. If you hold some, you should consider conducting your own investigation.

▎ Ask your plan manager for the names of the insurance companies backing your GICs. As a member of a 401(k) plan you are legally entitled to at least annual reports from your plan manager on how your investments are performing. If you don't find the names there, ask a representative of your pension plan for a list of companies.

▎ Check the firms' credit ratings. Most companies have begun including credit-rating information on the issuers of GICs they hold. If not, you can find that information from the rating companies described in the section on deferred annuities in this chapter. Few pension plans buy GICs from companies with less than an A rating. If you find one rated lower than A on your company's list, request an explanation of why the company is taking that additional risk.

▎ Look for diversification. Your pension manager should be buying GICs from at least three to five separate insurance companies—more if your firm is large enough. That way the risk is spread, reducing the chance your plan will be affected by the failure of one insurance company.

▎ Finally, if you are uncomfortable with the GIC offered by your 401(k), examine the plan's other investment options and consider putting your money in one of them instead.

Because GICs in an individual company's plan are most likely drawn from a number of insurance companies, the failure of one would not ordinarily mean a significant drop in your 401(k) assets. And in most states, GIC contract holders would be covered by guaranty insurance plans under the same terms as holders of life insurance policies, which means that the state would make good on at least some of the loss.

At any rate, the worry is probably overdone. Most of the major GIC sellers are holding only small amounts of noninvestment-grade junk bonds. A bigger worry for younger members of 401(k)

THE SAFETY OF 401(K)S

Q: *If a company fails, would the money I have in a 401(k) plan be lost?*

A: It shouldn't be. Under the Employee Retirement Income Security Act (ERISA), employers and pension plan trustees have a responsibility to safeguard employees' pension funds— and a company would be breaking the law if it tapped those funds. Generally, your account is as safe as its underlying investments. You could run into trouble if you've selected company stock for your 401(k) and the company goes under.

---

plans should be whether too much of your money is tied up in relatively low-yielding GICs. If you are in your 40s or younger, consider shifting a significant portion of your money—say, 50% or 60%—into a good stock mutual fund offered by the plan. But make sure the plan meets the standards described in Chapter 6.

Trading GICs for BICs. Some companies are shifting away from GICs to alternatives such as Treasury bills or to bank investment contracts, or BICs. As bank deposits, BICs are federally insured up to $100,000. BICs have pulled in $20 billion but now face competition from still more GIC alternatives—for example, a blend of BICs and short-term government securities.

Insurance companies themselves have joined the fray, issuing what have been dubbed "synthetic" or "separate account" GICs that give plan members a piece of the underlying portfolio of investments. Should the insurer become insolvent, the assets of these contracts would transfer directly to the pension fund. Besides offering a more active role to buyers, synthetic GICs shift the creditworthiness issue to the underlying investments and away from the insurance company.

Synthetic GICs carry no guaranteed return; interest rates are adjusted annually. And buyers assume at least some of the default risk of the underlying investments.

EMPLOYEE STOCK OWNERSHIP PLANS

Employee stock ownership plans, or ESOPs, let employees buy stock in their company through payroll withholding or some other way, or the corporation may contribute shares of its stock to funds that allocate the shares to employees based on their annual compensation. The advantage to employees is that they acquire stock of the company they work for at little or no cost. Employees must pay taxes on the value of the stock when they take possession of it when they leave the company, but in the meantime, the stock can appreciate tax-free. When employees receive it, they can continue the tax-favored treatment by rolling it over into an IRA.

An ESOP can be a great deal—if the company makes adequate contributions and the stock does well. But there are no guarantees. A recession, stock market slump or downturn in business at your company could savage your account. Examples of that aren't hard to find.

▪ In 1989, Thomson McKinnon, one of the nation's largest brokerage firms, sold its network of 158 branch offices and closed shop. The 2,800 members of the company's ESOP, who held about 75% of the stock, were left holding the bag.

▪ In 1990 the employees of Pan Am, who held large blocks of their company's stocks through an ESOP, were among the biggest losers when the airline filed for bankruptcy.

What can you do to make sure your retirement dollars don't go down the drain with your company? Read on.

How ESOPs work: the promise. The company contributes a certain amount for each participating ESOP employee, based on salary. ESOP contributions average between 8% and 15% of annual pay. At 10%, for example, $5,000 would be contributed to the account of an employee earning $50,000. Company contributions and earnings on them are not taxed until the employee quits or retires and receives the money.

But unlike other retirement plans, in which the trustees are obligated to diversify investments prudently, an ESOP invests primarily—sometimes entirely—in company stock. That can make an ESOP a high-stakes gamble.

The employer can contribute shares it owns to the ESOP, or it can give cash that the plan's trustees use to buy company stock. As a rule, though, the trustees get a company-backed loan to pay for the stock, and the employer's contributions go to repay the loan.

Once the shares are allocated to an employee's account, that employee has voting rights. In publicly traded companies, employees can vote on all issues put before the shareholders. In closely held firms—those owned by relatively few people and whose stock is not traded on an exchange—voting rights of ESOP shareholders can be limited to major issues, such as the sale or merger of the company.

In theory, a well-run ESOP can be good for everybody. Giving workers a direct financial stake in their company should make them more productive. If morale is high, the company is more likely to prosper, and if it does, so will its employees. And so will the other stockholders. Today, the plans are in place at dozens of blue-chip corporations, including Polaroid, Anheuser Busch, Lockheed, and Procter & Gamble, as well as hundreds of smaller concerns.

How ESOPs work: the worries. There are some concerns that companies are rushing into ESOPs more to cut costs and block takeovers than to give workers a bigger stake in the enterprise. And ESOPs apparently have had little or no impact on productivity or profits. Indeed, ESOPs offer unique advantages to the corporate sponsors. For one thing, the company gets the right to deduct dividends paid on shares allocated to ESOP accounts. ESOPs can also be used as a source of low-cost financing. Setting up an ESOP to borrow money to buy newly issued shares, for example, can provide a cash infusion for the company.

What you should do about an ESOP. It's crucial that you know just where you stand if your employer has an ESOP or is considering starting one. Federal law requires disclosure of the major provisions of the plan and values of the stock, but you should also get a full explanation from key company officers and assess the plan in light of your long-term financial goals.

An ESOP is a defined-contribution benefit plan, like a deferred profit-sharing plan or a 401(k) plan with a company match. An ESOP is riskier than some other defined-contribution plans, though, because its success is dependent entirely on the sponsoring company's success. Although a few plans are somewhat diversified, most are funded entirely with the company's stock. If the stock rises in value, everybody gains. But if it performs poorly, contributions taper off. If the company fails, ESOP members may wind up with nothing.

How can you find out whether an ESOP is in your best interest? First, take a critical look at any other long-term benefits your employer provides, such as a profit-sharing or pension plan. The principal disclosure document required by federal law is called a summary plan description. If your company has a good retirement-income plan with federally guaranteed benefits, much less will be riding on the ESOP.

The plan description for an ESOP must include information on the workings of the plan and the rights and obligations of employees. In addition, employers must furnish annual statements showing the balance of their accounts, the value of the stock and the extent to which each worker is vested—that is, how much you would get if you quit. The law requires that you be fully vested after no more than seven years in the plan.

The leading public companies are tracked by security analysts who forecast future performance. Sources of this kind of information are listed in Chapter 4. Unfortunately for your fact-gathering process, only about 10% of ESOPs active today are at public companies. The rest are at privately held concerns. Those firms are subject to the same benefit-disclosure rules but not the federal securities laws. Still, many do furnish workers with an abundance of financial and performance information, and you should be able to get what you need from the company benefits manager.

How to protect yourself. Don't make the mistake of confusing an ESOP with a pension plan. It's really an investment in the company you work for and should be evaluated as such—in light of other investments you have, your stage in life and your tolerance for risk.

As a participant in an ESOP, you have the right to diversify your account as you near retirement age. A worker reaching age 55 who has been in an ESOP for ten years can direct that 25% of the assets in his account be invested outside of company securities. At age 60, you can shift 50% of your account to noncompany investments.

The ability to diversify is a key point to study in the plan summary. What provisions does the ESOP make for diversification? Are alternative investments provided within the plan? Will the percentage you shift out of company stock be paid to you in cash so you can roll it over into an IRA? The decision whether to diversify should turn on both your view of the company's prospects and the way the ESOP fits into the rest of your investment plan.

PART 4

GETTING IT DONE

CHAPTER

CHOOSING & USING
A BROKER

I F YOU'RE GOING to buy individual issues of stocks and bonds, you're going to need a broker. A broker is your link to the exchanges on which securities transactions take place. A carefully selected broker can also supply you with valuable investment information and make profitable investment suggestions. Unfortunately, a lot of investors don't choose their broker; their broker chooses *them*. Typically it happens in one of two ways.

■ You get a phone call from a representative of SteadFast Brokerage, a national firm with a name you recognize. Stead-Fast, the broker tells you, is bringing to market a new issue of municipal bonds. They yield 7% completely free of federal income taxes. During the underwriting phase, the issue is available at no commission cost. Wouldn't you like to take advantage of this opportunity? You, who had been thinking about investing in municipal bonds but weren't quite sure how to go about it, say "Yes." Bingo, you've got yourself a broker.

■ You and your spouse have been discussing the wisdom of setting up an investment account and you finally decide to take some action. You saw a television commercial for SteadFast and liked its spokesman. So you stroll into the local office and announce to the receptionist, "I'd like to talk to someone about opening an investment account." The receptionist consults a piece of paper, picks up the phone and summons Mr. Smith. Bingo, you've got yourself a broker.

What's wrong with both of these scenarios is that you're trusting your fate to chance. In the first example, the SteadFast representative may be a perfectly fine broker, but you have no way of knowing that. He or she is probably fairly new on the job and prospecting for business, working from a list of club members or business magazine subscribers in the area—likely prospects for investment accounts. There's nothing wrong with that, as long as it's done honestly and politely, but it tends to serve the broker's interest more than it does yours.

In the second example, the broker that's summoned to meet with you is also a random choice. Each day, brokerage firms designate someone on the staff to handle walk-in business. The assignment rotates. You may get a good broker that way, one whose investment style and philosophy suit yours to a tee. Or you may get a commodities-trading specialist who is bored with buy-and-hold investors like you or whose recommendations are highly inappropriate for your investment goals and risk tolerance.

THE RIGHT WAY TO CHOOSE A BROKER

The first thing to know about stockbrokers is that they are hardly ever called that anymore. They have much more impressive names: financial consultant, account executive, financial counselor. Sometimes the title reflects extra schooling in the art and science of investing; sometimes the title just happens to be what the brokerage firm likes to call its brokers. Because the quality and experience of the individual matter more than the title on the business card, the best course is to ignore the title and concentrate on discovering whether you've found a good match.

The seeds of a potentially poor investor-broker relationship are planted when the broker picks the investor, rather than the other way around. To find the right broker, you have to take the initiative. It starts with some thinking about the kind of service you want. Your most important choice is between two kinds of brokerages: full-service firms and discount firms.

Full-Service Brokers

Do you want investment advice and recommendations? If so, you're in the market for a full-service broker. Mostly, these are the high-profile national firms with armies of analysts who crank out buy and sell recommendations for a long list of stocks and bonds. Their fee structures reflect the expense of maintaining those research departments. Commissions vary according to the number of shares and dollar amount involved, but on average you can expect to pay about 2% of the value of the shares each time you buy or sell. In general, the bigger the transaction the smaller the bite taken out of it by the broker's commission.

Full-service firms also pride themselves on their comprehensive asset-management services, the granddaddy of which is the Merrill Lynch Cash Management Account, or CMA. Other firms have followed suit, calling their comprehensive accounts by different names but offering the same kind of services under one roof. They vary in details, but all include a money-market account into which the firm automatically "sweeps" idle funds (such as from dividend payments, for example); check-writing privileges; a substantial line of credit; a debit card or credit card tied to the account; and a comprehensive monthly statement that makes investment record-keeping a breeze. Minimum account size that qualifies for such deluxe service ranges from $5,000 to $20,000, depending on the broker.

You know the names of most of the full-service brokers because they have offices all over the country: Merrill Lynch, Dean Witter Reynolds, Advest, PaineWebber, Prudential Securities, Shearson Lehman Brothers, and others. Smaller, more upscale firms that cater to a generally better-heeled clientele include Bear Stearns and Morgan Stanley. Depending on where you live, you may also be familiar with some of the full-service regional firms, which have offices in certain parts of the country—for instance, Piper Jaffray & Hopwood, which is based in Minneapolis; J.C. Bradford in Nashville; Alex. Brown & Sons in Baltimore; Scott & Stringfellow in Richmond.

Finding a good one. The best way to start your search for a broker who's right for you at a full-service firm is to ask friends who are investors who they use. Then quiz your friends as closely as you comfortably can about their investment goals and styles. Are they buy-and-hold types or do they trade frequently? Do they favor stocks or bonds? Small companies or large? Are they in contact with their broker frequently, or only once in a while? Are their phone calls returned? What do they think of the firm's account statements? Are they easy to understand or are they confusing? What about research reports—does the broker provide them and other backup for investment recommendations? Finally, knowing what they do about you, would your friends recommend their broker to be *your* broker?

This process will produce a few names for you to pursue. Call the most promising of the recommended brokers and tell them where you got their names. Briefly outline your investment goals and make an appointment to meet at their offices. At that meeting, inquire into the brokers' experience and educational background, both academic and professional. Ask about their approach to investments in general: Do they specialize in any particular area, or do they generalize?

Note what kinds of questions each broker asks about you and your financial situation. A broker should know your goals, your resources and your risk tolerance before he or she is in a position to advise you. Your interests and the broker's interests should be the same: to lay the seeds for a long-term, mutually beneficial relationship. If the broker shows little interest in finding out your financial position and goals and instead presses you with a sales pitch on getting rich, scratch that one off your list and make plans to interview the next one.

Discount Brokers

If you make your own investment decisions and don't need or don't want investment advice or recommendations from your broker, there's no need to pay for them. So-called discount brokers don't make specific buy and sell recommendations. What you get is fulfillment of your order, period (although some discounters offer a range of investor services, which will be described later). Because they don't have to support research departments and because most of their business is done over the phone, discounters can charge considerably less than full-service brokers to accomplish your transactions. On average, according to the *Mercer Stock Commission Survey*, discounters charge less than one-fourth the commissions charged by full-service brokers.

Despite their common devotion to bare-bones order-taking, it would be a mistake to think discount brokers are interchangeable. Some offer a limited amount of research, some have investment-oriented libraries open to their customers, and some even offer all-in-one accounts that rival those of the full-service firms. Fidelity, Schwab, and Quick & Reilly, for example, will set up accounts that automatically sweep idle cash into a money-market account. Fidelity's Ultra Service Account and the Schwab One asset management account provide comprehensive consolidated monthly statements that help you keep track of all investment transactions conducted there.

Still, it is cut-rate commissions that put discounters on the map and it is largely on that basis that they must be evaluated. A study done by *Kiplinger's Personal Finance Magazine* discovered that some very small trades are often cheaper at a full-service firm because discounters typically charge minimum commissions of at least $25, more often $35. Thus, buying or selling a few shares of a low-cost stock—10 shares of a $5 issue, for example—would normally cost you less at Merrill Lynch, where the minimum commission is $35 or 25% of the transaction amount, than it would at Charles Schwab, where the minimum is $39.

Handling large lots of high-priced stocks is where the discounters shine. At the time of the Kiplinger survey, buying or selling 500 shares of IBM at $125 a share cost $510 at Paine Webber, $485 at Merrill Lynch, a smidgen over $200 at Fidelity, Schwab, or Quick and Reilly, and only $65 at Brown & Co., a discounter based in Boston.

Use Both Kinds

There's not a thing wrong with using both a full-service broker and a discounter. But you may alienate your full-service representative if you rely on him or her for quality research and recommendations and use the discounter for all your biggest trades. Still, you can use the dual structure of the brokerage industry to your advantage.

■ If you need to sell several thousand dollars' worth of stocks or bonds to raise cash, look for a discounter to exercise the trade at the lowest possible cost. See the list in the box on the next page.

■ When you need investment advice and information, the quality of what you will find at full-service firms is usually excellent. If a full-service broker puts you on the trail of a good investment opportunity, it is only fair to throw your business in his or her direction. One or two solid recommendations can be worth several bargain-rate trades.

■ Whichever kind of broker you use, discuss commission rates on a regular basis. Don't hesitate to ask for a discount, even from a full-service broker, if you think you deserve it for some reason—the volume of your business, for example, or because your recommendation to a friend resulted in the broker acquiring another valuable customer.

WHICH KIND OF ACCOUNT?

When you have selected a broker, you'll be asked to fill out a new-account information form. On that form you'll have to make some choices about the kind of account you want.

■ *A single account* is one in which you, and only you, can

DISCOUNT BROKERS THAT DO BUSINESS NATIONWIDE

Before you choose a discount broker, call the number given and ask for descriptive literature about the firm. Examine it and note the differences in services offered by each firm. Then compare rates on a trade typical of your investment pattern. (The first number shown is the national toll-free number. For firms that have a different in-state toll-free number, that number is shown next. Most firms will also accept collect calls from customers whose location makes them unable to use the toll-free number.)

Andrew Peck Associates
800-221-5873
212-363-3770 (N.Y.)

Brown & Co.
800-225-6707
617-742-2600 (Mass.)

Bull & Bear Securities
800-262-5800
212-742-1300 (N.Y.)

Fidelity Brokerage Services
800-544-7272

First National Brokerage Services
800-228-3011
402-346-5965 (Neb.)

Jack White & Co.
800-223-3411
619-587-2000 (Cal.)

Kennedy, Cabot & Co.
800-252-0090
800-257-2045 (Cal.)

Marquette de Bary Co.
800-221-3305
212-644-5300 (N.Y.)

Muriel Siebert & Co.
800-872-0711
212-644-2400 (N.Y.)

Olde Discount Stockbrokers
800-225-3863
313-961-6666 (Mich.)

Pacific Brokerage Services
800-421-8395
213-939-1100 (Cal.)

Quick & Reilly
800-672-7220
800-522-8712 (N.Y.)

T. Rowe Price Discount Brokerage
800-638-5660
301-547-2308 (Md.)

Charles Schwab
800-648-5300
415-627-7000 (Cal.)

Spear Securities
800-695-4220
818-543-4400 (Cal.)

StockCross
800-225-6196
800-392-6104 (Mass.)

authorize purchases, sales and other transactions.

■ *A joint account* works in much the same way as a joint bank account and is often the choice for married couples because of its flexibility.

■ *A cash account* is the most sensible choice for new customers. It requires that all trades be settled on a cash basis, meaning that if you want to buy $1,000 worth of stock, you've got to deliver the $1,000 to the broker within a few days of the transaction.

■ *A margin account* permits you to trade "on margin," meaning with money borrowed from the brokerage firm. The size of the loan depends on the current "margin requirement," which for some years has been 50%. That means you can borrow up to 50% of the cost of the purchase. If the cash (nonmargined) portion of the securities you bought on margin dips below a certain level (usually about 30%), you have to come up with the difference, either by sending the broker more cash or by selling enough of the underlying securities to get your cash position back over the minimum. Meanwhile, you pay interest at a rate of 1% to 3% over the prime rate. Only experienced investors should consider trading on margin.

■ *A discretionary account* is one in which you authorize a full-service broker to buy and sell securities without getting your permission first. For most investors, this is a bad idea.

Street name or your name? When you open your brokerage account, you'll also be asked whether you want the broker to hold your stock and bond certificates at the firm in "street name" or send them to you, in which case you'll be responsible for their safekeeping. If you leave them at the firm, you won't actually have any certificates issued in your name. Instead, the firm will add up all the shares owned by its customers and have one certificate issued in its own name for the total number. Each customer's claim on the shares is kept track of through a book-entry system. When dividends are paid by the company, they are sent to the brokerage, which parcels them out according to its records of who owns what.

The main advantages of keeping your shares in street name are liquidity and safety. If you want to sell, all you have to do is call your broker and direct the sale of as many shares as you wish. That's it. Meanwhile, the shares are stored safely in the firm's vault. If something happens to them, it's the broker's responsibility to make good. If the broker goes broke, your share of the shares is protected by the Securities Investor Protection Corp., as explained later on in the chapter.

If you keep the shares yourself, you have to get them delivered to the broker within a few days in order to complete any transaction. Nevertheless, you are entitled to take possession of your shares, and many investors choose to do so. If you do, tell the broker so when you open your account, and arrange to rent a safety deposit box in which to store the certificates.

RECORDS YOU SHOULD KEEP

The paperwork generated by a brokerage account can be confusing if you don't keep it sorted out. Hang on to all purchase and sales slips, monthly account "activity" statements and annual 1099 forms that summarize the year's activity for tax purposes. Annual and quarterly reports from companies whose shares you own can also be kept in these files.

Set up a master file for each brokerage account, plus separate file folders within it for each stock, bond or mutual fund or other investment bought or sold through that firm. This will make transaction slips, income statements and other pertinent documents easy to find when you need them. After you get your yearly 1099, you can get rid of some interim reports, but hang on to the monthly account statements. Keep records of capital gains, dividend distributions and other payouts because you'll need them for tax purposes long after the transactions are completed.

It's especially important to keep records that show the cost of investments, such as transaction slips and canceled checks. Without them you may not be able to document profits and losses. It's also important to keep records showing amounts and dates of reinvested dividends, and amounts and dates of principal payments from unit trusts.

HOW TO DEAL WITH YOUR BROKER

In the best of all possible worlds, you and your broker work out a good investment plan—a nice mix of stocks and bonds and such—and the plan works beautifully. Your broker keeps you posted on the progress of your holdings and you chat amiably from time to time about the general direction of the market.

In the real world, if you own stocks, bonds, unit trusts, mortgage-backed securities or anything else sold by a broker, the person who sold it to you will eventually be calling to try to interest you in buying something else. The broker may or may not be doing you a favor. Individual investors have been known to snooze through opportunities to enhance their yield, take their profits or make other moves in their own interests.

A good broker will keep you informed about market developments that may affect your portfolio. But that doesn't mean you have to approve every suggestion, or even respond right away. Nothing is so urgent that a decision can't wait until you have time to investigate the broker's recommendation. Here's how to deal with unsolicited investment suggestions from a broker you know and trust. (If you get a call from a stranger you know nothing about, the question of what to do is simple: Tell the caller thanks very much but you already have a broker and you're quite satisfied with the service you're getting.)

■ *Give the topic your full attention.* If you're distracted, tell the broker to call you back or arrange to return the call. Don't be tempted to mutter "Okay" and authorize the transaction just so you can get back to what you were doing.

■ *Consider whether the suggestion fits into your investment plan.* The broker may be proposing that you leave a dividend-paying blue-chip stock in favor of a stock with more growth potential but less yield and more risk. A phone call out of the blue is not the time to change your plans. A broker with your interests in mind will know better than to push you in a direction you've said you don't want to go, but may genuinely feel that this is a superior opportunity. If it does seems appropriate, is fairly presented and you bite, you have no one to blame but yourself if things turn sour later on.

■ *Get more information.* Ask the broker to send you written research on the recommendation. With so many kinds of investments to handle, no broker can be expert on everything. Most rely on written analysis by others, either within the firm or independent of the firm. Ask the broker to share this research with you. If you don't understand it, let this one pass.

YOUR RIGHTS IF YOUR BROKER FOULS UP

Most brokers make an honest effort to serve their customers well. They don't "churn" customers' accounts by engaging in excessive trading just to generate commissions. They don't misrepresent the risks involved in the investments they recommend. They don't initiate transactions without the customer's authorization.

But all those things and worse *do* happen. If they happen to you, you have the right to strike back. If you feel you've been cheated, it's possible to battle your broker and win. The most common customers' complaints fall into these categories.

■ *Inappropriate investment recommendations.* A broker should know your financial situation and investment objectives and recommend only investments that fit them. Your retirement nest egg, for instance, doesn't belong in commodity futures contracts.

■ *Misrepresentation of risk.* This happens when a broker fails to inform you of the risks involved in an investment or misleads you about the nature of those risks.

■ *Churning your account.* It's illegal for brokers to trade excessively in order to run up commissions. Suspect churning if you find yourself paying 10% to 12% or more in stock commissions and the stocks in your portfolio are turning over six or more times a year.

■ *Unauthorized trading.* Unless you sign a contract giving your broker discretionary authority over your account (which you shouldn't do), the broker can make no trades without your permission. If it happens, don't waste any time before complaining. In the past, brokers' attorneys have argued successfully that a customer's failure to complain right away constitutes evidence that the customer "ratified" the broker's action.

■ *Failure to execute.* "Failure to obey" is how the industry describes a broker's failure to execute a trade you called in or a lengthy delay that caused you to miss an opportunity. Even if it's a mistake, you have grounds for a complaint.

What to do if you're wronged. If you suspect something illegal or unethical is going on with your account, the first step is to notify the broker. There may be an explanation or a way to resolve the matter to your satisfaction right away.

If that doesn't satisfy you, the next step is to complain to the broker's boss: the branch manager. Call and ask for an appointment and take along a written account of what happened. Take notes on what happens at that meeting.

Still not satisfied? The next level up is the firm's headquarters office. Address your complaint to the compliance director and send it by certified mail. Your success at this level will depend on how well you have documented your case. Determine ahead of time how much money it will take to make you whole again and be prepared to discuss a reasonable offer of settlement from the firm.

If the brokerage firm's compliance director can't or won't settle the matter to your satisfaction, your choice may well be predetermined. The agreement you signed when you opened your account at the firm probably restricts your avenue of complaint to the arbitration process set up by the industry to resolve such disputes. You can't sue in court if your agreement bars it—a legal restriction that has been upheld by the Supreme

Court. Nearly all brokerages include a mandatory arbitration clause in their customer contracts, whether you read it or not.

But the deck isn't necessarily stacked against you. Thousands of small investors have turned to arbitrators to settle disputes with the giants of the financial world, and many have come away winners.

Most contracts require you to take your case before one of the industry's ten self-regulatory organizations, or SROs. They are sponsored by the New York Stock Exchange (NYSE), the American Stock Exchange, several regional exchanges, the Chicago Board Options Exchange, the Municipal Securities Rulemaking Board and the National Association of Securities Dealers (NASD). Most investors wind up in the arbitration programs set up by the NYSE or the NASD. A few are heard by representatives of the American Arbitration Association (AAA), which has the advantage of having no direct affiliation with the securities industry.

The rules governing the forums are similar, although filing fees for AAA cases, starting at $300, are considerably higher than for SROs, which are subsidized by the industry and start as low as $15. Both hold hearings in most major cities, and both have streamlined procedures for small claims. To get information about the process, along with the forms you need to file a claim, write to either the National Association of Securities Dealers at 33 Whitehall St., New York, N.Y. 10004, or the New York Stock Exchange, 11 Wall Street, New York, N.Y. 10005.

What are your prospects for success? Quite good, actually. Small investors who bring arbitration actions against brokers win, on average, more than half the time.

WHAT IF YOUR BROKER GOES BROKE?

Since banks and savings and loan associations started toppling with regularity in the late 1980s, the unthinkable has become an everyday thought: What would happen if the brokerage firm where you do your business went *out* of business?

Just as banks and thrifts have the FDIC to bail them out, brokerage firms have the SIPC, the Securities Investor Protection Corporation. If that doesn't strike you as very reassuring, take comfort in the fact that by all accounts the SIPC is a lot healthier than the FDIC.

The SIPC is a federally chartered but private, nonprofit corporation that levies assessments on its members to protect brokerage customers in the event a member becomes insolvent. All broker-dealers are required by law to be members.

SIPC provides insurance for securities accounts of up to $500,000 per customer, with a $100,000 per customer limit on cash being held by the firm. Many brokerages purchase additional coverage, often up to a couple of million dollars. It's important to know that SIPC coverage applies only in the case of financial insolvency. It doesn't cover market-related losses from ill-advised or ill-timed investment decisions; those are considered part of the game. Nor does the SIPC cover you in case of broker theft or fraud; you must turn to the courts for redress in such cases.

Because it takes a lot of time to sort through a brokerage firm's records to determine who owns what, which securities are in customers' names and which in street name, which were in the process of being bought and sold but not yet settled on the day the doors closed, the SIPC generally takes much longer to settle matters than does the FDIC, which tries hard to minimize disruption to bank and s&l customers in the case of a shutdown. It can take weeks, even months, for SIPC to complete its business and get the proper securities distributed to the proper customers. In the meantime, the markets keep moving up and down but customers' assets are frozen. If the delay costs you money because the market moves against you, you're out of luck. SIPC protection is better than none, but it isn't perfect.

16

TAXES & YOUR INVESTMENTS

———— ▪ ————

"The art of taxation consists in so plucking the goose as to obtain the largest possible amount of feathers with the least possible amount of hissing."

THAT'S HOW Jean Baptiste Colbert, who was finance minister to Louis XIV, summed things up in the 1600s. As an investor in the 1990s, you must be aware that how you invest your money is crucial to how much of your earnings and profits will be plucked away by the Internal Revenue Service.

Different kinds of investments *are* treated differently by the IRS. As recently as 1980, earnings from some investments ran head-on into a 70% federal tax rate while earnings from other investments were taxed at the kindest and gentlest of all rates: 0%. Today, the official rates run from 0% to 31%. (Almost all states demand to share in your investment success, too.)

Understanding the rules can pay off handsomely, but keeping up with them is not easy. Congress is always tinkering, a tendency epitomized by the issue of capital gains. Capital gains are profits from stocks, bonds, real estate and other investments. Whether all or just part of such profits should be taxed is the subject of a never-ending battle in Washington. Not so long ago, 60% of capital gains were tax-free; now, 100% is taxed. Current law does provide a small break for higher-income taxpayers, though. That's discussed in detail later in this chapter.

Your investment success is going to depend in part on keeping your eye on the true bottom line: your after-tax return. That is what you get to keep after the government claims its share. And what you get to keep depends on where you put your money.

SAVINGS ACCOUNTS AND CERTIFICATES

The basic rules are mercifully simple. Interest you earn in a savings account is fully taxable in the year you earn it. It doesn't matter whether you withdraw the money or let it compound inside the account.

On certificates of deposit, the IRS also usually demands its share as the interest is earned. An exception lets you postpone the tax bill temporarily if you put your savings in a CD that matures in a year or less. In that case, the interest is taxed in the year the certificate matures. If you invest in a six-month CD in September, for example, the interest earned on it during the current year won't be taxed until the following year, when the certificate matures. For deposits with longer maturities, the interest is taxed in the year it is credited to your account.

Your bank, credit union or savings and loan will send you a notice each year showing how much interest to report to the IRS. (The IRS gets a copy, too.) The institution will also report as income to you the value of any inducement it gave you to get your business. The extra tax on such "income" isn't worth worrying about if all you got was a toaster or a videotape. But an expensive incentive could create a noticeable tax.

If you withdraw funds from a CD before it matures and have to pay an early-withdrawal penalty, the IRS will subsidize your loss. You can deduct such a penalty whether or not you itemize other deductions on your tax return.

Complications for children's accounts. The same rules generally apply to interest earned inside a custodial account set up for your children, but there's a complication: the so-called kiddie tax. It was created in 1986 because Congress worried that parents were stashing funds in kids' accounts so the interest would be taxed in the child's low tax bracket rather than the parents' higher one. To prevent such lamentable maneuvers, Congress declared that if a child under age 14 has *unearned* income over a certain amount, the excess is to be taxed at the parents' top rate. (Unearned income is basically earnings from investments while *earned* income is earnings from a job.)

As explained in Chapter 13, the kiddie tax applies the parents' tax rate to a child's income when unearned income passes $1,100. For a child under 14, the first $550 of investment income is tax-free, the next $550 is taxed at the child's rate, probably 15%. Only unearned income above $1,100 is nipped by the parents' rate, which is probably 28% or 31%. (The triggering point for the kiddie tax is indexed to rise with inflation.)

Although the kiddie tax was designed to prevent families from shifting income to children as a tax-saving strategy, it doesn't entirely eliminate the opportunities. In an account earning 8%, for example, savings in your child's name could reach almost $14,000 before the earnings would be threatened by the kiddie tax. Assuming $1,100 in interest is the child's only income, the first $550 would be tax-free and the 15% tax on the remaining $550 would cost $82.50. If that same money were invested in the parents' name, and the earnings taxed in the 31% bracket, the tax bill would be $341. That $250-plus savings is available year after year.

Remember that the kiddie-tax threat disappears on a child's 14th birthday. If your son or daughter turns 14 any time during the year, even on New Year's Eve, the kiddie tax does not apply to any income received during the year.

U.S. SAVINGS BONDS

As noted in Chapter 5, today's savings bonds are far superior to those issued in the past. Gone is the fixed, well-below-market interest rate. Series EE bonds are sold for half of face value and guarantee a minimum rate if the bonds are held for at least five years. The actual rate earned is set semiannually at 85% of the average yield on five-year Treasury notes. It has been as high as 11%; it was 6.57% in mid 1991.

EE bonds have three special tax appeals.

■ *No state or local tax.* The interest is free of state or local tax. That hikes your effective return. If your state tax rate is around 7%, for example, avoiding that tax adds about 0.5% to the taxable equivalent yield.

■ *Deferred federal tax.* Federal tax on the interest is deferred until you redeem the bond. This allows money that would otherwise go to the IRS to remain invested for further growth. (Series HH bonds, also described in Chapter 5, are free from state tax but the interest is paid out in semiannual installments and taxed in the year received.)

The tax-deferral feature makes Series EE bonds popular for college savings plans. Because tax is deferred until the bonds are cashed, bonds purchased in a child's name and used for college bills escape the kiddie tax described earlier. Assuming the bonds are not cashed until the child is 14 or older, the interest will be taxed in the child's bracket. (If the parent is a co-owner, however, the parent will be stuck with the tax bill.)

Sometimes it makes sense to forgo this tax-deferral, though, and report the interest each year as it is earned. For a child with little or no other income, reporting the interest year by year could render part or all of it completely tax-free because the child's total income is so low that no tax would be due.

To report interest annually, file a tax return for the child showing the amount of interest earned by the bonds during the first year. Banks have tables showing how much that will be. File the return even if no tax is due to show intent to report bond interest annually. Then you don't have to file another return for the child until his or her income is high enough to require it.

■ *Tax-free interest for college.* The third advantage of EE bonds is that you can make them totally tax-free without going through the annual-reporting rigmarole. Interest on bonds purchased by parents is tax-free if the money is used to pay a child's college bills. Freedom from both state and federal tax significantly boosts the true return on this investment. At 6%—the minimum guaranteed rate on EE bonds—the double-tax-free virtue gives the bonds a taxable-equivalent yield of between 8.5% and 9% in most states.

To qualify for this break, the bonds must be purchased and owned by the parents, who must be at least 24 years old when the bonds are purchased. The rules don't allow for grandparents to buy the bonds, but there's nothing to stop them from giving the money to the parents for that purpose. (Bonds purchased before 1990 do not qualify.)

For qualifying bonds, the interest is tax-free if, in the year the parents redeem the bonds, they also pay qualifying educational expenses—basically that's tuition and fees for a dependent child—equal to the value of the bonds. If you pay $10,000 in tuition and fees and redeem bonds worth $10,000 or less, for example, all interest would be tax-free. If you cash in $10,000 worth of bonds and pay $7,500 for a child's qualifying expenses, only 75% of the interest would be tax-free. Parents must also meet certain income tests. See Chapter 13 for more information on using EE bonds as part of a college savings plan.

THE BASICS OF BASIS

When you move beyond savings to stocks, mutual funds and other investments that give you the potential for greater rewards in exchange for the risk of losing part or all of your money, your tax life gets much more complicated. On the bright side, the complications are generally beneficial if you know the rules and understand how to take advantage of them.

The beginning point is an understanding of *tax basis*. Your basis is basically the amount of your investment in a piece of property such as a share of stock, a bond, or a mutual fund share. It's the amount you compare with what you get when you sell the property to determine if you have a profit or a loss.

Sounds simple enough, but it's not, really. Not only does how you acquire an investment affect the basis, but the basis of different investments can change while you own them. You must keep track of the basis of every investment you own, and that means keeping good records. Your basis depends in part on how you obtained the property in the first place.

■ *If you bought it,* you've got the simplest job of figuring your basis. When you buy a stock, bond or mutual fund share, for example, your basis begins as what you pay, including any commissions. If you buy 100 shares of SureThing, Inc., for $40 a share and pay a $100 commission, your tax basis in each share is $41—the full $4,100 acquisition cost divided by the number of shares purchased. Keep the purchase confirmation form in your files.

■ *If you got it as a gift,* the basis depends in part on whether you eventually sell it for a gain or a loss. If you sell for a profit, your basis is the same as the basis of the previous owner—he or she passes on the basis along with the property. But if the sale results in a loss, the basis is either the previous owner's basis or the value at the time of the gift, whichever is lower. In other words, you don't get to deduct any decline in value that occurred before you got the gift.

If at the time of the gift the property is worth more than the benefactor's basis, all you need in your records is his or her basis. It becomes your basis. But if the property has declined in value, your records need to show both the previous owner's basis and the value at the time of the gift.

Say, for example, that a rich and generous uncle gives you 200 shares of stock for which he paid $10,000 but which are worth just $8,000 at the time of the gift. If the stock rises in price so that you eventually sell it for $12,000, your basis for

FIGURING THE BASIS ON INHERITED STOCK

Q: *My sisters, brother and I each received a gift of stock from our parents. The shares were purchased in small amounts over a long time; some are a result of stock splits and some were inherited by them from their parents as long ago as 1935. How do we figure the basis?*

A: If your parents don't have good records, you'll have to spend some time in the library with old newspapers looking up stock prices for the dates the shares were purchased. If you do not know the exact dates of the purchases, you could check the high and low for the year and use the midpoint.

The basis for shares that your parents gave you is their purchase price plus the commission. Since you plan to sell all the shares, the effect of stock splits doesn't matter. Once you've reconstructed what your parents paid for the shares they purchased, you need to pinpoint the basis of those they inherited. That's the stock's value on the date of death of the previous owner. If you sell for a gain, adding the basis of the stocks your parents purchased with those they inherited gives you your basis. If you sell the stock at a loss, however, the basis is either the amount just figured or the value of the stock at the time of the gift, whichever is lower.

determining gain is $10,000—your uncle's basis. If the share value continues to fall and you sell for less than $8,000, however, the basis for figuring your loss is the $8,000 value of the stock at the time of the gift. If you sell for an amount between $8,000 and $10,000, you have neither a gain nor a loss.

One additional complication: If the gift is large enough to trigger the federal gift tax, which generally applies to gifts over $10,000 and is owed by the donor, your basis is increased by part of the tax the donor incurs.

▮ *If you inherited it,* your basis is "stepped up" to the value of the asset on the date of death. (When large estates are involved, the value on a date within six months after death is sometimes used.) This rule means that the tax on any profit that built up during the previous owner's lifetime is forgiven. You will be taxed only on income and capital gains you realize after you inherit the asset. If its value falls and then you sell, you can deduct the loss. This rule also applies if you become the sole owner of property after the death of a joint owner. When a husband and wife jointly own stock and one spouse dies, for example, the survivor's basis becomes his or her half of the original basis plus half of the stock's value at the time the joint owner died. If you inherit property, be sure to pinpoint the stepped-up basis to hold down your tax bill.

∎ *If you get it as part of a divorce settlement,* your basis is whatever the basis of the property is at the time of the settlement. In other words, your basis is the same as your ex-spouse's. That means that when you sell you are responsible for the tax on any appreciation both before and after the transfer.

CAPITAL GAINS AND LOSSES

In addition to tracking the basis of your investments, you also have to keep an eye on the calendar. How long you own an asset before you sell it *might* affect how much tax you owe. *Might* is emphasized because it depends on Congress's ever-changing attitude about capital gains.

Figuring gains. The law segregates investment profits into two classes: Long-term and short-term capital gains, with one year as the dividing line. Assets owned one year or less produce short-term gains or losses; those owned more than one year get long-term treatment.

All of either variety is taxed, but higher-income taxpayers get a break. Although the current top tax rate is 31%, Congress set a special maximum rate for long-term gains of 28%. This benefits those whose income from salary, short-term gains and other sources falls in the 31% tax bracket—which begins at about $50,000 on a single return and about $82,000 on a joint return.

If your income is lower, there's no difference in the taxation of short- and long-term gains.

But you still need to watch the holding period of your investments. The IRS demands that you separate long- and short-term results on your tax return, and there's always a chance that Congress will extend a long-term capital gains break to everyone. One plan, to index capital gains for inflation—so that the longer you own an investment, the smaller the portion of profit that would be taxed—would create new record-keeping demands.

Deducting losses. If your investments produce a loss, the government will help absorb it—up to a limit. Losses can be used to offset any amount of capital gains, but no more than $3,000 of losses beyond that can be deducted against other income, such as your salary. But leftover losses can be carried forward and deducted in future years.

Say, for example, that during the year your investments produce $10,000 of capital gains and $14,000 of capital losses. The losses would offset all the gains, so you'd owe no tax at all on the profits. But only $3,000 of the excess $4,000 in losses could be deducted against other income. In the 28% bracket, that would save you $840 in taxes. The leftover $1,000 loss could be carried over to the next year.

The deductibility of capital losses makes your portfolio fertile ground for tax maneuvering, especially at year-end. Although you should not let the "tax tail wag the investment dog" by allowing tax factors to control buy or hold decisions, neither should you ignore the possibility of converting a paper loss to a real one to offset gains on other income.

Avoiding the wash-sale trap. Say you own stock showing a big paper loss. You expect the shares to recover, but you could use a tax deduction this year. So you sell the stock to take the loss, then buy it right back. Result: You get the tax deduction you sought *and* you still own the stock.

Pretty clever—provided you waited more than 30 days after the sale before you bought back the shares. Buy them back any sooner and the IRS will deny the tax loss. It considers the deal a wash since you wind up with the same stock in your portfolio.

You trigger the wash-sale rule if you buy "substantially identical" securities within 30 days *before or after* the sale of securities showing a loss. There's no precise definition of substantially identical, but it definitely covers shares in the same company whose shares you just sold.

You can skirt the wash-sale rules fairly easily by using mutual funds with similar objectives but different portfolios. You could sell a Scudder growth fund at a loss, for example, and immediately buy a Twentieth Century growth fund to position yourself for an anticipated market upturn.

STOCKS

Unlike interest on savings, which is generally taxed as it is earned, profits from stocks are shielded from the IRS until you sell. This gives you important flexibility. Postponing a sale from December to January, for example, allows you to delay reporting the profit by a full year. Accelerating a sale, on the other hand, might allow you to use a loss in a year when it would be most beneficial.

Making the most of this advantage requires keeping careful records so you can calculate your basis correctly and pinpoint the profit or loss from a potential sale.

As noted earlier, the basis can change while you own an investment. If a company in which you have invested declares a stock split, for example, your basis in each share will drop because your original basis will be spread over both the old and new shares. Assume you own 100 shares, each with a $40 basis, and the company declares a two-for-one split. That suddenly makes you the owner of 200 shares. Your original $4,000 investment does not change, however, so your basis in each share drops to $20 ($4,000 ÷ 200). The holding period for the shares you received in the split is the same as for the original shares. If you have owned the shares for more than a year at the time of the split, the new shares immediately qualify for long-term treatment.

When you buy additional shares through a dividend reinvestment plan (see Chapter 4), the basis of those shares is their actual cost to you. If you reinvest $300 in dividends and it buys you 25 shares, for example, your basis in each share would be $12 ($300 ÷ 25). The holding period for the newly purchased shares begins on the date they are purchased.

Controlling the shares you sell. Carefully recording the basis of all your shares pays off when you're confronting the decision of what and when to sell. Say you bought 100 shares of SureThing three years ago for $25 a share. Two years ago you bought 100 more shares, this time for $30 each. One year ago you bought another 100 shares at $35.

Now the stock has climbed to $45 a share and you decide to take some profits. If you just tell your broker to sell 100 shares, you'll find yourself penalized by what's called the FIFO rule. FIFO stands for first in, first out. It assumes that the first shares you purchased, the ones that cost you $25, are the first ones you sell. That would give you a taxable capital gain of $20 per share, or $2,000. In the 28% bracket you'd pay $560 of your profit to Uncle Sam. But if you told your broker to sell the shares you purchased a year ago, you'd sell the ones with a basis of $35. You'd still realize $4,500 on the sale, but your gain would be just $10 a share and your tax bill would be cut in half.

You'll usually want to sell the shares that produce the smallest taxable profit. But sometimes it could pay to sell the shares with the lowest basis—if you have sufficient losses to offset the larger gain, for example, or if you have big investment expenses that can be written off only if they are matched by investment income. The key to controlling the choice is a well-maintained set of records of your cost basis.

Controlling the tax bite on dividends. Dividends you receive from stock you own are usually fully taxable. And, odd as it sounds, sometimes you owe tax on dividends you never see. For instance, dividends invested through a dividend reinvestment plan (See Chapter 4) count as taxable income even though you never lay hands on the money. What's more, if the plan allows you to buy shares at a discount from market value, the discount counts as taxable income, too. It is also added to your cost basis for those shares. Thus the basis of the new shares would be what you actually paid for them plus the amount of the discount.

When companies pay dividends in shares of stock instead of cash, the value of the stock dividends is generally not taxable. Instead, the new shares dilute your basis in the shares. Say you have 100 shares of stock with a basis of $2,500, or $25 a share, and you get a stock dividend of ten shares. The $2,500 basis is then spread over the 110 shares, giving each one a basis of $22.73. The practical effect is that you'll pay tax on the value of the stock dividend when you sell the shares because you report a higher profit due to the reduced basis.

If you have the choice of taking a dividend in stock or in cash, the dividend is taxable in the year you receive it, even if you take the shares. The market value of the shares counts as income, but the basis of your original shares stays the same.

From time to time shareholders receive payments that don't come out of company earnings but are actually a return of part of their original investment. These payments, which will be labeled capital distributions by the company, aren't taxable. But they do reduce your basis in the stock, which will increase your profit or reduce your loss when you sell.

BONDS

Investing in bonds can bring you steady income and, if you're not careful, steady tax headaches. Corporate bonds generally pay interest every six months and it is taxable in the year you receive it. If you buy a bond at face value and hold it to maturity, tax on the interest is all you owe. But as discussed in Chapter 5, you can buy bonds at a premium (more than face value) or at a discount (below face value). Either situation complicates your taxes, particularly when it comes to keeping track of your basis.

Bonds bought between interest payments. The price of bonds sold between semiannual interest dates includes the interest accrued since the last payment date. For the seller, that part of the price is interest income and should be reported as such rather than being counted as part of the price of the bond when determining gain or loss on the sale. For the buyer, the "purchased interest" is not part of the basis. Rather, when you receive your first interest payment on the bond, part of it is considered a nontaxable return of part of your investment rather than taxable interest.

Say you purchase a $10,000, 9% bond midway between semiannual $450 interest payments and that you pay $10,225 for the bond and the $225 of accrued interest. When you receive the first $450 interest payment, half of it is considered return of your investment. (You report the full amount on your tax return, though, then subtract $225 as "accrued interest." If you fail to do so, you'll overpay your tax.) Your basis in the bond is $10,000.

Discounted bonds. When you buy bonds at a discount from face value, the tax rules that apply depend on the type of discount involved and when the bond was issued.

■ *Original issue discount (OID) bonds* are, as the name suggests, issued for less than face value. This basically means part of the interest will be paid when the bond is redeemed for more than its original price rather than in regular payments over the life of the bond. You have to wait for your money, but the IRS doesn't want to wait for its share of it. Each year that you own the bond, you have to report as interest income a portion of the original discount amount. (The method you must use to calculate how much to report depends on when the bond was issued, but each year the issuer should send you a 1099-OID form showing the taxable amount.) Good records are critically important here. The portion of the original-issue discount you report as income each year increases your basis in the bond. If you fail to keep track, you could wind up paying tax on the same income twice—once as original-issue discount interest and later as part of the profit on the bond.

■ *Market-discount bonds* usually sell at a discount because interest rates have risen since they were issued, or because the safety-rating agencies have downgraded the issuing company's rating (See Chapter 5). For bonds issued after July 18, 1984, the difference between what you pay for a market-discount bond and its redemption value is considered to be interest that will accrue between the time you buy the bond and the time it matures. You can wait until you dispose of the bond via sale or redemption to report that interest income, or if you prefer, you can figure how much interest accrues each year and report it annually. If you opt to report a portion of the market discount annually, your basis in the bond increases by the amount reported as interest income. You're probably better off waiting.

■ *Zero-coupon bonds,* as discussed in Chapter 5, pay no interest until maturity. Issuers compensate investors for their patience by issuing zeros at steep discounts from their redemption value. A new 30-year zero with a face value of $10,000 and a yield to maturity of 10%, for example, would sell for $535 today.

Because a zero-coupon bond is really nothing more than the OID idea carried to its extreme, the OID rules apply. Even though you don't see the money, interest is taxed as it accrues so each year you must report and pay tax on the interest your investment is assumed to have earned that year. The bond issuer or your broker should send you a notice showing how much to report.

This "imputed" interest hikes your basis in the bonds and,

again, it's up to you to keep track. Consider this example: You buy zeros for $7,000 that are called (redeemed early by the issuer) three years later for $8,600. During the intervening years, you report $2,000 of imputed interest. That raises your basis to $9,000, so even though the bonds are called for $1,600 more than you originally paid, you have a $400 loss. (On zero-coupon municipal bonds, accruing interest raises your basis even though the imputed interest is not taxable.)

Premium-priced bonds. When you buy a bond for more than its face value, as you might to capture above-market rates, the IRS gives you a choice of how to deal with the premium. You can spread it over the life of the bond, claiming a tax-saving deduction each year. Or you can wait until you sell or redeem the bond to crank the premium into your tax calculations.

(One problem with amortizing the premium is that you have to figure out how much to deduct each year. Exactly how you do that depends on when the bond was issued. Basically, for bonds issued before September 27, 1985, the annual deduction can be determined by dividing the premium by the number of years to maturity. A more complicated method applies to more recently issued bonds. You'll probably need an accountant's help to figure it out.)

If you do amortize the premium, your basis in the bond decreases by the amount of the deductions you claim. (If you buy a tax-exempt bond at a premium, amortizing the premium doesn't generate any tax deductions but it does reduce your basis.)

A simpler alternative to amortizing the premium is to wait until you sell or redeem the bond and report the premium all at once. If you redeem the bond at face value, you can claim a capital loss equal to the size of the premium.

U.S. government bonds. When you invest in U.S. government obligations, you get a break compared with corporate bonds: The interest on Treasury bills, notes and bonds is exempt from state and local income taxes. You have to take this benefit into account when comparing yields.

Assume you live in a state with an 8% state tax rate and can choose between investing $10,000 in a corporate bond yielding 10% or a $10,000 Treasury bond yielding the same. Either investment will generate $1,000 of interest annually and will cost you $280 in federal taxes if you are in the 28% bracket. On the T-bond, that's all you'd have to pay. With the corporate bond, however, your state would want its 8%, or $80. Because the state tax is deductible on your federal return, you get back 28% of that $80, so the actual extra cost would be $57.60. Still, the after-tax yield of the Treasury bond works out to 7.2%, compared with 6.62% on the corporate bond.

Treasury bills, which are issued with 13-week, 26-week and 52-week maturities, offer the chance to defer income from one year to the next. The bills are issued at a discount, with the interest paid when they are redeemed at face value. The tax isn't due until the year the bill matures. If you sell a T-bill before maturity, part of the sales price is accrued interest and must be reported as interest income rather than being counted in the capital gain or loss.

The interest on Treasury notes and bonds, which is paid every six months, is taxable in the year you receive it. When T-bonds and notes are purchased at a market discount or premium price, the same basic rules apply as for corporate bonds.

Ginnie Maes. If you invest in bonds guaranteed by the Government National Mortgage Association (GNMA), part of each payment you receive will be totally tax-free. As discussed in Chapter 10, Ginnie Maes represent an investment in a pool of home mortgages. As homeowners make their monthly payments, you get your share of the interest and principal. The principal portion is a return of your investment and therefore tax-free. You should get a statement showing a breakdown between taxable interest and nontaxable return of principal.

Municipal bonds. Municipal bonds are discussed in detail in Chapter 5. These are the investments that enjoy the gentlest of all federal tax rates: 0%. Although you must report municipal bond interest to the IRS each year, it is almost never taxed. (One exception allows the IRS to tax interest from "private-activity" bonds owned by a taxpayer subject to the alternative minimum tax.)

Although the interest on these bonds is tax-free, the IRS wants its cut if you sell municipal bonds for a profit. Capital gains are fully taxable. By the same token, if you sell a municipal bond for less than your basis, the loss is deductible.

Cost basis is usually figured the same way as with taxable bonds. However, if you buy a tax-exempt bond at a premium, you must amortize the premium over the period you own the bond. This gradually shrinks your basis in the bond but you can't deduct the amortized amount, as you can with taxable bonds. If you buy a bond originally issued at a discount—including a zero-coupon municipal—you increase your basis each year by the amount of the interest accruing on the bond, but you don't have to report that amount as income. When you buy a municipal bond at a market discount, however, different rules apply. Your basis doesn't change. When you redeem the bond at face value, the difference between your purchase price and the face value is a taxable capital gain.

Bond Swaps

Bond swapping is a maneuver that may allow bond investors to generate a tax loss without affecting the income stream from their fixed-income investments. What's involved is selling bonds that have fallen in value—due to rising market interest rates—and reinvesting the proceeds in other bonds. Consider this example:

Assume you own $100,000 worth of AA-rated bonds with a 7% coupon yield, a maturity date in 2016, and a current market value of $84,750. You bought the bonds at par, so selling at the current price would produce a $15,250 capital loss. Suppose, too, that you can buy $100,000 face value of AAA-rated bonds with a 7% coupon and a 2015 maturity, for $83,612.

Consider the result if you sell one set of bonds and buy the other: Since they have the same par value and coupon rate, your annual income remains the same. Your bond rating increases from AA to AAA. You pull $1,138 out of the investment—the difference between what you got for the old bonds and what you paid for the new ones. And you can claim a $15,250 tax loss. If it offsets gains that otherwise would have been taxed at 28%, you save $4,270.

If you have bonds that show a paper loss, your broker should be able to help you find attractive candidates for swapping that won't run afoul of the wash-sale rule discussed earlier in this chapter.

TAXES AND YOUR MUTUAL FUNDS

The professional management you get when you invest in mutual funds handles some of the tax work for you. The fund worries about the fluctuating basis of the stocks or bonds it owns. That spares you the hassle of amortizing bond premiums, for example, or adjusting your basis to account for stock splits. But funds don't spare you all the tax-related work.

Except for money-market funds, the price of mutual fund shares fluctuates just like the price of individual stocks and bonds. When you redeem shares, you need to know your tax basis in order to calculate your taxable gain or loss. You also need to know how long you've owned the shares to know whether you have long- or short-term gains or losses.

To protect yourself from overpaying your taxes on fund income, set up a separate file for each fund you own and faithfully keep it up to date.

Your basis in shares begins as what you pay for them. When you invest in a no-load fund, your basis is the share's net asset value on the day you buy. If you buy into a load fund, include the commission in your basis.

Undistributed capital gains. From time to time, funds declare capital gains but retain the profits and pay tax on them rather than distributing the profit to shareholders. Such undistributed capital gains increase your basis in the shares. Even though you didn't get a dime, you have to report the gain as income. You also get to claim a credit for the amount of tax paid by the fund on your behalf. Finally, you raise your basis in the shares by the difference between the undistributed gain and the credit you claim. If all this sounds like a lot of trouble for nothing, take comfort in the fact that claiming the credit cuts your tax bill now and raising the basis reduces your tax bill when you sell.

Nontaxable distributions. Funds occasionally make a payment that doesn't come out of earnings or profits. Such "return of capital" distributions are sometimes called tax-free dividends or nontaxable distributions, but they do reduce your basis in the shares, thus increasing the gain or diminishing the loss when you sell.

Reinvested dividends. Mutual fund investments demand especially careful attention because you will likely be buying shares at different times and at different prices. If you have your dividends reinvested in additional shares, you'll be buying new shares monthly or however often the fund distributes income. Your basis in the new shares is their cost at the time of purchase. Thus, if $72.75 in dividends buys you 5.89 shares, for example, the basis of each share is $12.35 ($72.75 ÷ 5.89).

It's important to keep careful track of all this. If you don't, here's the potential threat: Say you invest $5,000 in a fund and each year have $500 of dividends reinvested in additional shares. After five years, you redeem all your shares for $10,000. What's your gain? An investor who simply compared the redemption amount to the original investment would pay twice as much tax as necessary. Because the $2,500 of reinvested dividends raised your basis by that amount, the gain is just $2,500, not $5,000.

Partial sales. Good record-keeping habits really pay off when you sell only part of your fund holdings. In deciding which shares to sell, you can pick the ones that will produce the best tax result.

Redeeming shares with the highest basis will produce the lowest taxable gain. But since your shares are pooled in a single account by the mutual fund, who knows which ones got sold? You do, if you've kept good records. If you direct the fund to sell specific shares, the basis of those shares determines the tax consequences of the sale. (Keep records of your sale order, including a copy of a letter to the fund identifying the shares to be sold by the date of purchase and price paid, and a copy of the fund's confirmation of the sale. If you order the sale by phone, keep a copy of a letter to the fund confirming your instructions.)

If you just tell the fund to sell a certain number of shares without specifying which ones, the FIFO rule described earlier will govern which ones those are. FIFO assumes that the first shares you bought are the first ones sold. If the shares have been appreciating gradually, that insures that those with the lowest basis are assumed to be sold—and that leaves you with the highest taxable profit.

If you prefer, you can use the *average basis* method for figuring gain or loss on the sale of your shares. There are actually two average basis methods: single- and double-category. With the former, you find the total basis of all the shares you own of a fund, then divide it by the number of shares and arrive at the average basis. The double-category method is similar, but you divide the shares according to whether you have owned them long-term (more than one year) or short-term (one year or less). To use the short-term average basis, you must have written confirmation that you advised the fund at the time of the trade that you were redeeming shares from the short-term group. Otherwise you use the long-term average basis.

The specific-identification method gives you the most flexibility but if you normally use the FIFO method, you should check whether the average-basis method can work to your benefit. Note, however, that once you start using it, you must apply it to all funds run by the same mutual fund family.

Switching funds. Switching from one fund to another, even within the same family, creates what the tax people like to call a "taxable event." To switch, you must sell the shares in the fund you're leaving. Unless you're moving out of a money-market fund, the switch is likely to produce a taxable capital gain or a deductible loss.

Accounting for annual fund income. Knowing how fund income is treated by the IRS can save you both trouble and money.

■ Income from money-market and taxable bond funds is considered dividend income for tax purposes, even though the source of the income is interest. If you accidently report such income as interest, you'll probably hear from the IRS, which has been told by the fund that it paid you dividends.

■ Interest from a tax-free municipal bond fund escapes federal income tax. It may be taxed by your state, however, although interest from bonds issued within your state may be state-tax exempt, too. The fund statement should show what percentage of the income you received was attributed to homegrown issues. That statement should also alert you if the fund owned any so-called private-activity bonds that might be subject to the alternative minimum tax.

■ You may get some state tax savings on income from a fund that invests solely or predominately in U.S. government securities. That interest would be free of state tax if you owned the obligations directly, and most states allow it to retain its tax-free status when it comes from a fund. Check with your state tax department.

■ Ordinary dividends are taxable in the year paid, whether you take them in cash or have them reinvested in new shares. Knowing when a stock fund declares dividends, its ex-dividend date, is important. When the dividend is declared, the share value drops by about the same amount. If you invest in the fund just before the ex-dividend date, the dividend you get amounts to a refund of part of your purchase price. But you'll also owe taxes on it. Better to buy *after* the ex-dividend date. The price of the shares will be lower by the amount of the dividend, and you won't owe taxes on the dividend.

■ Capital-gains distributions—your share of profits from portfolio trades during the year—are considered long-term gains regardless of how long you have owned the fund. Investors in tax-free bond funds are sometimes confused by capital-gains distributions. Such payouts are taxable because they represent your share of the profits realized when bonds within the portfolio were sold.

■ If you own shares in a fund holding foreign securities, you may be in line for a foreign tax credit. Your year-end statement from the fund will show the amount of foreign tax paid on your behalf. You must include that amount in your taxable income for the year, but you can either write it off as an itemized deduction or claim a foreign tax credit.

LIFE INSURANCE AND ANNUITIES

Cash-value life insurance, including whole-life and universal-life policies, is often promoted more as an investment than as insurance. Sometimes a very substantial part of the premiums are used by the company to pay not for insurance but for investments that build cash value. Policy owners may be able to invest their cash value in a choice of stock and bond mutual funds and other investments. The key tax break is that earnings within the policy are allowed to grow tax-free. Taxes aren't due until you cash in the policy, and you owe taxes only on the amount by which the cash value exceeds your premiums.

The more insurance companies promote their products as tax shelters, the more Congress cracks down on the tax benefits. Still, carefully structured policies can deliver important tax benefits.

Annuities are another insurance product sporting tax advantages. When you invest in an annuity, the contract serves as an

---

COMBINING ROLLOVER ACCOUNTS

Q: *Later this year, my company's pension plan and 401(k) plan will be terminated. Because I will not yet be 59½, I plan to roll the funds over into an IRA. Can I put both payouts into a single IRA?*

A: Yes, you can combine your payouts and roll them over into a single IRA, as long as all of your contributions were made from pretax earnings. If you made any after-tax contributions, they cannot be rolled over. But because you've already paid taxes on them, you can invest or spend that amount however you like. Be sure to roll the distribution over within 60 days of receiving it.

---

impenetrable wrapper that keeps the tax collector's hands off your earnings. No tax is due until you withdraw your funds, presumably in retirement. In exchange for that tax break, you have to agree to leave your money invested until you reach age 59½. Pull the money out early and the earnings are not only taxed but also subject to a 10% penalty. The penalty does not apply to taxpayers who are disabled, nor to any payment that is part of a series of periodic payments based on your life expectancy.

The penalty is designed to dissuade investors from trying to use annuities as short-term tax shelters. If you are at least 59½, though, you don't have to worry about the tax penalty. Note, though, that insurance companies generally apply stiff penalties of their own if annuity buyers withdraw funds during the early years of a contract. See Chapter 14 for more on annuities.

DEDUCTIBLE INVESTMENT EXPENSES

If you borrow money to make an investment, the interest on the loan is usually deductible if the purpose of the investment is to generate taxable income. But if you borrow in order to invest in tax-free bonds, the interest is not deductible. Nor do you get the deduction if you borrow to buy a single-premium life insurance policy or an annuity. The government doesn't want to subsidize loans used to purchase tax shelters. Interest on money borrowed to invest in a passive investment activity, such as a real estate limited partnership, is an expense of the passive activity and therefore deductible only to the extent of passive income (See Chapter 9).

The deduction for investment interest you pay is limited to the amount of investment income you report. If your investment income for the year is $5,000, your investment interest deduction cannot exceed that amount. For this test, investment income includes interest, dividends and capital gains. Any interest you are unable to deduct because of the cap can be carried forward to future years and deducted when you have sufficient investment income.

Other expenses of investing that may be tax deductible in whole or in part include the following.

■ Rental fees for a safe-deposit box used to store taxable securities.

■ Investment counselor or management fees.

■ Subscriptions to investment-advisory newsletters.

■ Cost of books (including this one) and magazines purchased for investment advice.

■ State and local transfer taxes on the sale of securities.

■ Fees paid to a broker or other agent to collect bond interest or stock dividends. (Commissions paid to brokers when you purchase stock aren't deductible. They are added to the basis of the shares.)

■ Cost of travel to see your broker to discuss investments. If you drive your own car, you can deduct the actual cost or the IRS standard rate, which was 27½ cents per mile for 1991 and changes from time to time. In either case, you can add in what you pay for parking or tolls.

■ Computer expenses. If you use a home computer to investigate investments and track your portfolio, you may be able to depreciate part of the computer's cost. If you can show that your computer is used 40% for investment purposes, for example, 40% of the cost could be depreciated as an investment expense. The cost of investment software and of using a computer database for investment purposes can also qualify as a deductible expense.

Although all of the above expenses are deductible, it's not easy to get a tax benefit from any of them. All have been branded as "miscellaneous" expenses, which means you can deduct them only to the extent that all of your miscellaneous expenses exceed 2% of your adjusted gross income (that is, your gross income minus "adjustments," such as IRA contributions, but before itemized deductions). If your AGI is $50,000, for example, the first $1,000 of your miscellaneous expenses don't count.

USEFUL NUMBERS EVERY INVESTOR CAN USE

$\mathbf{I}$NVESTING IS A QUEST to make dollars grow, and an important tool for achieving such a goal is the ability to anticipate what will happen to those dollars as the years go by, given different assumptions about how much you can invest and on what schedule. On the pages that follow, you'll find a collection of tables and formulas you can use to do just that.

HOW REGULAR INVESTMENTS WILL GROW

The table on page 346 shows how a specific amount of money invested on a monthly schedule at various rates of return will grow as the years pass. The table uses $10 as the sum because multiples of $10 convert easily to actual amounts you might put aside. For instance, say you can invest $150 a month. How much would you have after ten years if your investment earned an average annual return of 12%? The intersection of 10 years and 12% on the table shows that $10 would grow to $2,323. You'll be investing 15 times $10, so you multiply the result by 15. Answer: You'd have $34,845.

The table can also be used to determine how much you will need to invest in order to have a specific amount on hand at some future date. For example, suppose you want to accumulate $50,000 by the time your daughter starts college in 15 years. Assuming you could earn 14% on your investments, how much should you be socking into your investment account? Find the place in the table where 15 years intersects with 14%. Divide that number—$6,129—into your goal of $50,000. That tells you that your goal is 8.16 times the total generated by $10 monthly deposits, meaning you'll have to set aside $81.60 each month to reach your goal on time, assuming a 14% return.

YEAR	5%	6%	7%	8%	9%	10%	11%	12%	13%	14%	15%
1	$123	$124	$125	$125	$126	$127	$127	$128	$129	$130	$130
2	253	256	258	261	264	267	270	272	275	278	281
3	389	395	402	408	415	421	428	435	442	449	457
4	532	544	555	567	580	592	605	618	632	646	660
5	683	701	720	740	760	781	802	825	848	872	897
6	841	868	897	926	957	989	1,023	1,058	1,094	1,132	1,171
7	1,008	1,046	1,086	1,129	1,173	1,220	1,268	1,320	1,374	1,430	1,490
8	1,182	1,234	1,289	1,348	1,409	1,474	1,543	1,615	1,692	1,773	1,859
9	1,366	1,435	1,507	1,585	1,667	1,755	1,849	1,948	2,054	2,168	2,288
10	1,559	1,647	1,741	1,842	1,950	2,066	2,190	2,323	2,467	2,621	2,787
15	2,684	2,923	3,188	3,483	3,812	4,179	4,589	5,046	5,557	6,129	6,769
20	4,128	4,644	5,240	5,929	6,729	7,657	8,736	9,991	11,455	13,163	15,160
25	5,980	6,965	8,148	9,574	11,295	13,379	15,906	18,976	22,714	27,273	32,841
30	8,357	10,095	12,271	15,003	18,445	22,793	28,302	35,299	44,206	55,571	70,098

HOW COMPOUNDING AFFECTS YOUR RETURN

When you're shopping around for a certificate of deposit or a similar savings instrument, comparing "nominal" (stated) rates of return is a waste of time. What you need to know is the real yield, usually called the effective yield, which takes into account the effects of compounding.

The difference between the nominal yield and the effective yield depends on the frequency of compounding, as shown in the table below. For example, an 8% nominal interest rate produces an 8.45% effective yield if interest is compounded

Nominal annual percentage rate	EFFECTIVE YIELD if compounded quarterly	if compounded daily
5.00%	5.0945%	5.1997%
5.50	5.6145	5.7343
6.00	6.1364	6.2716
6.50	6.6602	6.8116
7.00	7.1859	7.3543
7.50	7.7136	7.8998
8.00	8.2432	8.4481
8.50	8.7748	8.9992
9.00	9.3083	9.5530
9.50	9.8438	10.1096
10.00	10.3813	10.6691
10.50	10.9207	11.2314
11.00	11.4621	11.7966
11.50	12.0055	12.3646
12.00	12.5509	12.9355

daily, but only 8.24% if interest is compounded quarterly. For an account containing $5,000 the difference amounts to only about $10 per year, but over a span of several years, it can have a substantial impact.

Warning: How often your compounded return is credited to your account has an effect on your yield, too. For example, if the interest isn't credited to your daily compounded account until the end of the quarter and you withdraw $1,000 five days before the quarter ends, you usually lose all of the interest earned on that amount up to that point. The ideal account is one that pays the highest rate, compounds interest daily (or "continuously," a formula that yields a little more) and credits interest daily.

HOW MUCH MONEY YOU'LL NEED

An important key to determining how much you'll have to accumulate for a goal such as retirement is knowledge of how long the money will last when you start drawing it down for living expenses or some other purpose. The table on the next page lets you do just that.

Your nest egg won't stop earning money when you start to deplete it, so the first step is to estimate how much you think you can earn. In retirement, you'll probably pull back a bit (but not completely) from the kinds of investments that can produce handsome returns over the long run but may be a bit risky for your current circumstances. Thus it's best to assume a more modest rate of return than you have reason to expect during the wealth-accumulation phase of your life. Here's how to use the table:

Find the number of years you plan to draw on your savings in the left-hand column and choose an estimated annual rate of return from the row across the top. The point at which the two figures intersect is the amount you'll need to draw $100 a month for the number of years selected. (At the end of the period, the $100 will be exhausted.) Divide your actual nest egg by the amount shown there, then multiply it by 100 to see how much you'll be able to draw per month before you deplete your savings.

For example, assume you've accumulated $200,000 and you plan to draw it down over a 25-year period. How much can you take out each month? Assume you can earn 9% on the money. Where the 25-year column intersects with the 9% column, you see $11,916. That would yield you $100 a month. Dividing $11,916 into $200,000 gives you a multiplier of 16.78. Because your fund is 16.78 times larger than $100, you can draw out $1,678 a month for 25 years before your nest egg is gone.

The table can also be used to figure things the other way around: to calculate how much capital you'd need to yield $100 a month for various periods. For example, say you want to be able to have $1,000 a month for 20 years and you think that you can earn 9% on the money during the draw-down phase. The 9% and 20-year columns intersect at $11,114. That means you'd need ten times that amount, or $111,140, to draw $1,000 a month for 20 years.

YEAR	5%	6%	7%	8%	9%	10%	11%	12%	13%	14%	15%
5	$5,299	$5,173	$5,050	$4,932	$4,817	4,706	$4,559	$4,496	$4,395	$4,298	$4,203
10	9,428	9,007	8,613	8,242	7,894	7,567	7,260	6,970	6,697	6,441	6,198
15	12,646	11,850	11,125	10,464	9,860	9,306	8,798	8,332	7,904	7,509	7,145
20	15,153	13,958	12,898	11,955	11,114	10,362	9,688	9,082	8,536	8,042	7,594
25	17,106	15,521	14,149	12,956	11,916	11,005	10,203	9,495	8,867	8,307	7,807
30	18,628	16,679	15,030	13,628	12,428	11,395	10,501	9,722	9,040	8,440	7,909

HOW A LUMP SUM WILL GROW

The table on the following page is useful for anticipating how money you've already accumulated will grow over various lengths of time at various rates of return, compounded annually. Simply read down the left-hand column to the number of years and across the top for the assumed rate of return, and multiply the starting amount by the factor that's shown at the intersection of the two columns. For example, say you have $4,000 in a mutual fund that you expect to pay 15% per year. How much will you have after 10 years? Where the 15% and 10-year columns intersect, the factor is 4.05. Multiplying that by $4,000 gives you $16,200.

YEAR	5%	6%	7%	8%	9%	10%	11%	12%	13%	14%	15%
1	1.05	1.06	1.07	1.08	1.09	1.10	1.11	1.12	1.13	1.14	1.15
2	1.10	1.12	1.14	1.17	1.19	1.21	1.23	1.25	1.28	1.30	1.32
3	1.16	1.19	1.22	1.26	1.29	1.33	1.37	1.40	1.44	1.48	1.52
4	1.22	1.26	1.31	1.36	1.41	1.46	1.52	1.57	1.63	1.69	1.75
5	1.28	1.34	1.40	1.47	1.54	1.61	1.69	1.76	1.84	1.93	2.01
6	1.34	1.42	1.50	1.59	1.68	1.77	1.87	1.97	2.08	2.19	2.31
7	1.41	1.50	1.61	1.71	1.83	1.95	2.08	2.21	2.35	2.50	2.66
8	1.48	1.59	1.72	1.85	1.99	2.14	2.30	2.48	2.66	2.85	3.06
9	1.55	1.69	1.84	2.00	2.17	2.36	2.56	2.77	3.00	3.25	3.52
10	1.63	1.79	1.97	2.16	2.37	2.59	2.84	3.11	3.39	3.71	4.05
15	2.08	2.40	2.76	3.17	3.64	4.18	4.78	5.4	6.25	7.14	8.14
20	2.65	3.21	3.87	4.66	5.60	6.73	8.06	9.65	11.52	13.74	16.37
25	3.39	4.29	5.43	6.85	8.62	10.83	13.59	17.00	21.23	26.46	32.92
30	4.32	5.74	7.61	10.06	13.27	17.45	22.89	29.96	39.12	50.95	66.21

HOW TO ACCOUNT FOR INFLATION

The same kind of compounding has a negative effect as well. To see how inflation could erode your investment results, choose a number of years in the future from the left-hand column in the table below and follow that row across to where it intersects with a rate of inflation listed across the top. Multiply your anticipated nest egg by the number to see how much you'll need to have the equivalent amount in the future. For instance, assuming 4% inflation (a reasonable assumption for the next decade or so), a $10,000 nest egg today would have to be $14,800 to have the equivalent purchasing power 10 years from today.

YEAR	3%	4%	5%	6%	7%	8%	9%	10%	11%	12%	13%
5	1.16	1.22	1.28	1.34	1.40	1.47	1.54	1.61	1.69	1.76	1.84
10	1.34	1.48	1.63	1.79	1.97	2.16	2.37	2.59	2.84	3.11	3.39
15	1.56	1.80	2.08	2.40	2.76	3.17	3.64	4.18	4.78	5.47	6.25
20	1.81	2.19	2.65	3.21	3.87	4.66	5.60	6.73	8.06	9.65	11.52
25	2.09	2.67	3.39	4.29	5.43	6.85	8.62	10.82	13.59	17.00	21.23
30	2.43	3.24	4.32	5.74	7.61	10.06	13.27	17.45	22.89	29.96	39.12

TAX-FREE vs. TAXABLE YIELDS

Municipal bonds and other investments that pay tax-free interest make sense for you only if their yields top what you could earn in after-tax interest from taxable investments. The table on the following page shows the taxable-equivalent yields of tax-exempt investments for various brackets. (The income levels that fall into each bracket are those in effect for 1991. Because they are indexed to inflation, the levels will rise a little each year.)

Here's how to use the table. Say you're in the 28% bracket

and are considering investing in a municipal bond paying 6% interest. Find the column where your tax bracket and the tax-free yield intersect. It shows a taxable-equivalent yield of 8.33%. If you can find a taxable yield higher than that, then you're better off taking it and paying the taxes. Remember that if you also escape state income taxes, your taxable equivalent yield would be higher.

TAX FREE VS. TAXABLE YIELDS

Taxable Income	Tax Bracket	TAX-FREE YIELD						
		4%	5%	6%	7%	8%	9%	10%
Single Return		TAXABLE-EQUIVALENT YIELD						
Up to $20,350	15	4.71	5.88	7.06	8.24	9.41	10.59	11.76
$20,350-$49,300	28	5.56	6.94	8.33	9.72	11.11	12.50	13.89
Over $49,300	31	5.80	7.25	8.70	10.14	11.59	13.04	14.49
Joint Return		TAXABLE-EQUIVALENT YIELD						
Up to $34,000	15	4.71	5.88	7.06	8.24	9.41	10.59	11.76
$34,000-$82,150	28	5.56	6.94	8.33	9.72	11.11	12.50	13.89
Over $82,150	31	5.80	7.25	8.70	10.14	11.59	13.04	14.49

If the tax-free yield falls in between the numbers on the table, you can get a pretty good idea of the taxable equivalent by estimating. For instance, 6.5% falls halfway between 6% and 7%, so in the 28% bracket, the taxable equivalent would be halfway between 8.33 and 9.72, or about 9.03%.

If you prefer a more precise answer, use the formula from Chapter 5:

$$\frac{\text{tax-free rate}}{1 - \text{federal tax bracket}} = \text{taxable-equivalent yield}$$

HOW TO FIGURE BOND YIELDS

Enough bond-yield tables have been published over the years to fill your living room, each volume the size of an unabridged dictionary. But in the age of handheld calculators, it's probably faster to apply the simple formulas for figuring yields yourself than to heft one of those weighty tomes.

To calculate the current yield of a bond, divide the annual interest payment of the bond by its purchase price and multiply the result by 100.

$$\text{Current yield} = \frac{\text{Annual interest payment}}{\text{Purchase price}} \times 100$$

Example: Say you pay $920 for a $1,000 bond issued to pay 9%. What's you current yield?

$$\text{Current yield} = \frac{90}{920} = .0978 \times 100 = 9.78\%$$

The yield to maturity, which takes into account the fact that you'll receive the full face value of a discounted bond at maturity even though you paid less than full value at purchase,

$$\text{Yield to maturity} = \frac{\text{Annual interest payment} + \text{annualized discount}}{\text{Average of face value and current price}}$$

is more complicated. The shorthand formula produces only an approximate answer, but when you're comparing alternatives, this will lead you in the right direction (See Chapter 5).

Example: You buy a $1,000 bond with six years to go until maturity. Its stated interest rate is 7% and it costs you $880. Thus, your discount is $120, or $20 per year on an annualized basis.

$$\text{Yield to maturity} = \frac{\dfrac{70 + 20}{1,000 + 880}}{2} = \frac{90}{940} \times 100 = 9.6\%$$

HISTORIC MARKET HIGHS AND LOWS

In addition to patience, an investor needs perspective. Here's some perspective on important indicators of where the market is and where it might be going.

	Historic high	Historic low
One-year total return of S&P 500	37.16% (1975)	-26.39% (1974)
Price-earnings ratio of S&P 500	23.50 (1961)	3.57 (1946)
Average yield, long-term corporate bonds	16.62% (1981)	2.82% (1950)
Average yield, municipal bonds	13.14% (1982)	1.22% (1946)
Yield of U.S. savings bonds	11.09% (1983)	2.90% (1941)

100 INVESTMENT TERMS YOU SHOULD KNOW

Account executive. The title given by some brokerage firms to their stockbrokers. Other variations on the title include *registered representative,* financial counselor and financial consultant.

Accrued interest. Interest that is due but hasn't yet been paid. It most often comes into play when you buy bonds in the *secondary market.* Bonds usually pay interest every six months, but it is earned (accrued) by bondholders every month. If you buy a bond halfway between interest payment dates, you must pay the seller for the three months' interest accrued but not yet received. You get the money back three months later when you receive the interest payment for the entire six-month period.

Alpha. A mathematical measure of price volatility that attempts to isolate the price movements of a stock from those of the market. A stock with a high alpha is expected to perform well regardless of what happens to the market as a whole. (See also *beta.*)

American Depository Receipt. Certificates traded on U.S. stock

exchanges or *over the counter,* representing ownership of a specific number of shares of a foreign stock.

Annuity. A series of regular payments, usually from an insurance company, guaranteed to continue for a specific time, usually the annuitant's lifetime, in exchange for a single payment or series of payments to the company. With a deferred annuity, payments begin sometime in the future. With an immediate annuity, payments begin right away. A fixed annuity pays a fixed income stream for the life of the contract. With a variable annuity, the payments may change according to the relative investment success of the insurance company.

Arbitrage. An attempt to profit from momentary price differences that can develop when a security or commodity is traded on two different exchanges. To take advantage of such differences, an arbitrageur would buy in the market where the price is lower and simultaneously sell in the market where the price is higher.

At-the-market. When you buy or sell a security "at-the-market," the broker will execute your trade at the next available price.

Back-end load. A fee charged by mutual funds to investors who sell their shares before owning them for a specified time.

Back office. The support operations of a brokerage firm that don't deal directly with customers. "Back office problems" usually refers to slow paperwork or other bottlenecks in the execution of customers' orders.

Bearer bond. Also called a coupon bond, it is not registered in anyone's name. Rather, whoever holds the bond (the "bearer") is entitled to collect interest payments merely by cutting off and

mailing in the attached coupons at the proper time. Bearer bonds are no longer being issued.

Bearish. A bear thinks the market is going to go down. This makes bearish the opposite of *bullish*.

Beta. A measure of price volatility that relates the stock or mutual fund to the market as a whole. A stock or fund with a beta higher than 1 is expected to move up or down more than the market. A beta below 1 indicates a stock or fund that usually jumps up and down less than the market.

Bid/asked. Bid is the price a buyer is willing to pay; asked is the price the seller will take. The difference, known as the *spread,* is the broker's share of the transaction.

Blue chips. There is no set definition of a blue-chip stock, but most would agree it has at least three characteristics: It is issued by a well-known, respected company, has a good record of earnings and dividend payments, and is widely held by investors.

Boiler room. A blanket term used to describe the place of origin of high-pressure telephone sales techniques, usually involving *cold calls* to unsuspecting customers who would be better off without whatever is being offered to them.

Bond. An interest-bearing security that obligates the issuer to pay a specified amount of interest for a specified time, usually several years, and then repay the bondholder the face amount of the bond. Bonds issued by corporations are backed by corporate assets; in case of default, the bondholders have a legal claim on those assets. Bonds issued by government agencies may or may not be collateralized. Interest from corporate bonds is taxable; interest from municipal bonds, which are issued by state and local governments, is free of federal income taxes and, usually, income taxes of the issuing jurisdiction. Interest from Treasury bonds, issued by the federal government, is free of state and local income taxes but subject to federal taxes.

Bond rating. A judgment about the ability of the bond issuer to fulfill its obligation to pay interest and repay the principal when due. The best-known bond-rating companies are Standard & Poor's and Moody's. Their rating systems, although slightly different, both use a letter-grade system, with triple-A being the highest rating and C or D being the lowest.

Book value. For investing purposes, this is the net asset value of a company, determined by subtracting its liabilities from its assets. Dividing the result by the number of shares of common stock issued by the company yields the book value per share, which can be used as a relative gauge of the stock's value.

Brokered CD. A large-denomination *certificate of deposit* sold by a bank to a brokerage, which slices it up into smaller pieces and sells the pieces to its customers.

Bullish. A bull is someone who thinks the market is going to go up, which makes bullish the opposite of *bearish*.

Call. See *Options*.

Capital gain or loss. The difference between the price at which you buy an investment and the price at which you sell it. Adding the capital gain or loss to the income received from the investment yields the *total return*.

Certificate of deposit. Usually called a CD, a certificate of deposit is a short- to medium-term instrument (one month to five years) that is issued by a bank or savings and loan association to pay interest at a rate higher than that paid by a passbook account. CD rates move up and down with general market interest rates. There is usually a penalty for early withdrawal.

Charting. Another name for *technical analysis*.

Churning. Excessive buying and selling in a customer's account undertaken to generate commissions for the broker.

Closed-end investment company. Also called a closed-end fund, it is a pooled investment fund that issues a set number of shares and then no more. When the initial offering of shares is sold out, the closed-end fund trades on the *secondary market* at a price determined by investor supply and demand. For contrast, see the definition of *mutual fund*.

Cold calling. The practice of brokers making unsolicited calls to people they don't know in an attempt to drum up business.

Commercial paper. Short-term IOUs issued by corporations without collateral. They are bought in large quantities by *money-market funds*.

Common stock. A share of ownership in a corporation, which entitles its owner to all the risks and rewards that go with it. In case of bankruptcy, common stockholders' claims on company assets are inferior to those of bondholders. For contrast, see *preferred stock*.

Contrarian. An investor who thinks and acts in opposition to the conventional wisdom. When the majority of investors are bearish, a contrarian is bullish, and vice versa.

Convertible bond. A bond that is exchangeable for a predetermined number of shares of common stock in the same company. The appeal of a convertible is that it gives you a chance to cash in if the stock price of the company soars. Some *preferred* *stock* is also convertible to common stock.

Debenture. A corporate IOU that is not backed by the company's assets and is therefore somewhat riskier than a *bond*.

Discount broker. A cut-rate firm that executes orders but provides little if anything in the way of research or other investment aids.

Discretionary account. A brokerage account in which the customer has given the broker the authority to buy and sell securities at his or her discretion—that is, without checking with the customer first.

Dividend. A share of company earnings paid out to stockholders. Dividends are declared by the board of directors and paid quarterly. Most are paid as cash, but they are sometimes paid in the form of additional shares of stock.

Dividend reinvestment plan. Also called DRIPs, these are programs under which the company automatically reinvests a shareholder's cash dividends in additional shares of common stock, often with no brokerage charge to the shareholder.

Dollar-cost averaging. A program of investing a set amount on a regular schedule regardless of the price of the shares at the time. In the long run, dollar-cost averaging results in your buying more shares at low prices than you do at high prices.

Dow Theory. A belief that a major trend in the stock market isn't signaled by one index alone, but must be confirmed by two—specifically, a new high or low must be recorded by both the Dow Jones industrial average and the Dow Jones transportation average before it can safely be declared that the market is headed in one direction or the other.

Due diligence. The work performed by a broker or other

representative in order to investigate and understand an investment thoroughly before recommending it to a customer.

Earnings per share. A company's profits after taxes, bond interest and preferred stock payments have been subtracted, divided by the number of shares of common stock outstanding.

Ex-dividend. The period between the declaration of a dividend by a company or a mutual fund and the actual payment of the dividend. On the ex-dividend date, the price of the stock or fund will fall by the amount of the dividend, so new investors don't get the benefit of it. Companies and funds that have "gone ex-dividend" are marked by an X in the newspaper listings.

Fannie Mae. The acronym for the Federal National Mortgage Association, which buys mortgages on the *secondary market,* repackages them and sells off pieces to investors. The effect is to infuse the mortgage markets with fresh money.

Fixed-income investment. A catch-all description for investments in bonds, certificates of deposit and other debt-based instruments that pay a fixed amount of interest.

401(k) plan. An employer-sponsored retirement plan that permits employees to divert part of their pay into the plan and avoid current taxes on that income. Money directed to the plan may be partially matched by the employer, and investment earnings within the plan accumulate tax-free until they are withdrawn. The 401(k) is named for the section of the federal tax code that authorizes it.

403(b) plan. Similar to *401(k) plans,* but set up for public employees and employees of nonprofit organizations.

Freddie Mac. The acronym for the Federal Home Loan Mortgage Corporation, which operates similarly to *Fannie Mae.*

Front-end load. The sales commission charged at the time of purchase of a mutual fund, insurance policy or other product.

Full-service broker. A brokerage firm that maintains a research department and other services designed to supply its individual and institutional customers with investment advice.

Fundamental analysis. Study of the balance sheet, earnings history, management, product lines and other elements of a company in an attempt to discern reasonable expectations for the price of its stock. For contrast, see *Technical analysis.*

Futures contract. An agreement to buy or sell a certain amount of a commodity (such as wheat, soybeans or gold) or a financial instrument (such as Treasury bills or deutsche marks) at a stipulated price in a specified future month, which may be as much as nine months away. As the actual price moves closer to or further away from the contract price, the price of the contract fluctuates up and down, thus creating profits and losses for their holders, who may never actually take or make delivery of the underlying commodity.

Ginnie Mae. The acronym for the Government National Mortgage Association, which buys up mortgages in the *secondary market* and sells them to investors via securities known as pass-through certificates.

Good-til-canceled order. An order to buy or sell a security at a specified price, which stays in effect until it is executed by the broker because that price was reached, or until it is canceled by the customer.

Individual retirement account. A tax-sheltered account ideal for retirement investing because it permits investment earnings to accumulate untaxed until they are withdrawn. The contribution limit is $2,000 per year, and penalties usually apply for withdrawals before age 59½. Taxpayers whose income is below certain levels can deduct all or part of their IRA contributions, making the IRA a double tax shelter for them.

Initial public offering. A corporation's first public offering of an issue of stock. Also called an IPO.

Institutional investors. Mutual funds, banks, insurance companies, pension plans and others that buy and sell stocks and bonds in large volumes. Institutional investors account for 70% or more of market volume on an average day.

Junk bond. A high-risk, high-yield bond rated BB or lower by Standard & Poor's or Ba or lower by Moody's. Junk bonds are issued by relatively unknown or financially weak companies or they have only limited backing from reasonably solvent companies.

Keogh plan. A tax-sheltered retirement plan into which self-employed individuals can deposit up to 20% of earnings and deduct the contributions from current income. Investments within the Keogh grow untaxed until they are withdrawn. Withdrawals from the plan are restricted before age 59½.

Leveraging. Investing with borrowed money in the hope of multiplying gains. If you buy $100,000 worth of stock and its price rises to $110,000, you've earned 10% on your investment. But if you leveraged the deal by putting up only $50,000 of your own money and borrowing the rest, the same $10,000 increase would represent a 20% return on your money, not counting interest on the loan. The flip side of leverage is that it also multiplies losses. If the price of the stock goes down by $5,000 on the all-cash deal, your loss would be 5% of your $100,000 investment. On the leveraged deal, your loss would be 10% of the money you put up and you'd still have to pay back the $50,000 you borrowed.

Leveraged buyout. The use of borrowed money to finance the purchase of a firm. Often, an LBO will be financed by raising money through the issuance and sale of *junk bonds*.

Limited partnership. A business arrangement put together and managed by a general partner (which may be a company or an individual) and financed by the investments of limited partners, so called because their liability is limited to the amount of money they invest in the venture. Limited partnerships can invest in virtually anything, but real estate is the most common choice. They have often been characterized by high fees for the general partners, complicated tax reporting requirements and elusive payouts for the limited partners.

Limit order. An order to buy or sell a security if it reaches a specified price. A *stop-loss order* is a common variation.

Liquidity. The ability to quickly convert an investment portfolio to cash without suffering a noticeable loss in value. Stocks and bonds of widely traded companies are considered highly liquid. Real estate and limited partnerships are illiquid.

Load. See *Back-end load* and *Front-end load*.

Margin buying. The act of financing the purchase of securities partly with money borrowed from the brokerage firm. Regulations permit buying up to 50% "on margin," meaning an investor can borrow up to half the purchase price of an investment. See *Leveraging*.

Money-market fund. A *mutual fund* that invests in short-term corporate and government debt and passes the interest payments on to shareholders. A key feature of money-market funds is that their market value doesn't change, making them an ideal place to earn current market interest with a high degree of *liquidity*.

Mutual fund. A professionally managed portfolio of stocks and bonds or other investments divided up into shares. Minimum purchase is often $500 or less, and mutual funds stand ready to buy back their shares at any time. The market price of the fund's shares, called the net asset value, fluctuates daily with the market price of the securities in its portfolio.

Nasdaq. Pronounced Naz-dak, it is the acronym for the National Association of Securities Dealers Automated Quotations System, a computerized price reporting system used by brokers to track *over the counter* securities as well as some exchange-listed issues.

Odd lot. A stock trade involving fewer than 100 shares. For contrast, see *round lot*.

Opportunity cost. The cost of passing up one investment in favor of another. For instance, if you pull money out of a *money-market fund,* where it is earning 7% interest, to invest it in a stock that has promise but yields just 4%, your opportunity cost while you're waiting is 3%.

Option. The right to buy or sell a security at a given price within a given time. The right to buy the security is called a "call." Calls are bought by investors who expect the price of the stock to rise. The right to sell a stock is called a "put." Puts are purchased by investors who expect the price of the stock to fall. Investors use puts and calls to bet on the direction of price movements without actually having to buy or sell the stock. One option represents 100 shares and sells for a fraction of the price of the shares themselves. As the time approaches for the option to expire, its price will move up or down depending on the movement of the stock price.

Options can also be used to wring a little income out of stock you own without selling it. By writing (selling) a "covered call," you collect the premium and, assuming the stock price stays under the call price, get to keep the stock. The risk, of course, is that the stock will get called away and you will miss out on the price rise.

Over the counter. The place where stocks and bonds that aren't listed on any exchange (such as the New York or American Stock Exchange) are bought and sold. Despite the small-stock, small-town image conjured up by its name, in reality the over-the-counter market (OTC) is a high-speed computerized network called *Nasdaq*, which is run by the National Association of Securities Dealers.

Par. The face value of a stock or bond. Also called par value.

Penny stock. Generally thought of as a recently issued stock selling for less than $5 a share and traded *over the counter*. Penny stocks are usually issued by small, relatively unknown companies and lightly traded, making them more prone to price manipulation than larger, better-established issues. They are, in short, a gamble.

Preferred stock. A class of stock that pays a specified dividend set when it is issued. Preferreds generally pay less income than *bonds* of the same company and don't have the price appreciation potential of *common stock*. They appeal mainly to corporations, which get a tax break on their dividend income.

Price-earnings ratio. Usually called the P/E, it is the price of a stock divided by either its latest annual earnings per share (a "trailing" P/E) or its predicted earnings (an "anticipated" P/E). Either way, the P/E is considered an important indicator of investor sentiment about a stock because it indicates how much investors are willing to pay for a dollar of earnings.

Price-sales ratio. The PSR is the stock's price divided by its company's latest annual sales per share. It is favored by some investors as a measure of a stock's relative value. The lower the PSR, according to this school of thought, the better the value.

Program trading. A complex computerized system designed to take advantage of temporary differences between the actual value of the stocks composing a popular index and the value represented by *futures contracts* on those stocks. To simplify, if the stocks' prices are higher than the futures contracts reflect, computer programs issue orders to sell stocks and buy futures contracts. If the stocks are lower than the futures contracts reflect, program traders buy stocks and sell the futures. The result is virtually risk-free profits for the program traders and more volatility for the market because of the vast numbers of shares needed to make the system work.

Prospectus. The document that describes a securities offering or the operations of a mutual fund, a limited partnership or other investment. The prospectus divulges financial data about the company, background of its officers and other information needed by investors to make an informed decision.

Proxy. The formal authorization of a stockholder that permits someone else (usually company management) to vote in his or her place at shareholder meetings or on matters put to the shareholders for a vote at other times.

Real estate investment trust. A *closed-end investment company* that buys real estate properties or mortgages and passes virtually all the profits on to its shareholders.

Registered representative. The formal name for a stockbroker, so called because he or she must be registered with the

National Association of Securities Dealers as qualified to handle securities trades.

Return on equity. An important measure of investment results that is obtained by dividing the total value of shareholders' equity—that is, the market value of *common* and *preferred stock*—into the company's net income after taxes.

Return on investment. Often abbreviated ROI, this is a company's net profit after taxes divided by its total assets, which include *common stock, preferred stock* and *bonds*.

Round lot. A hundred shares of stock, the preferred number for buying and selling and the most economical unit when commissions are calculated.

Sallie Mae. Acronym for the Student Loan Marketing Association, which buys up student loans from colleges, universities and other lenders and packages them into units to be sold to investors. Sallie Mae thus infuses the student loan market with new money in much the same way that *Ginnie Mae* infuses the mortgage market with new money.

Secondary market. The general name given to stock exchanges, the over-the-counter market and other marketplaces in which stocks, bonds, mortgages and other investments are sold after they have been issued and sold initially. Original issues are sold in the primary market; subsequent sales take place in the secondary market. For example, the primary market for a new issue of stock is the team of underwriters; the secondary market is one of the stock exchanges or the over-the-counter market. The primary market for a mortgage is the lender, which may then sell it to *Fannie Mae* or *Freddie Mac* in the secondary mortgage market.

Short selling. A technique used to take advantage of an

anticipated decline in the price of a stock or other security by reversing the usual order of buying and selling. In a short sale, the investor (1) borrows stock from the broker and (2) immediately sells it. Then, if the investor guessed right and the price of the stock does indeed decline, he can replace the borrowed shares by (3) buying them at the cheaper price. The profit is the difference between the price at which he sells the shares and the price at which he buys them later on. Of course, if the price of the shares rises, the investor will suffer a loss.

Sinking fund. Financial reserves set aside to be used exclusively to redeem a bond or preferred stock issue and thus reassure investors that the company will be able to meet that obligation.

Specialist. A member of the stock exchange who serves as a market maker for a number of different stock issues. A specialist maintains an inventory of certain stocks and buys and sells shares as necessary to maintain an orderly market for those stocks.

Spread. The difference between the *bid* and *asked* prices of a security, which may also be called the broker's markup. In *options* and *futures* trading, a spread is the practice of simultaneously buying a contract for the delivery of a commodity in one month and selling a contract for delivery of the same commodity in another month. The aim is to offset possible losses in one contract with possible gains in the other.

Stop-loss order. Instructions to a broker to sell a particular stock if its price ever dips to a specified level.

Street name. The description given to securities held in the name of a brokerage firm but belonging to the firm's customers. Holding stocks in street name facilitates trading because there is no need for the customer to pick up or deliver the certificates.

Technical analysis. An approach to market analysis that

attempts to forecast price movements by examining and *charting* the patterns formed by past movements in prices, trading volume, the ratio of advancing to declining stocks and other statistics. For contrast, see *Fundamental analysis.*

Tender offer. An offer to shareholders to buy their shares of stock in a company. Tender offers are usually a key element of a strategy to take over, or buy out, a company and thus are usually made at a higher-than-market price to encourage shareholders to accept them.

10-K. A detailed financial report that must be filed by a firm each year with the Securities and Exchange Commission. It is much more detailed than a typical annual report published and sent to shareholders.

Total return. A measure of investment performance that starts with price changes, then adds in the results of reinvesting all earnings, such as interest or dividends, generated by the investment during the period being measured.

Triple witching hour. A phrase made popular by *program trading,* it is the last hour of stock market trading on the third Friday of March, June, September and December. That's when *options* and *futures contracts* expire on market indexes used by program traders to hedge their positions in stocks. The simultaneous expirations often set off heavy buying and selling of the options, futures and the underlying stocks themselves, thus creating the "triple" witching hour.

12b-1 fees. An extra fee charged by some *mutual funds* to cover the costs of promotion and marketing. In practice, 12b-1 fees are often used to compensate brokers for selling low-load and no-load funds. The effect of the fee is reflected in the performance figures reported by the funds.

Yield. In general, the return earned by an investment. In discussing *bonds,* yield can be any of several kinds. "Coupon yield" is the interest rate paid on the face value of the bond, which is usually $1,000. "Current yield" is the interest rate based on the actual purchase price of the bond, which may be higher or lower than the face amount. "Yield to maturity" is the rate that takes into account the current yield and the difference between the purchase price and the face value, with the difference assumed to be paid in equal installments over the remaining life of the bond.

Zero-coupon bond. A bond that pays all its interest at maturity but none prior to maturity. Called "zeros," these bonds sell at a deep discount to face value and are especially suitable for long-term investment goals with a definite time horizon, such as college tuition or retirement.

INDEX

A

B

C